# GUERNSEY
## THROUGH TIME
### Amanda Bennett

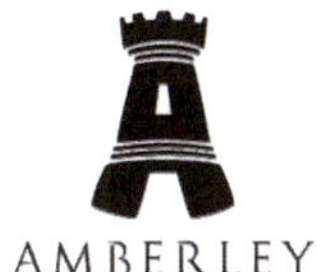

AMBERLEY

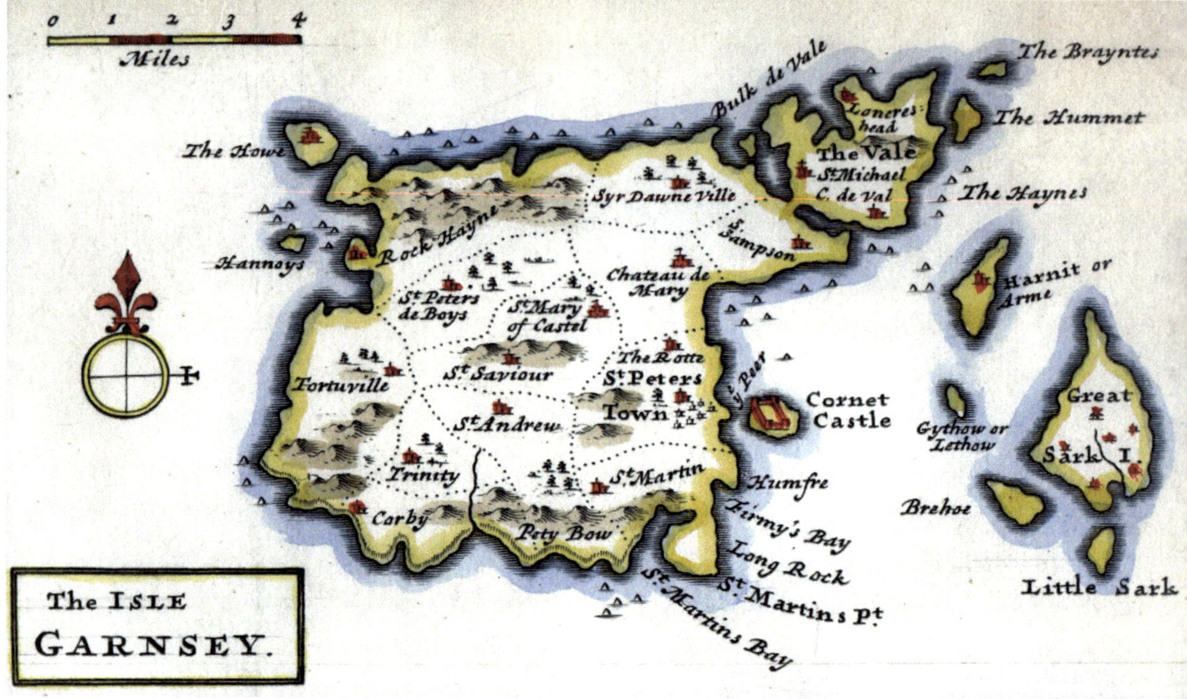



Herman Moll, 1721.

*For Zoë and Finlay Sneddon.*
*May you appreciate the past, and thrive in the future.*




First published 2014

Amberley Publishing
The Hill, Stroud, Gloucestershire, GL5 4EP
www.amberley-books.com

Copyright © Amanda Bennett, 2014

The right of Amanda Bennett to be identified as the Author of this work has been asserted in accordance with the Copyrights, Designs and Patents Act 1988.

ISBN 978 1 4456 3488 3 (print)
ISBN 978 1 4456 3509 5 (ebook)

British Library Cataloguing in Publication Data.
A catalogue record for this book is available from the British Library.

Typesetting by Amberley Publishing.
Printed in Great Britain

. Appointed GPSR EU Representative: Easy Access System Europe Oü, 16879218
Address: Mustamäe tee 50, 10621, Tallinn, Estonia
Contact Details: gpsr.requests@easproject.com, +358 40 500 3575

# Introduction

Guernsey is the second largest of the Channel Islands – an archipelago off the coast of Normandy made up of eight permanently inhabited islands and at least fifty other uninhabited islands and islets. Each island has its own distinct character, landscape and history.

Guernsey's unique character lies not just in its geography, but in its cultural and political history. The great French writer Victor Hugo lived in exile on Guernsey for more than fifteen years and said of the islands, 'little pieces of France, fallen into the sea, and picked up by Britain...' The Channel Islands are, in fact, the last remnants of the Duchy of Normandy – the great state ruled over by William the Conqueror and, for several generations, the Anglo-Norman Plantagenet kings. According to ancient tradition, the islands owe allegiance to the Queen in her role as Duke of Normandy. The blending of a French cultural background and a fierce loyalty to the British Crown has created a unique heritage.

The Guernsey character is formed by its landscape. The islanders are a hardy bunch, dependent on the sea, yet wary of its moods – the island is small enough to forge community spirit, but large enough to foster self-sufficiency and independence. The Guernsey people are said to be stubborn. I would rather say that they are deeply pragmatic and unsentimental – you cannot be otherwise in an island ruled by the waves and the weather. Victor Hugo again, 'There is an industrious human anthill here. The work of the sea, which has brought destruction, has been supplanted by the work of man, which has created a people.' It is pragmatism that has enabled the island to thrive across the centuries  – finding and exploiting a commercial market and making themselves indispensable, be it through knitting, privateering, quarrying, tomato growing, or international finance! It is the unsentimental streak that allows them to look to the future and not live in the past.

Guernsey is a beautiful island, but it is not a museum. With that in mind, this book looks at Guernsey through time with that unsentimental eye, but with an appreciation and respect for its cultural heritage. Photographs are moments frozen in time, but life continues to move beyond them, and seeing how places, people and buildings have changed tells us a unique and fascinating story. All of the old photographs in this book come from the local studies collections of the Priaulx Library. The library holds around 25,000 photographic images, many of which were taken or collected by Carel Toms, a *Guernsey Press* photographer for many decades before his death in 2002. The early and mid-Victorian photographs were collected by antiquarian Edith Carey and have been in the library since the 1930s.

The tour of the island will be roughly geographical, beginning with the town and harbour of St Peter Port – Guernsey's major port and its financial and commercial hub. Home to more than 20,000 souls, this quirky and hilly town has seen many dramatic changes, but has managed to retain its essential charm. Yet concentrating solely on what has changed physically on Guernsey does not do justice to its people, and a small central section of the book will look at how its people have adapted to change – how traditional crafts can be continued using modern methods, and how ancient traditions can be just as relevant today. The last section will be a tour of the remaining nine parishes, covering both coast and country, from the beauty of the cliffs and beaches, to the tranquillity of the lanes and the sometimes startling transformations caused by the modern world.

The profits from this book will go to support the work of the Priaulx Library in collecting and making accessible the documents, newspapers, images and maps that make up Guernsey's story. To find out more about the library, and more about the history of the island, please visit our website at www.priaulxlibrary.co.uk.

Amanda Bennett
Priaulx Library

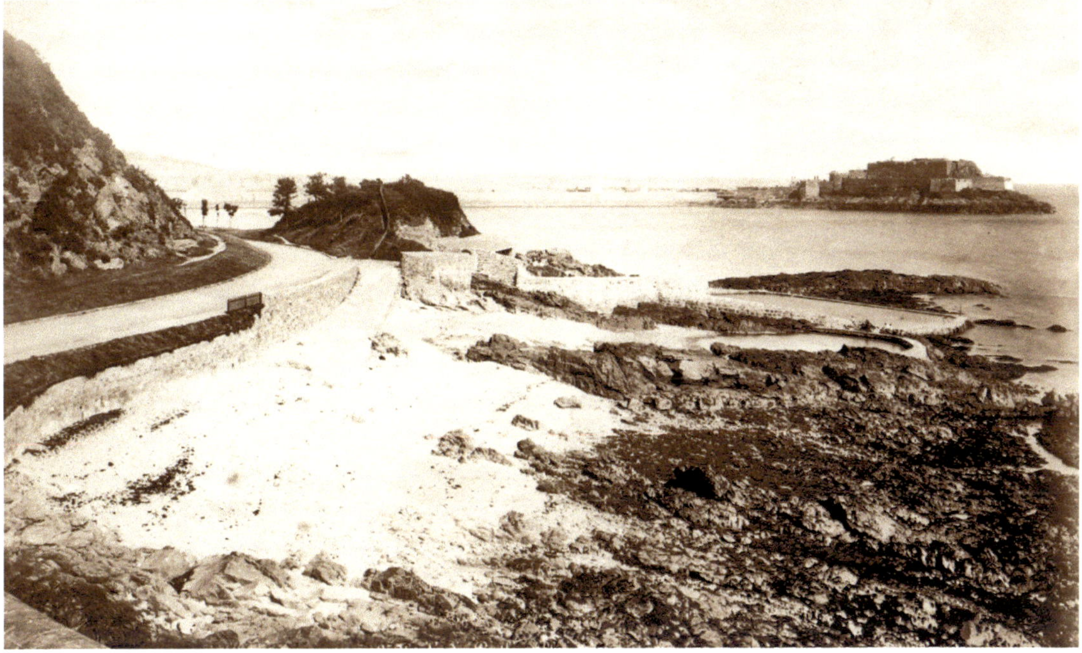

## The Bathing Pools, 1880

At La Vallette, south of Castle Cornet, lies a series of seawater bathing pools, created in the nineteenth century to accommodate the craze for sea bathing, and much beloved by many generations of town dwellers. The first pool was built in 1843, and three others were added over the decades. This photograph shows the Ladies' Pool (now a mixed pool) and the Children's Pool in front. The scene is little changed, but the winter storms of 2014 caused considerable damage to the structure, forcing their temporary closure.

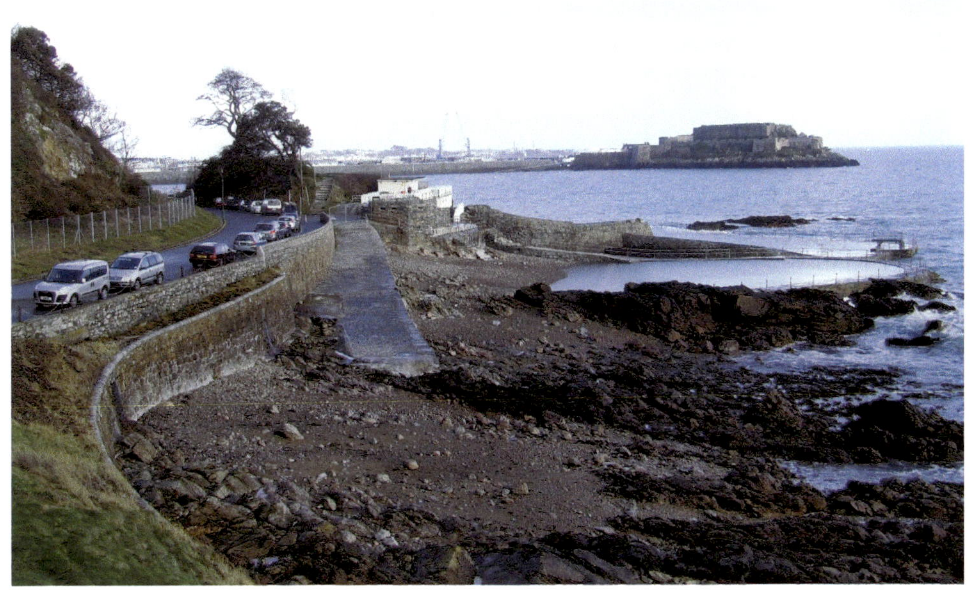

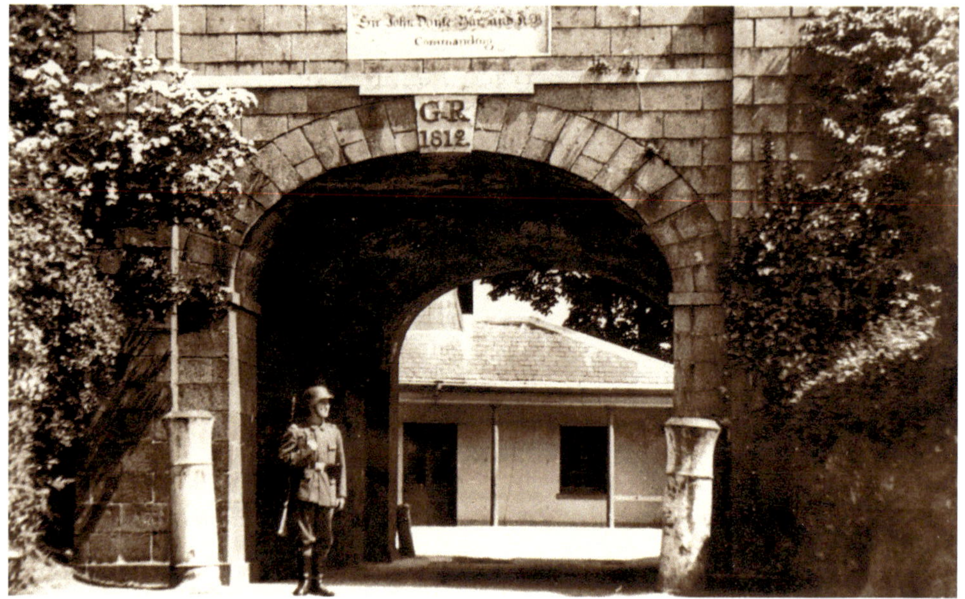

### Entrance Gate to Fort George

Photographs of Guernsey during the German occupation of 1940–45 often throw up startling juxtapositions. A German soldier guards the entrance to the English garrison fort with the initials of George III carved at the top of the arch. The fort was completed in 1812 under the direction of Sir John Doyle, and was used continuously for nearly 150 years. The fort was sold by the British Crown in 1958, and shortly afterwards became a very exclusive development of luxury houses. The archway today is unchanged, but the buildings beyond could not be more different.

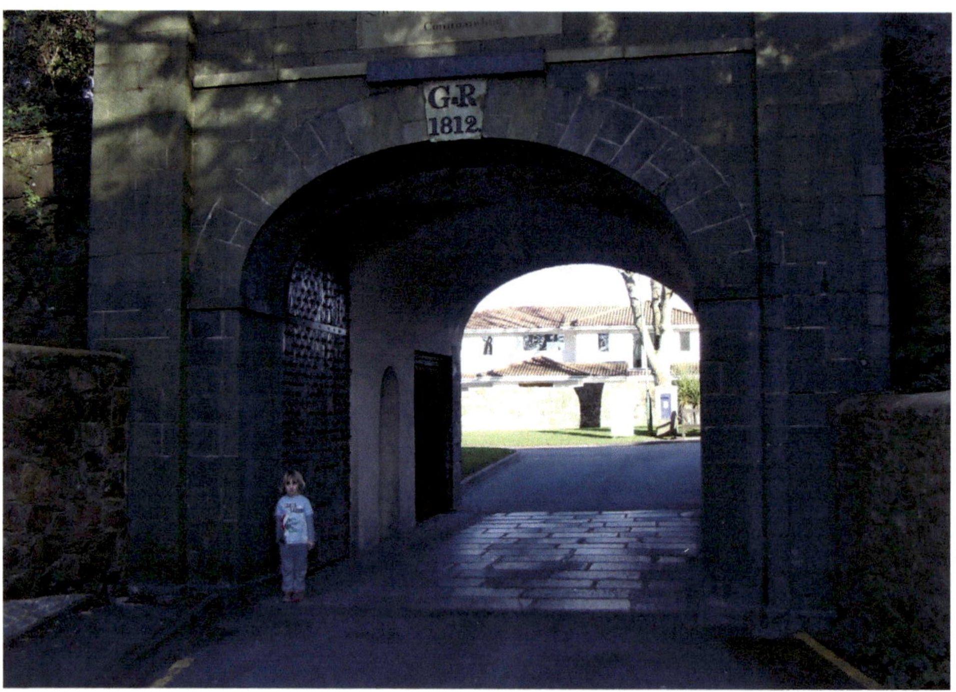

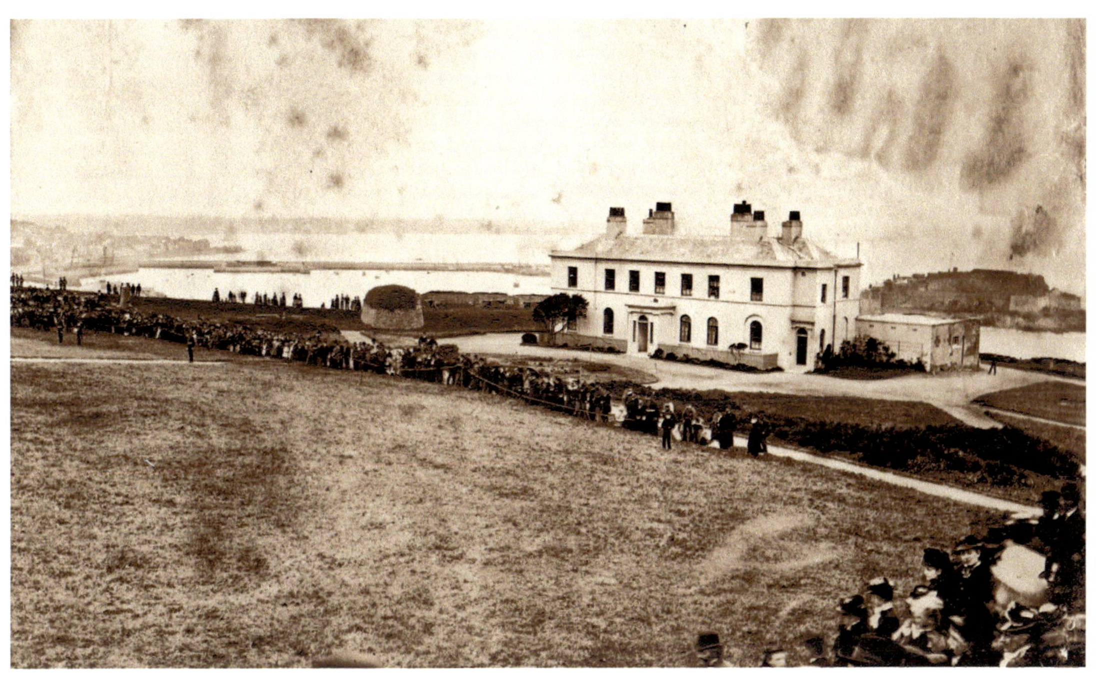

### Belvedere Field and House, Fort George

The British Army kept a garrison in Guernsey at Castle Cornet for many centuries. However, by 1780, the threat of French attack had become very real and work began on a new garrison – Fort George – capable of holding many more soldiers. Among the buildings was this very fine Regency-style house, built to house the Regimental Colonel. The field in front was used for parades, which in their day drew huge crowds of interested islanders. The house is still as grand today, but is now in private hands.

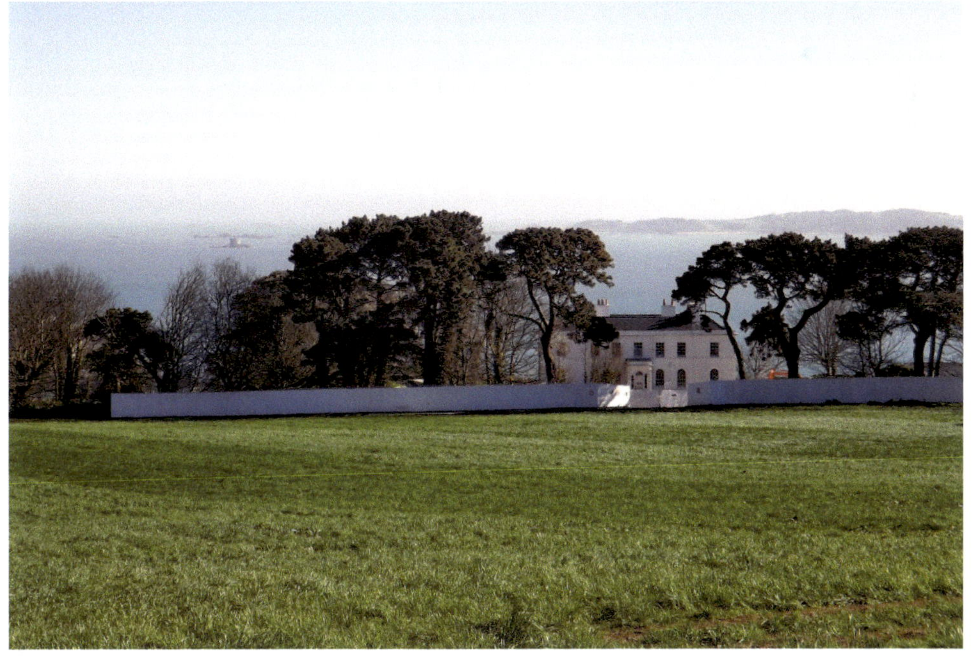

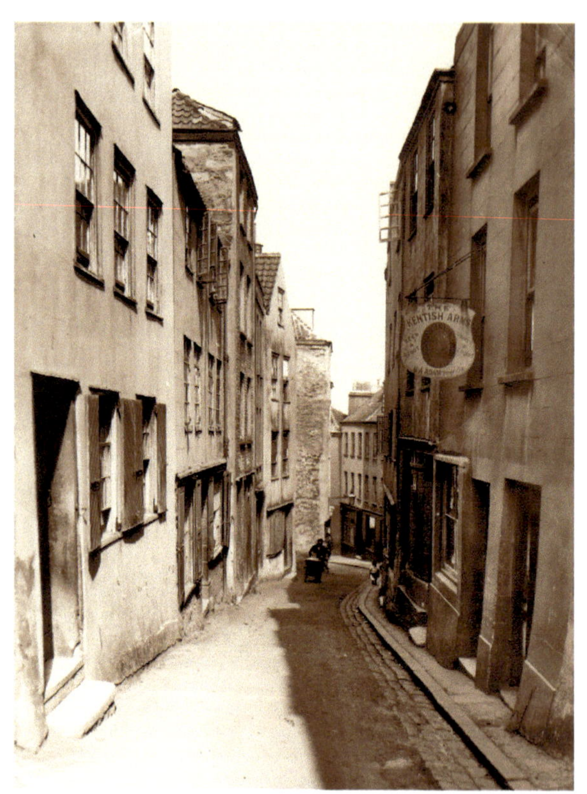

### Cornet Street

By the beginning of the twentieth century, Cornet Street was considered the worst and poorest street in St Peter Port. The 1901 census shows two, sometimes three, families sharing one house, and on the ground floors are beer retailers, pawnbrokers, and other less respectable trades. In 1929, the north-east side of the road was condemned and pulled down, never to be replaced. This opened out the road to great effect, and the street is now a pleasant mixture of houses, offices and pubs.

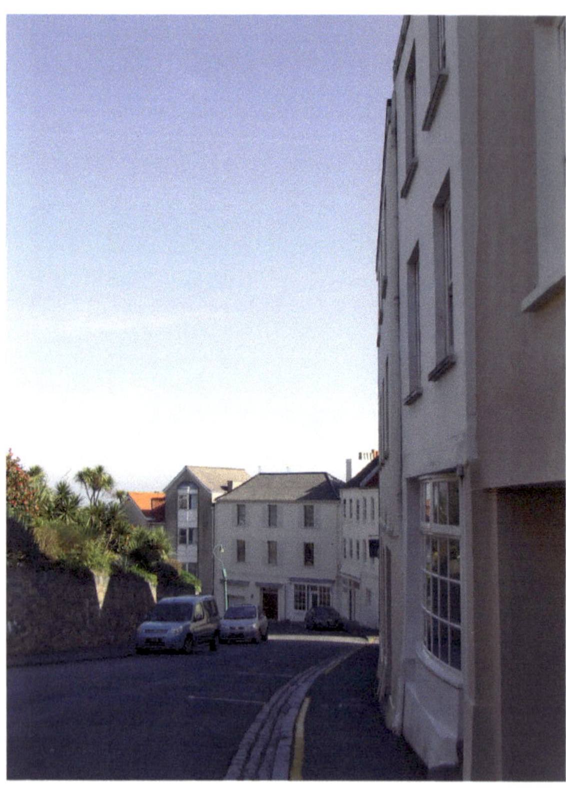

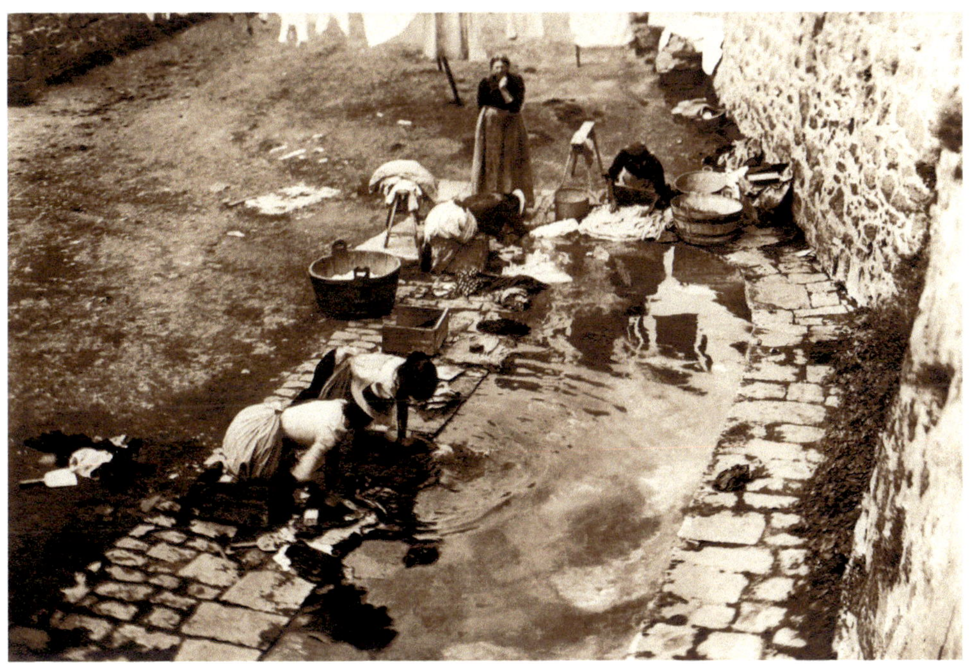

## Lavoir at Ruette Braye

A lavoir is a communal washing place, and many such places existed in Guernsey down the centuries. Usually built around a spring or pool, the users of these public facilities were also responsible for their upkeep. The washing must have been back-breaking work. This lavoir at the junction of Ruette Braye and La Charroterie was the last to be in regular use, and this photograph of French washerwomen dates from around 1900. When the land was developed by an investment bank, the lavoir was beautifully restored.

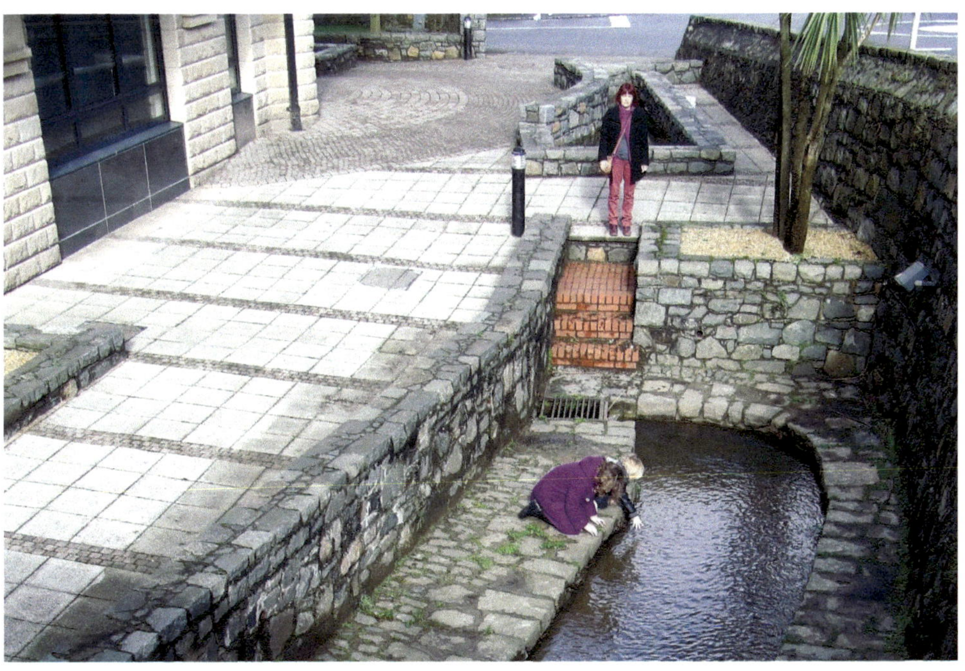

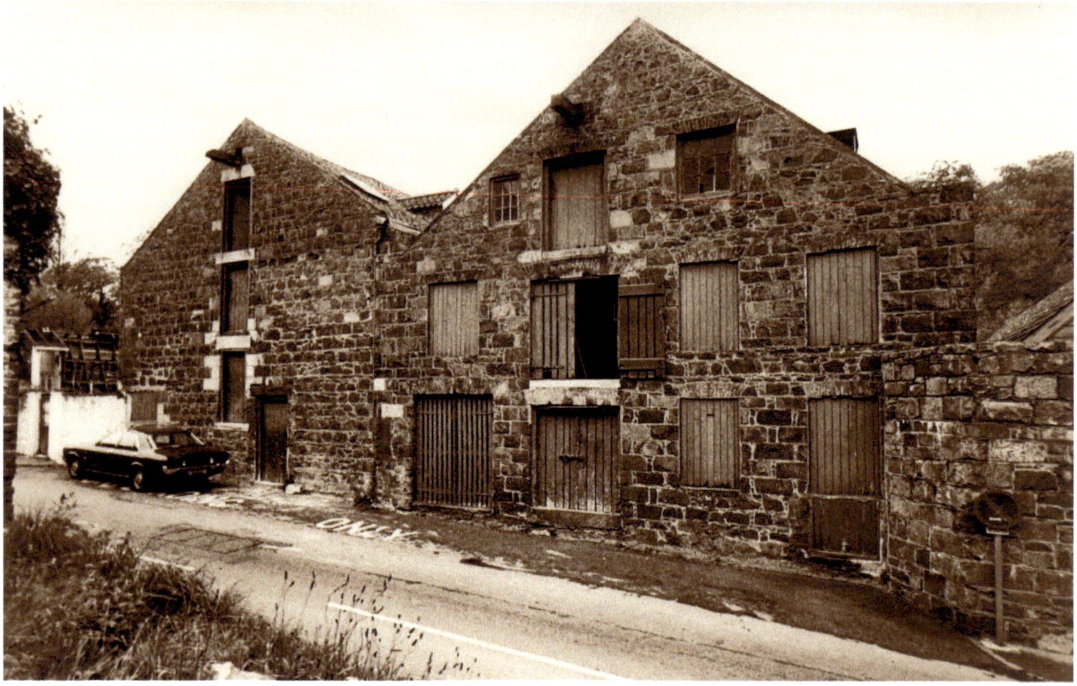

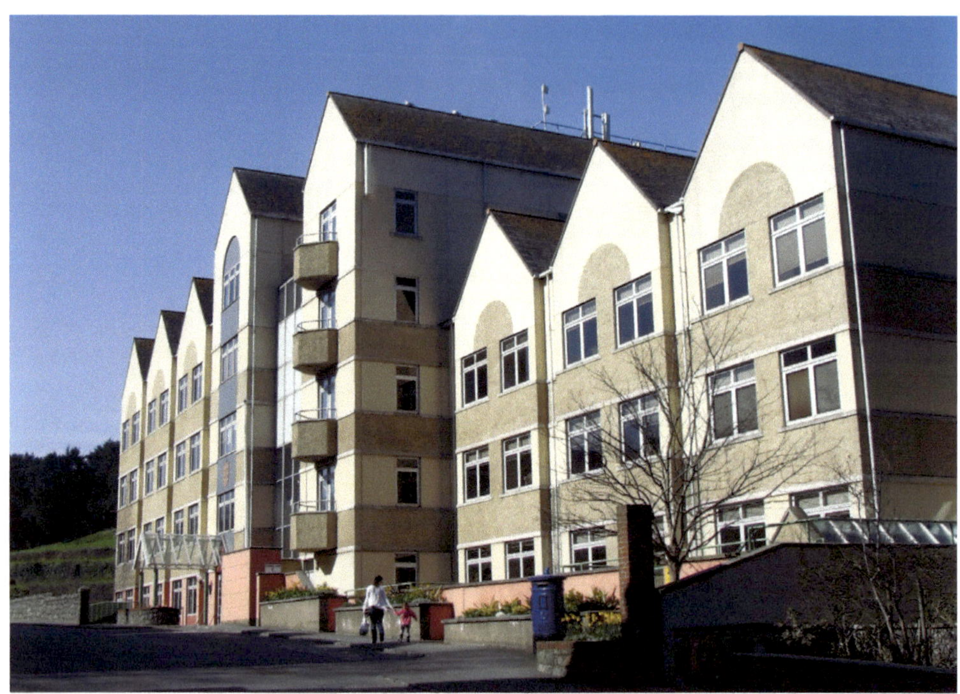

## Phoenix Mills, La Charroterie

One of several of the St Peter Port mills, the Phoenix Mill in La Charroterie was among the last to be demolished. On 30 November 1989, the States of Guernsey allocated £9 million to build a new office block – Sir Charles Frossard House – on the site, capable of accommodating several of the States' departments.

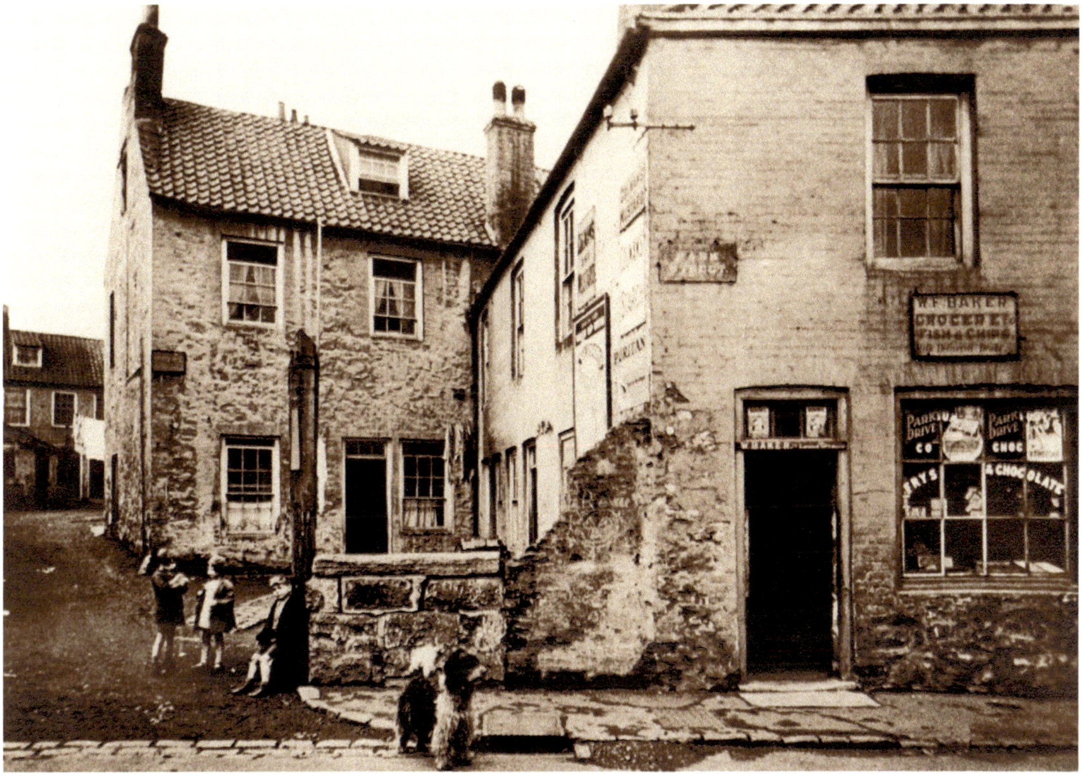

## Park Street

The three children, with their pet dog as guard, stand in a deserted Park Street against a background of rather grimy houses. W. F. Baker's grocery shop in Park Street is listed in local directories from 1929–36. These houses have long since vanished, having been demolished in the early 1960s. On 30 January 1963, the States of Guernsey gave its approval for the construction of the Cour du Parc – a mini-tower block of flats. Now shrouded in scaffolding, the building is being given a twenty-first-century makeover.

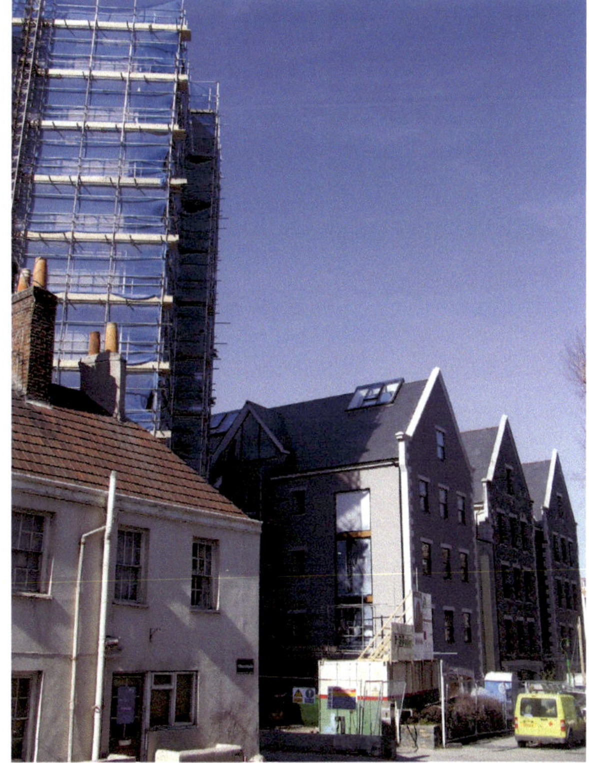

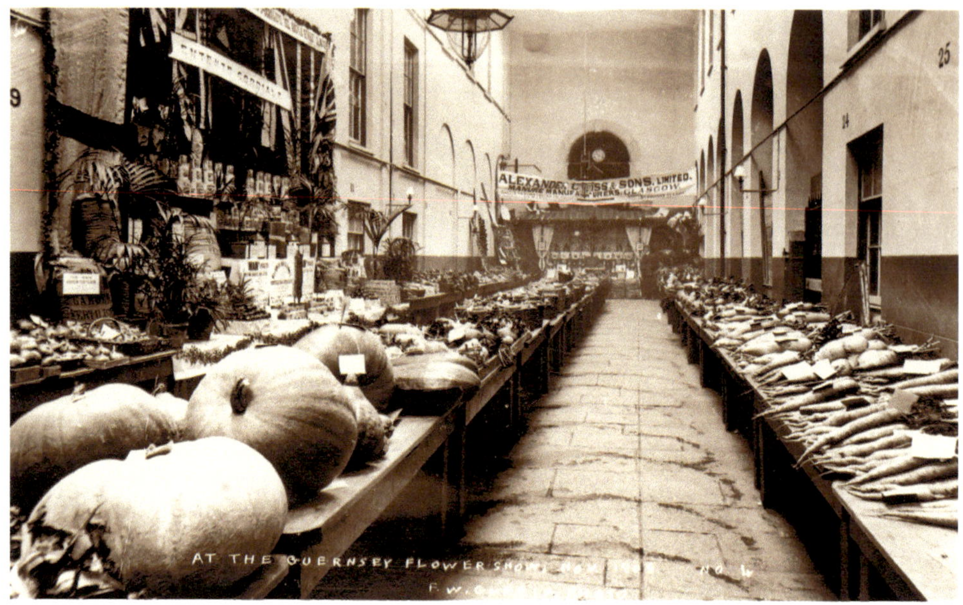

## At the Guernsey Flower Show, 1905

This photographic postcard by F. W. Guerin from 1905 shows the Inner Street of the Town Market laid out with some magnificent vegetable displays. The Inner Street linked the meat and fish markets with the lower Vegetable Market, and was usually full of fruit and flower stalls. Since the markets were redeveloped at the beginning of the twenty-first century, fresh produce is no longer sold there, except by a local supermarket. The Inner Street, though, has been beautifully restored.

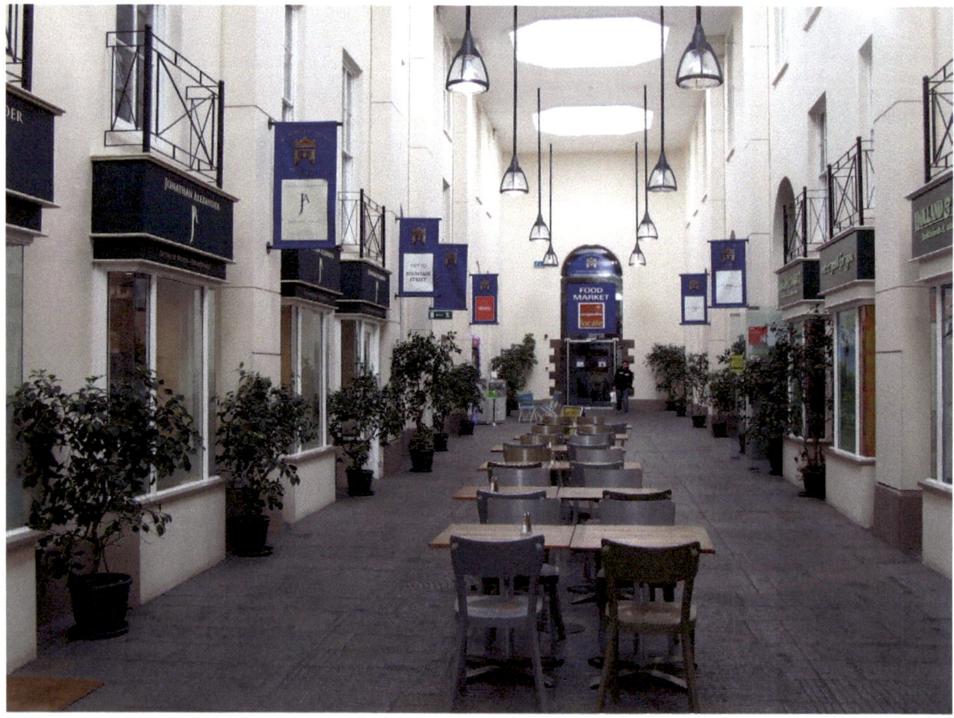

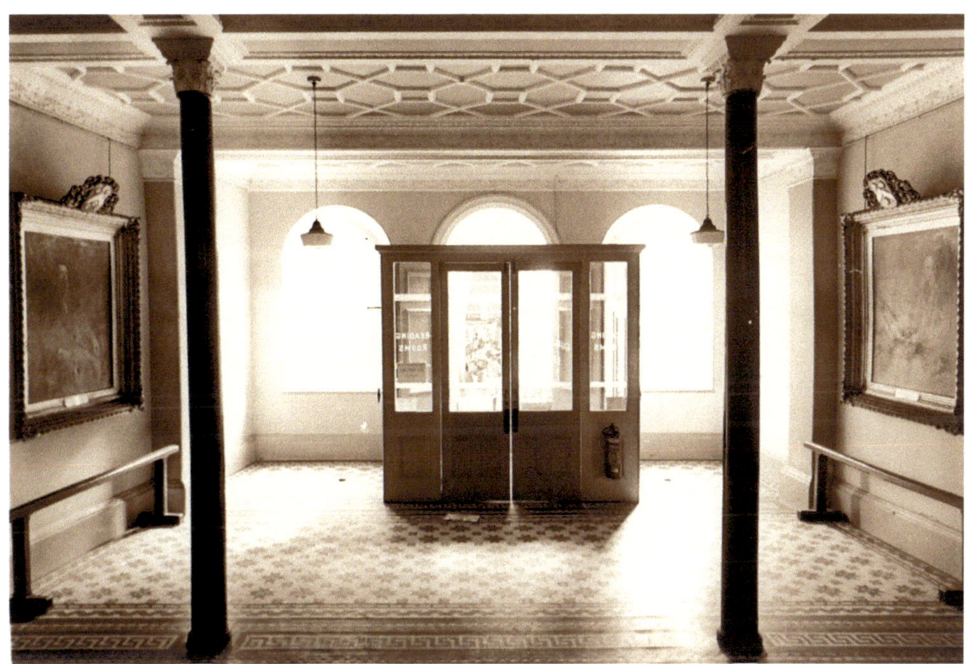

### Guille-Allès Library Entrance Hall

When Thomas Guille and Frederick Mansell Allès visited the United States in the 1830s, they were so impressed with the libraries in New York that they were determined on their return to Guernsey to open a public library. They purchased the Assembly Rooms in Market Street and considerably extended the building, including adding this fine new entrance hall, which greeted library users in 1888. Today, the Guille-Allès is Guernsey's main public library and welcomes around 200,000 people every year. In 2011, the entrance hall was restored to its Victorian splendour.

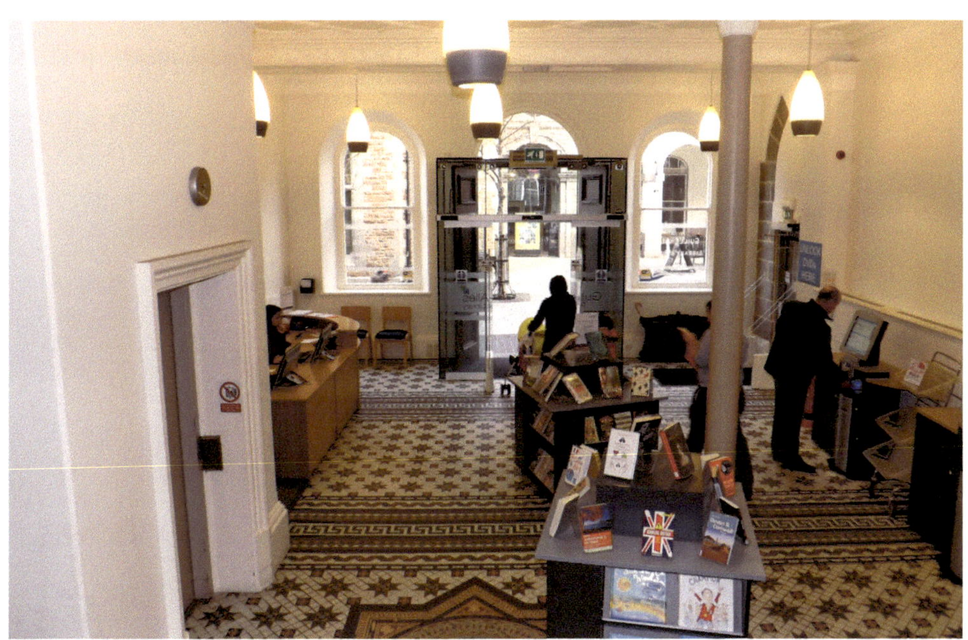

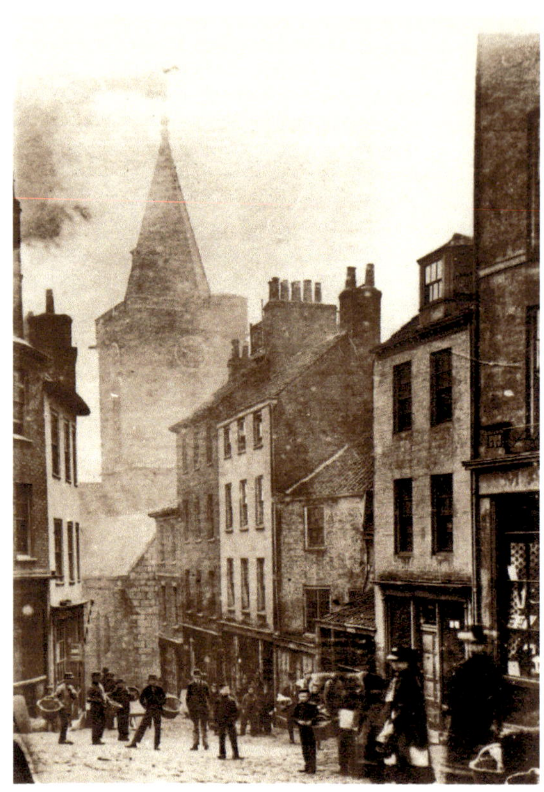

## Market Hill

None of the houses in this early photograph survived the building of the Bonded Store and lower Vegetable Market in 1879. It cannot be denied that the new buildings opened up the area considerably – a crowded medieval maze replaced by High Victorian town planning. The Guernsey markets were developed over more than fifty years and have undergone yet more work recently, including this terrace above the Bonded Store.

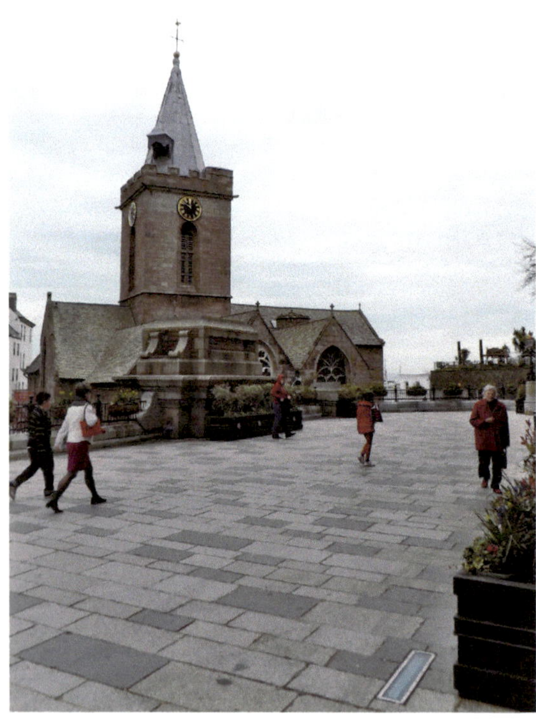

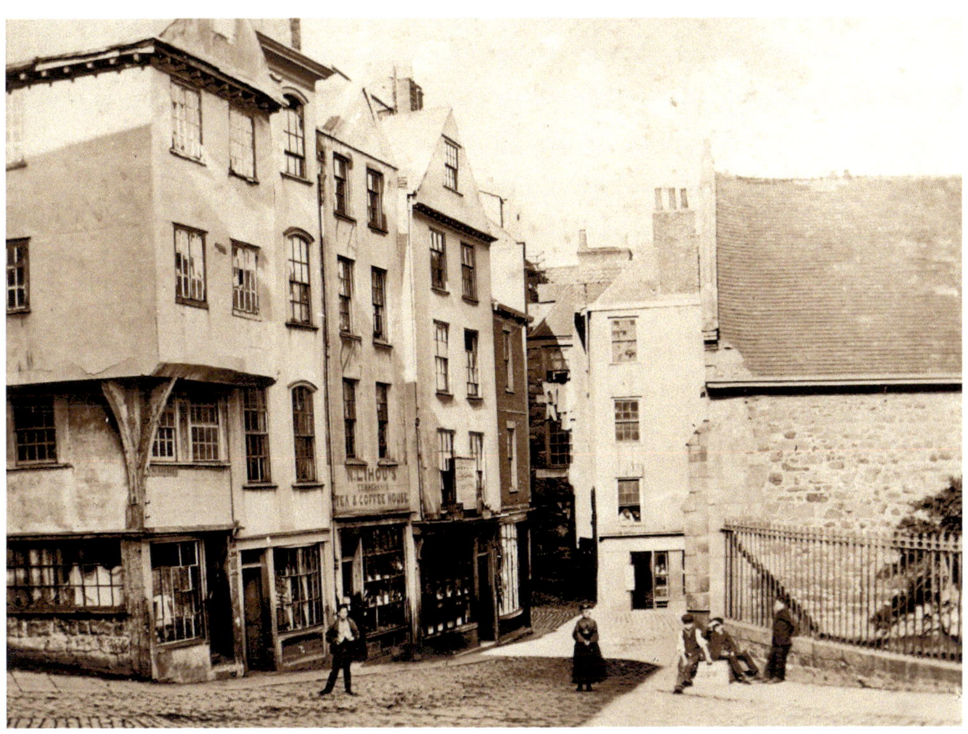

## Church Street

In the 1860s, Church Street was a narrow passage passing the west door of the Town church and then turning up into Market Hill. The Town church was hemmed in tightly on three sides by narrow, cobbled streets and tall, closely packed houses, some of great antiquity; the medieval origins of the house on the left corner can be seen in the jettied upper story. The buildings were swept away as part of the continuing redevelopment of the markets and the new photograph shows the Bonded Store, with terrace above, which was completed in 1879.

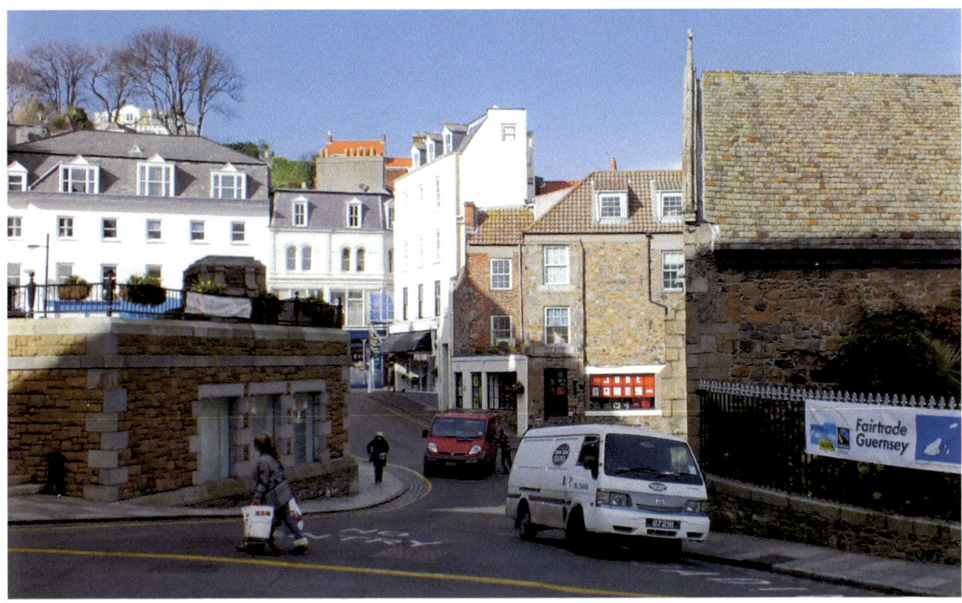

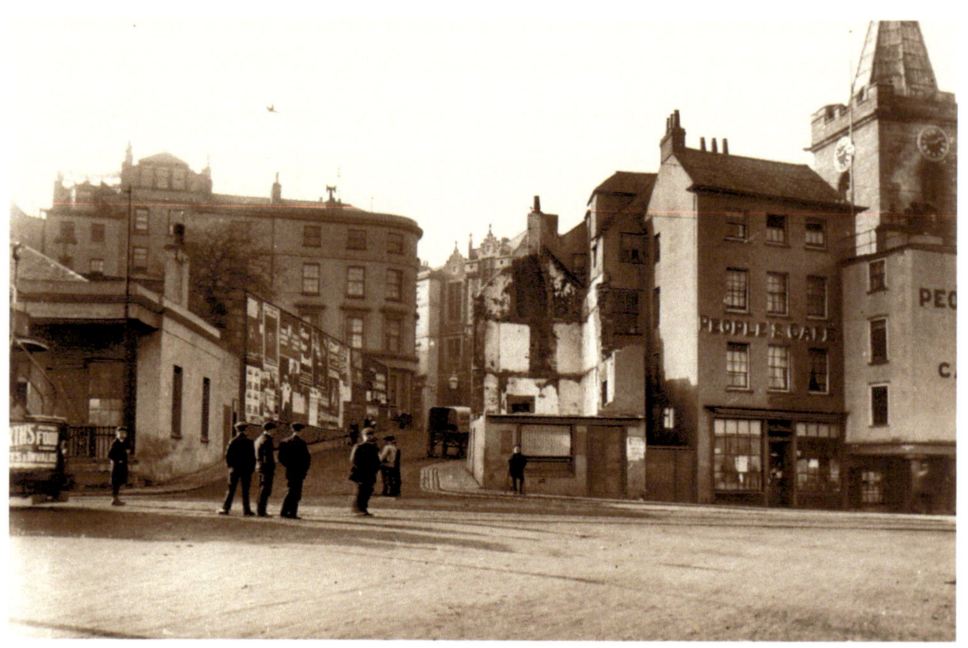

## Demolition Begins in Front of the Town Church, 1913

A group of men inspect the beginning of the demolition of the buildings in front of the Town church. They were taken down in 1913 so that the road to the quay could be widened. Once called Pier Hill, the narrow road next to the demolished building was merged with Cornet Street, which curves up a steep hill to the south, and Fountain Street was opened up to the seafront. Today, the open area in front of the church is a pleasant spot with benches and cobbles, and an old municipal pump.

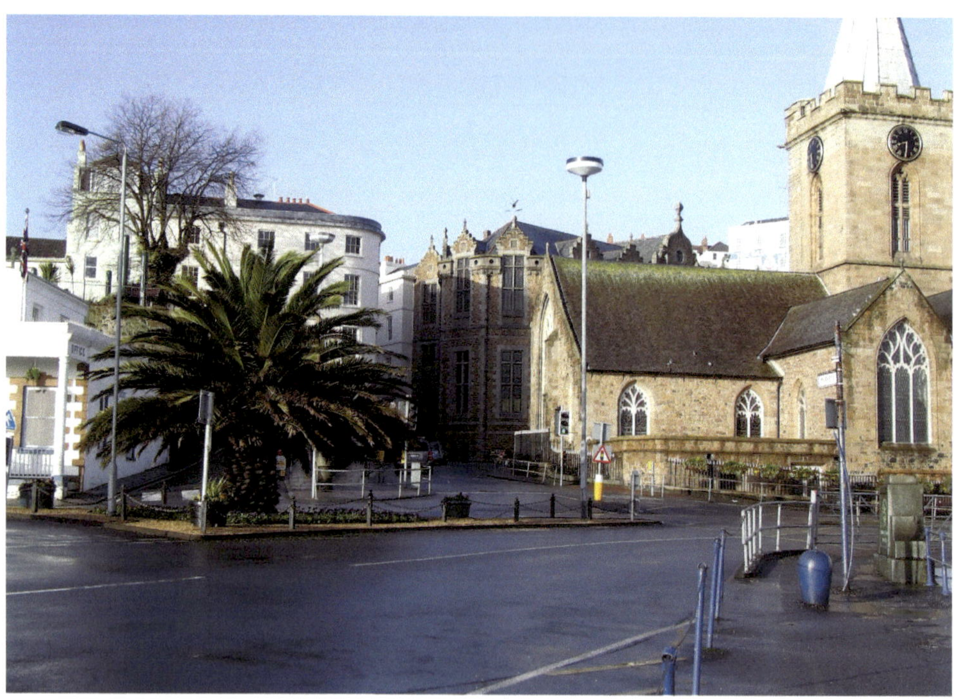

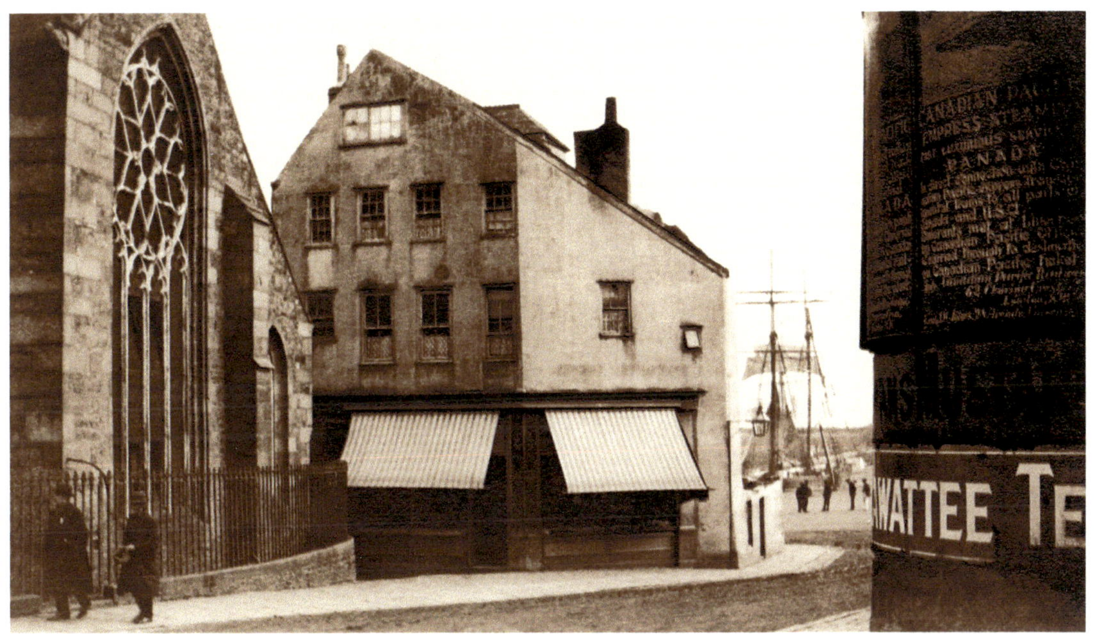


## Pier Hill

A reverse view of the demolition of buildings in front of the Town church. The view down Pier Hill shows the back of the People's Café and the rear wall of the newly demolished property that was once the Maritime Inn, which was run by Geoffrey Knight. The modern view clearly shows how much the road was widened, with a lovely open view down to the Victoria Marina. The wall covered in advertising to the right of the 1913 photograph was partly taken down, and a set of granite steps installed, creating a pedestrian junction with Cornet Street.

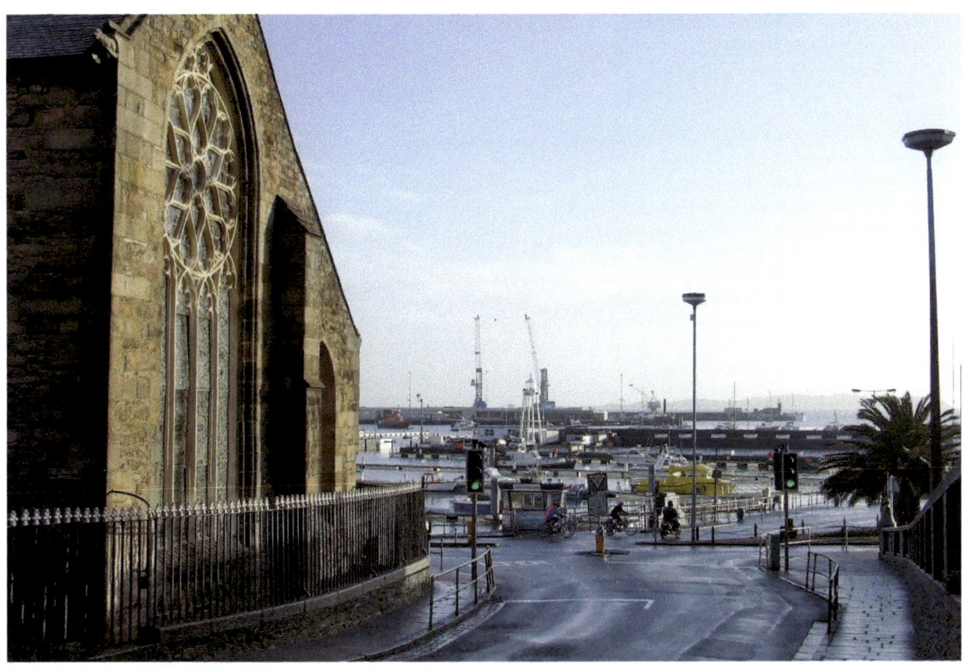

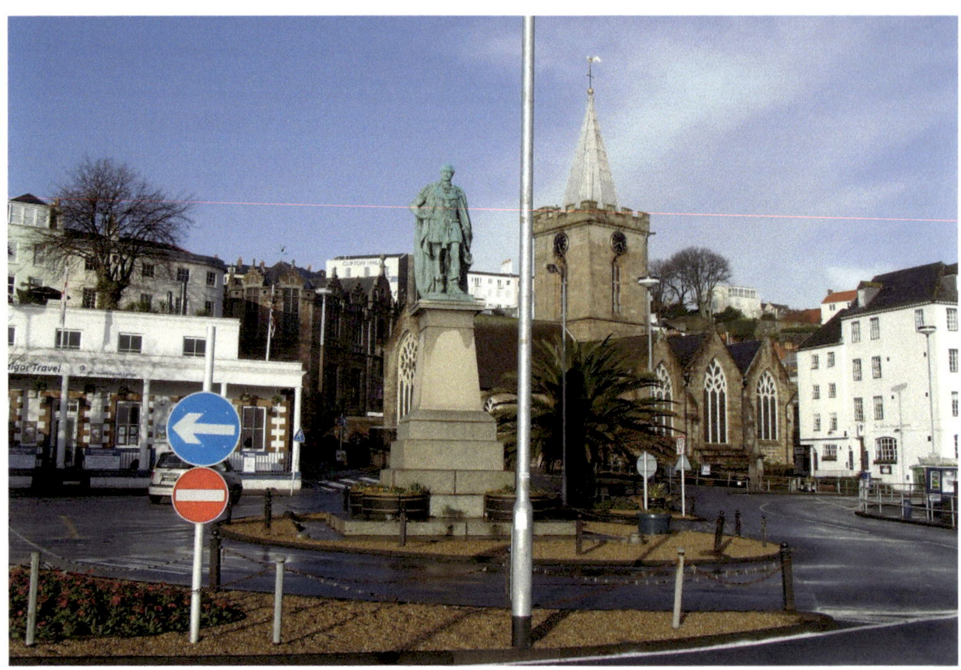

### The Albert Statue

The modern chaos of road signs, street lights and cars could not be more of a contrast to the tranquillity of the scene 100 years ago. The Albert Statue was erected in 1863 to commemorate the death of Prince Albert in 1861, and was paid for by public subscription. He has been a familiar figure for generations of islanders, despite the fact that his name on the plinth is now faded.

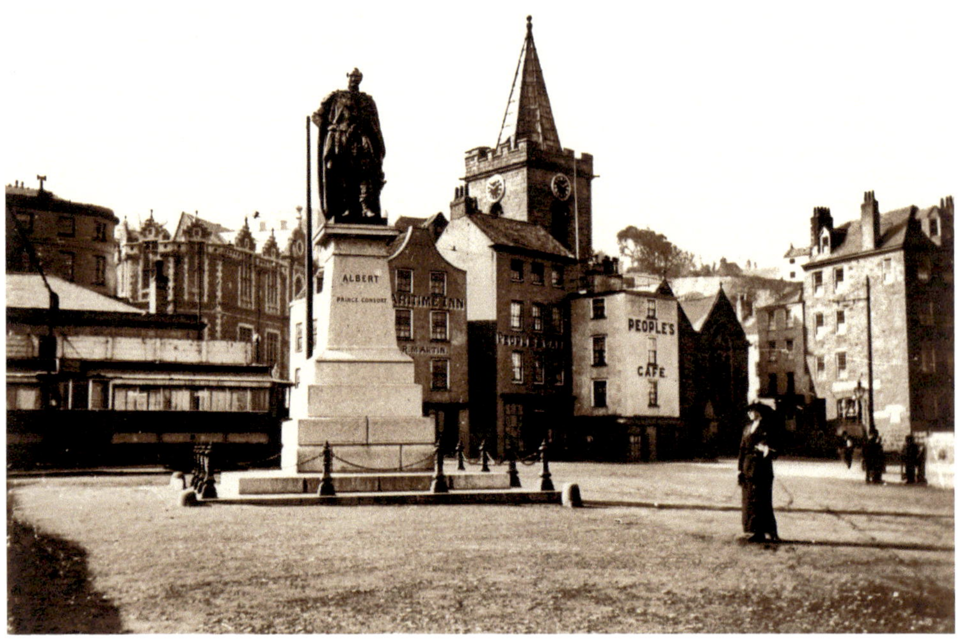

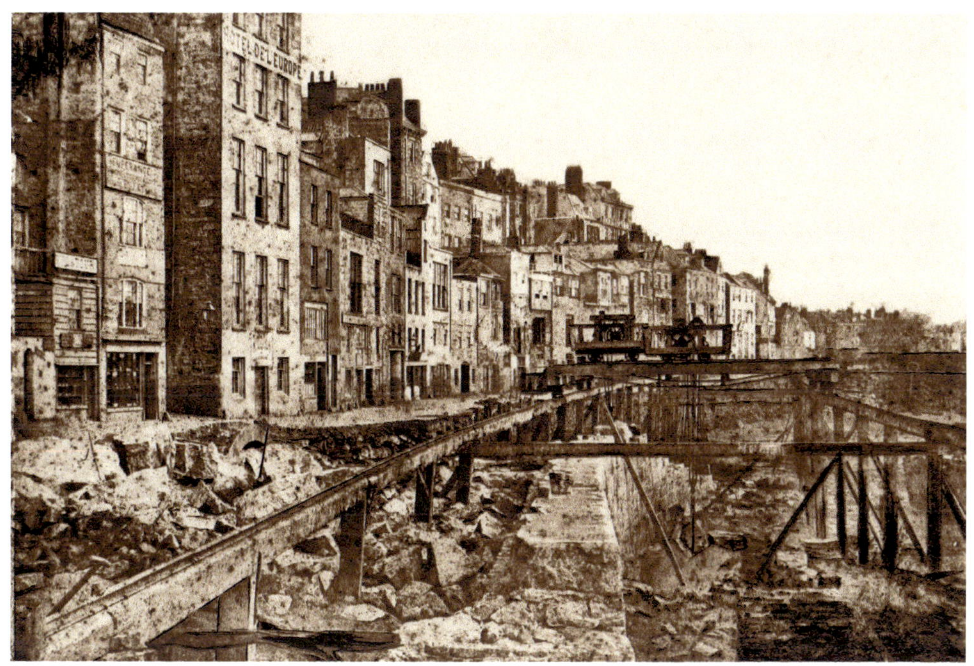

## The New Quay

Photographs of the old quay at St Peter Port are extremely rare, but it is obvious, even in this grainy image, that the original was very narrow indeed – no more than 18 feet wide. Yet, there had only existed a quay at all since 1779, and the sea would wash up against the houses on the seafront on a regular basis. In 1853, the foundation stone of a new harbour was laid, and among many improvements, the quay was widened. It has survived the test of time, but flooding still occasionally occurs.

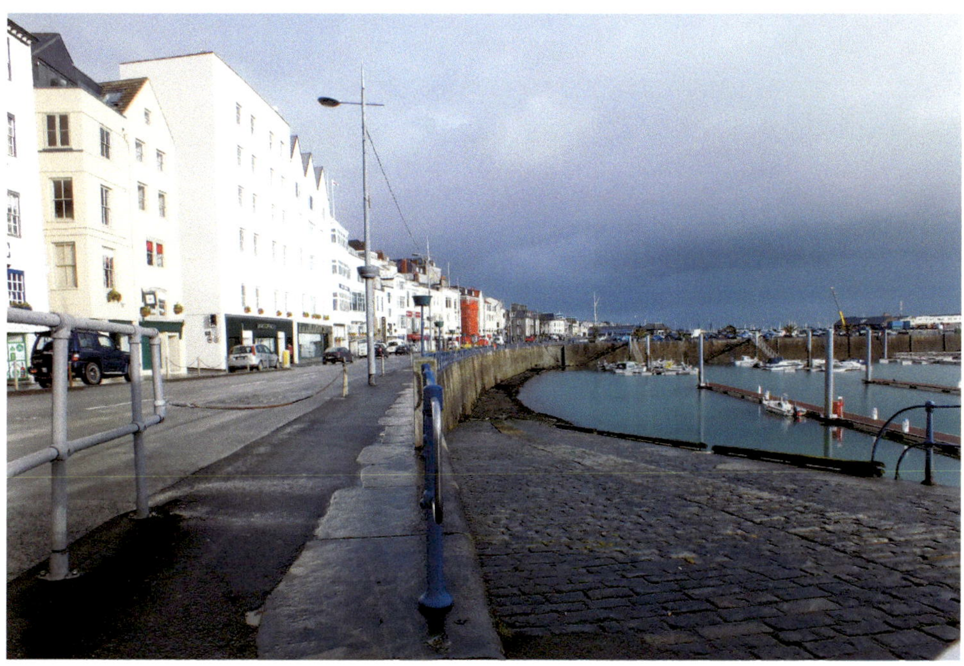

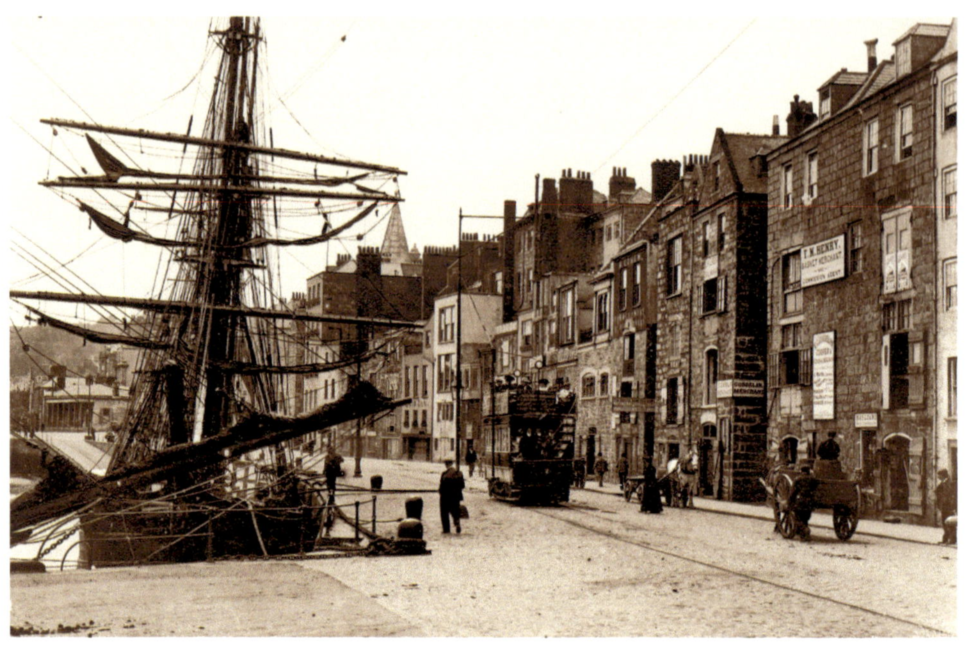

## The Quay Looking South

In 1900, the quay was a jumbled row of buildings of many different types and periods, and is very little changed today. A glance at the shopfronts immediately shows the commercial nature of St Peter Port Harbour: a basket merchant, commission agent, ships' chandler, merchants, and even a sailmaker. Today, they are supplanted by banks, shops and restaurants. In the centre of the picture is the tram that travelled the 2½ miles from St Peter Port to St Sampson's. Electrified in 1892, it ran until 1934. These days, buses and cars make the trek between the harbours.

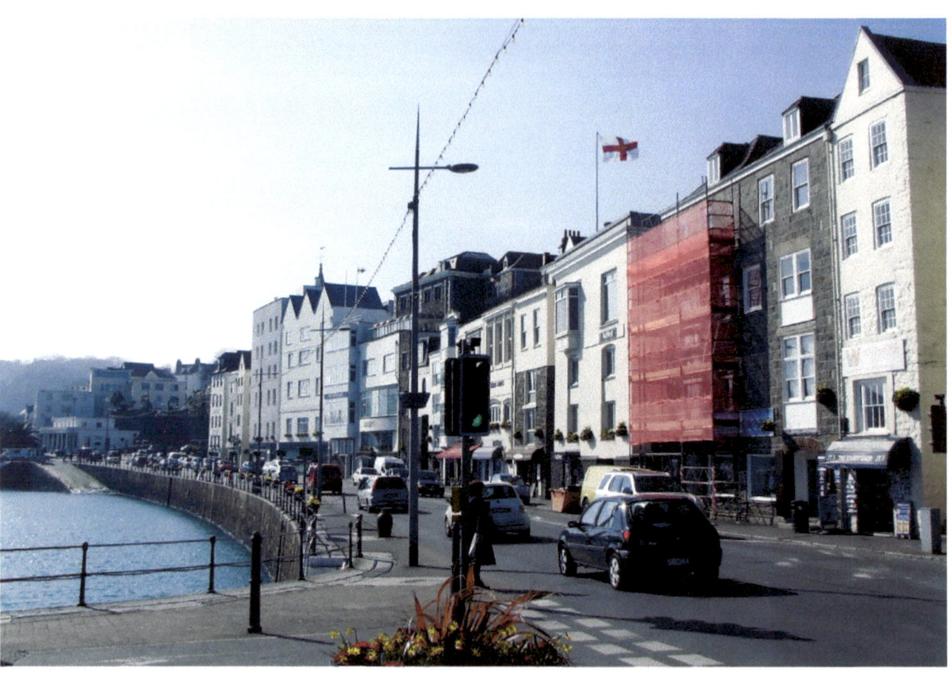

## Careening Hard

The Careening Hard at the Victoria Pier was constructed in 1870, not long before this photograph was taken. It began life as a patent slipway in which boats could enter shallow cradles in the water and then be hauled up the slip by a winch. The patent slip went into disuse in 1921, and a simple careening beach was left in its place. The boat on the Careening Hard today is the *Sark Belle*, purchased by the Sark Shipping Company in 2011 to carry visitors to Sark from April to October.

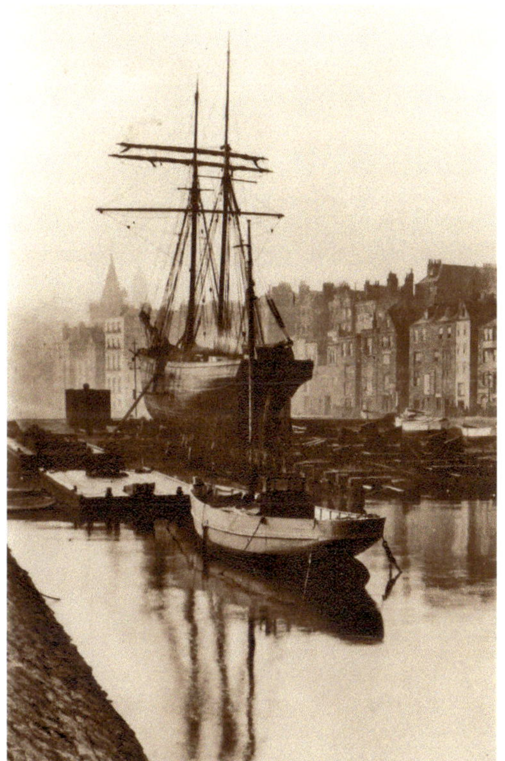

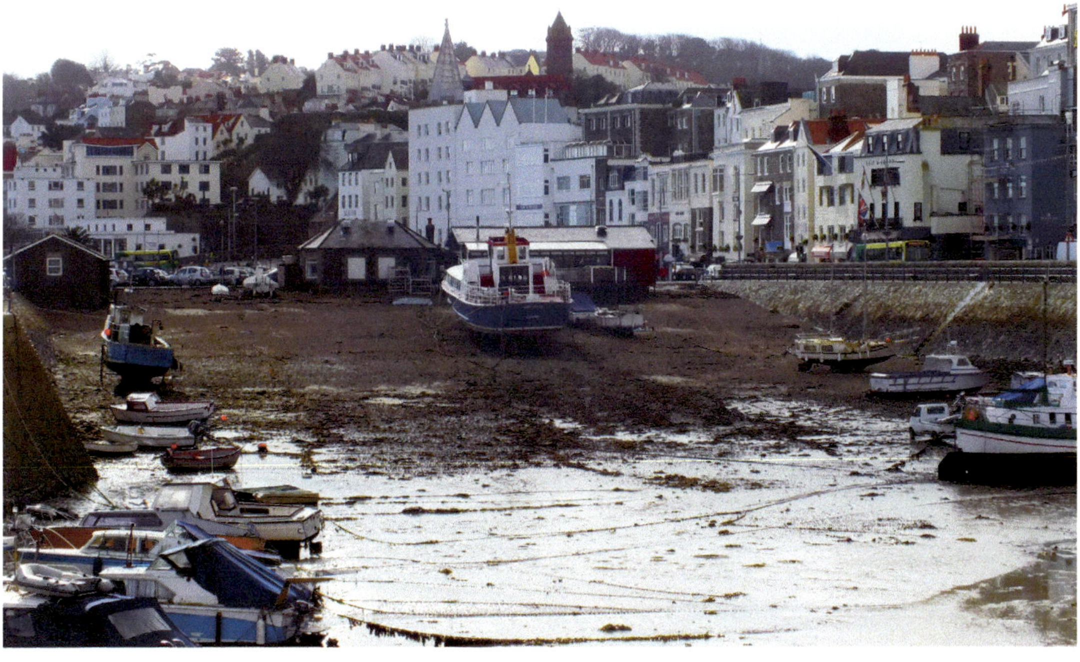

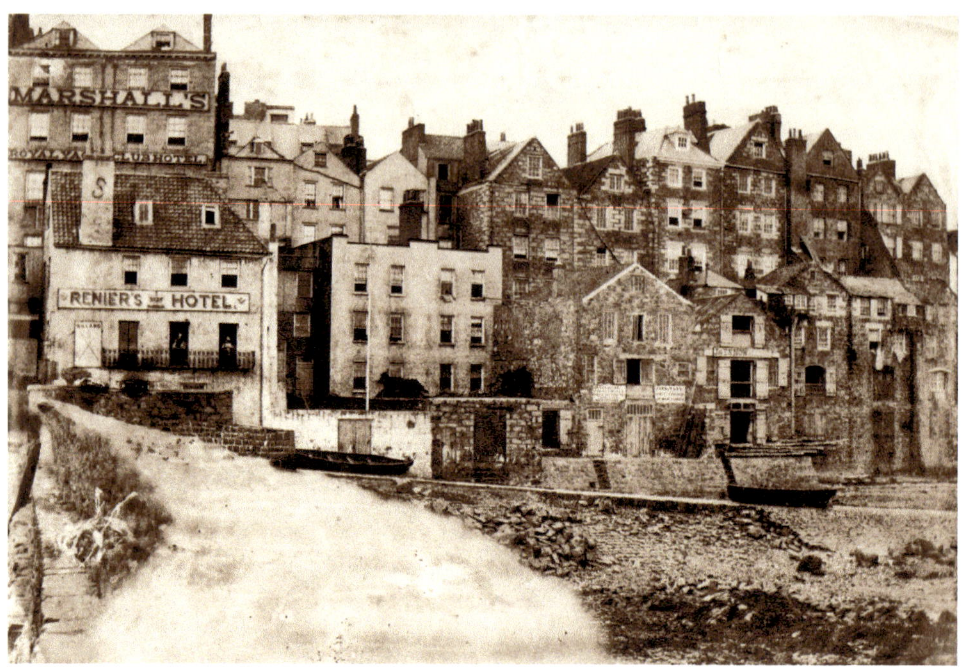

## The Beach Behind Pollet Street

An extremely rare photograph from the 1850s shows the buildings on what is now the North Quay, with their distinctive warehouse doors, ready to receive goods directly from the ships. In the foreground is the old North Pier of the harbour, which was rebuilt in the 1850s. A proper quay was built behind the Pollet Street buildings, and the beach behind became the Careening Hard. The ghost of the old buildings can be seen today, although the view is obscured by a modern restaurant built on the pier, and the ubiquitous cars.

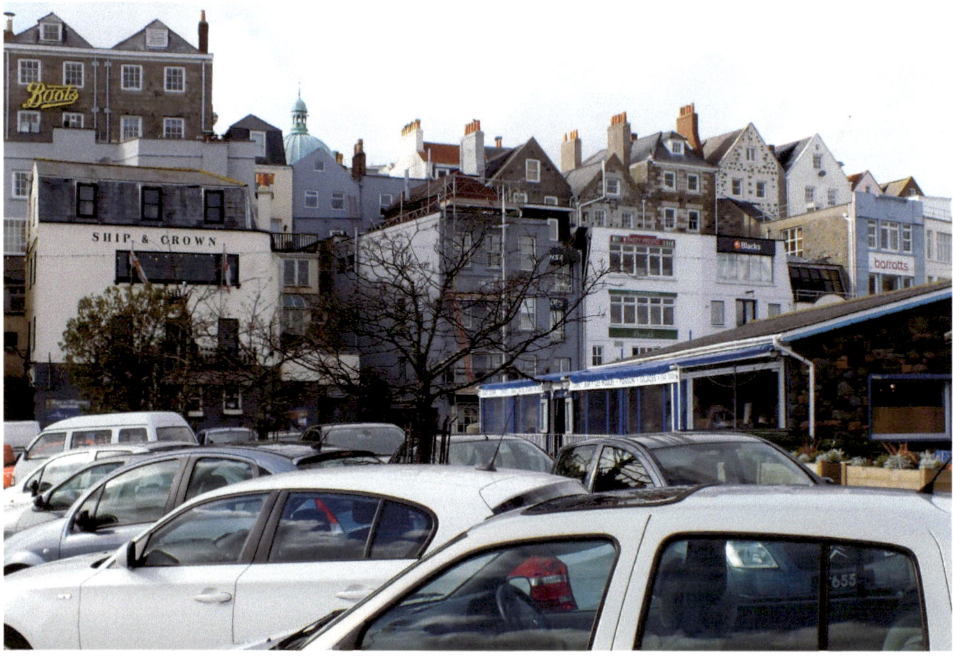

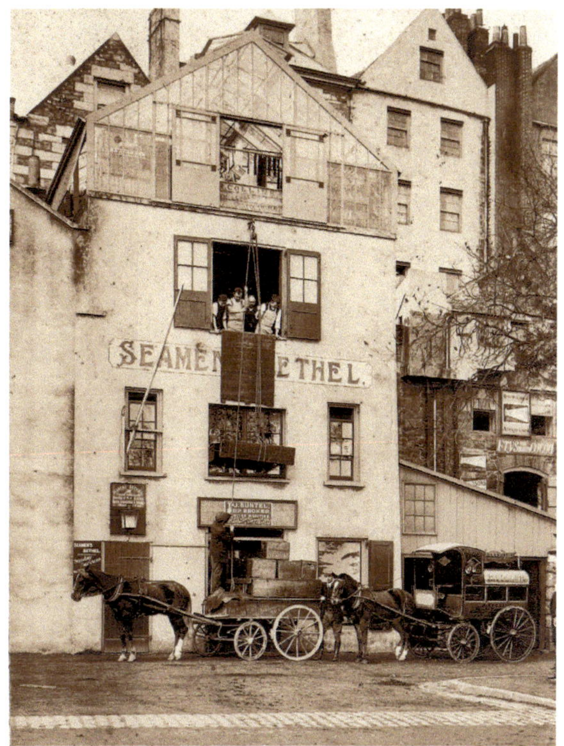

## A Delivery to Collins Sweet Shop

A more detailed look at the back of one of the old houses that fronts Pollet Street in 1890. A delivery of sugar is winched up to Mr R. Collins' sweet factory. The shop opened in 1879 and remained a family business for three generations, closing in the early 1970s. The company were renowned for their 'Guernsey Sweets', a curious confection containing cloves and cinnamon. Today, the building houses a number of different businesses.

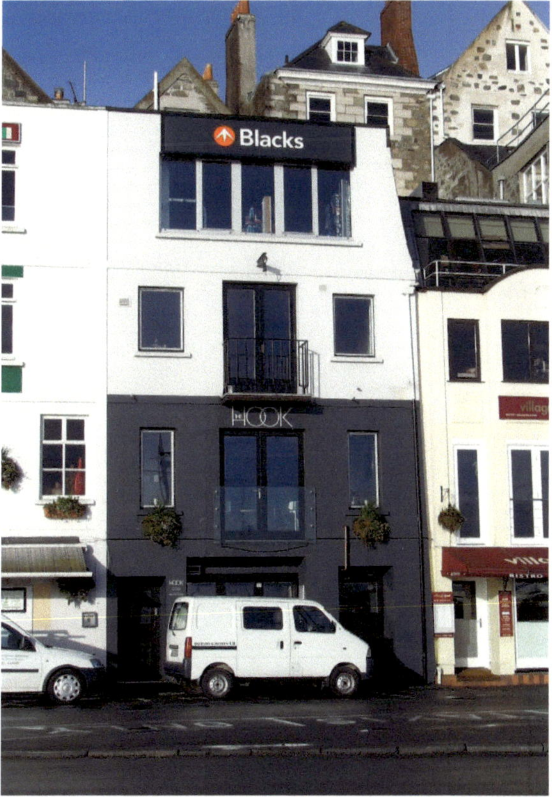

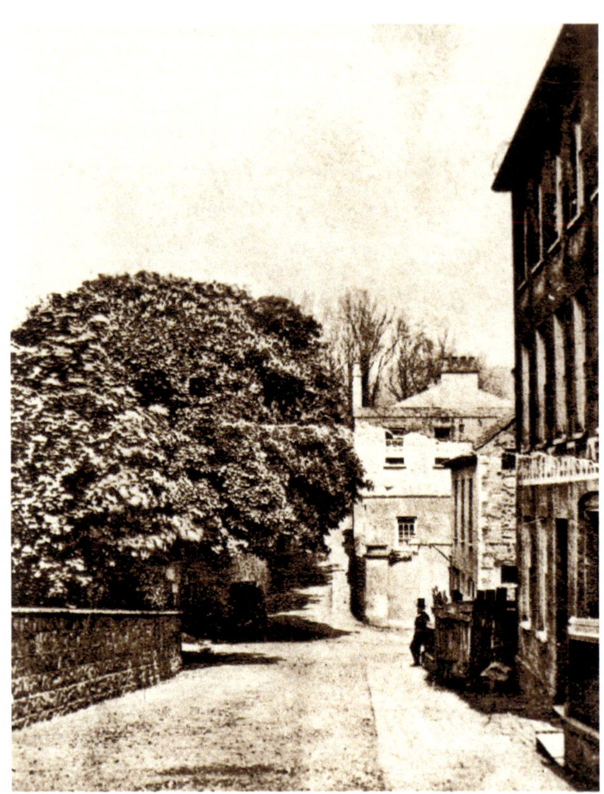

### College Street

College Street was created in the early nineteenth century and linked the thoroughfare of the Grange to the narrow routes of Le Profond Rue and La Chasse Vassal (now Candie Road and St Ann's Place). Today, the only part of the road that remains entirely recognisable is the low granite wall on the left, which marks the eastern boundary of Elizabeth College. In the 1870s, the house at the end of College Street, known as the Old Court House, was demolished to make way for St Julian's Avenue, thus changing the character of this part of town entirely.

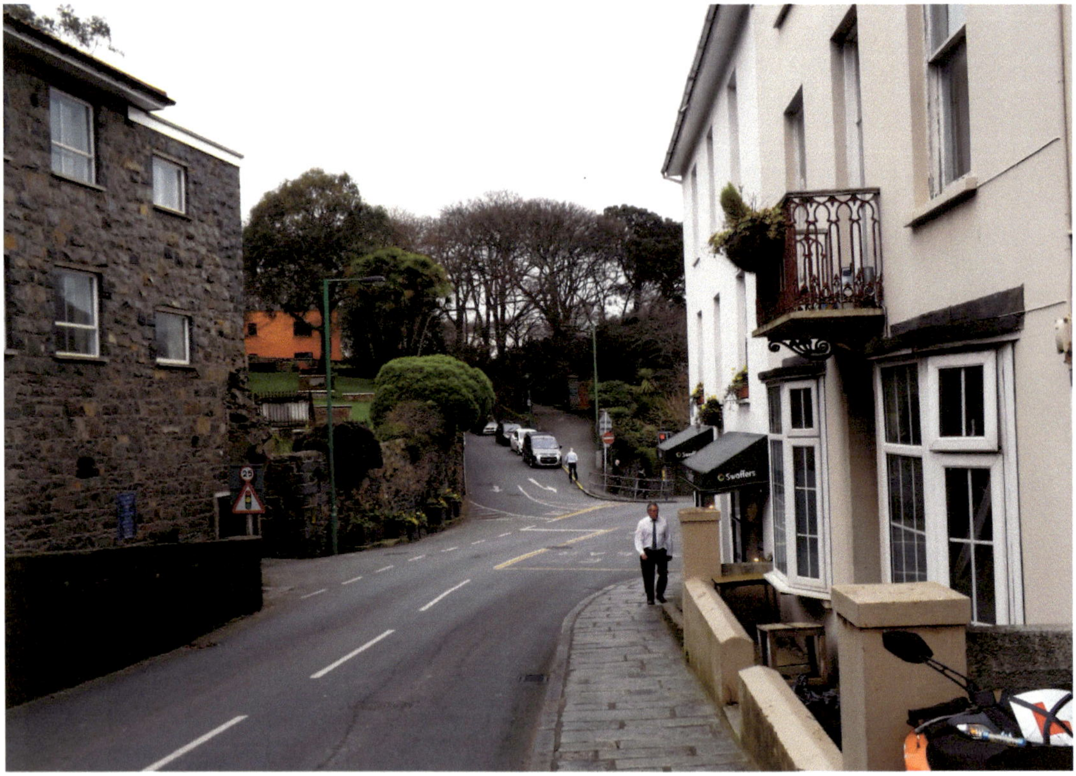

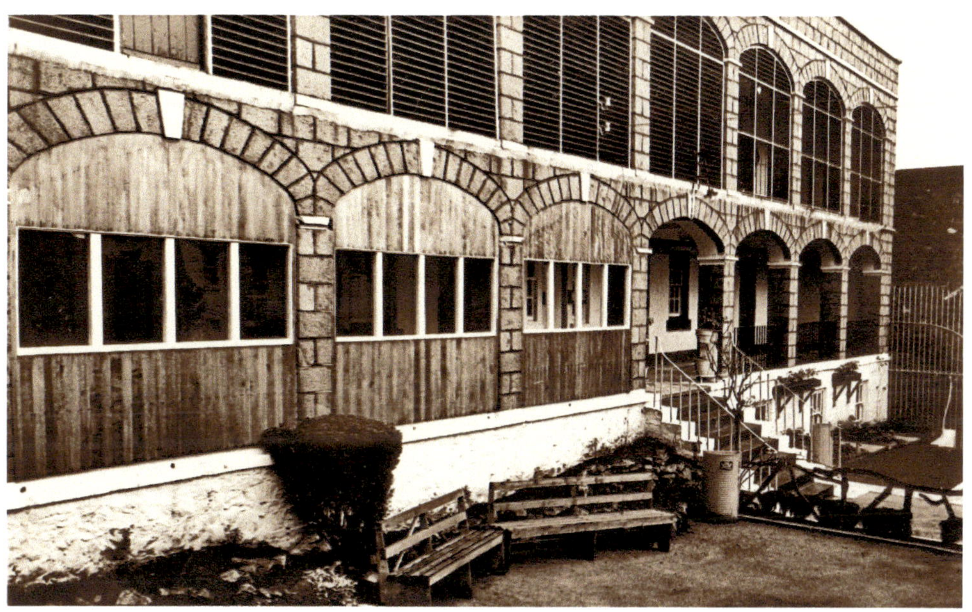

## The Town Prison

Built in 1811 at a cost of £11,000, this interesting building, although not seen by the majority of islanders behind its high wall in St James's Street, was considered to have architectural merit. It had certainly seen its share of history, including being the site of Guernsey's last execution in 1854. It was demolished to make way for a £17.5-million extension to the Royal Court. The new building used the granite from the 1811 building and reconstructed the arches inside the new Royal Court to great effect in 2005.

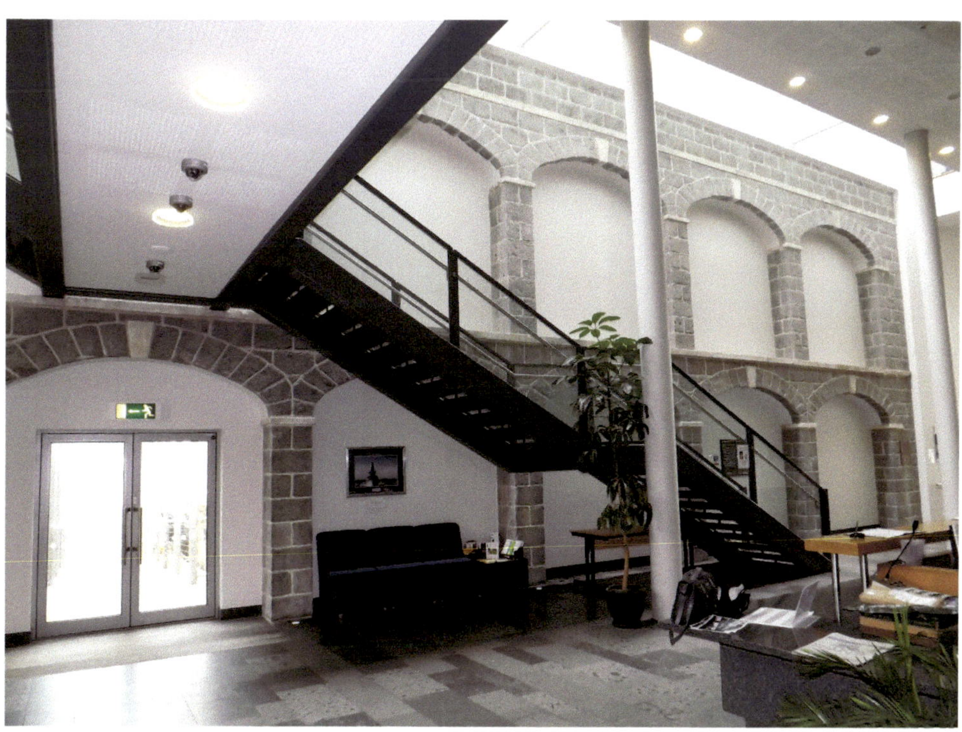

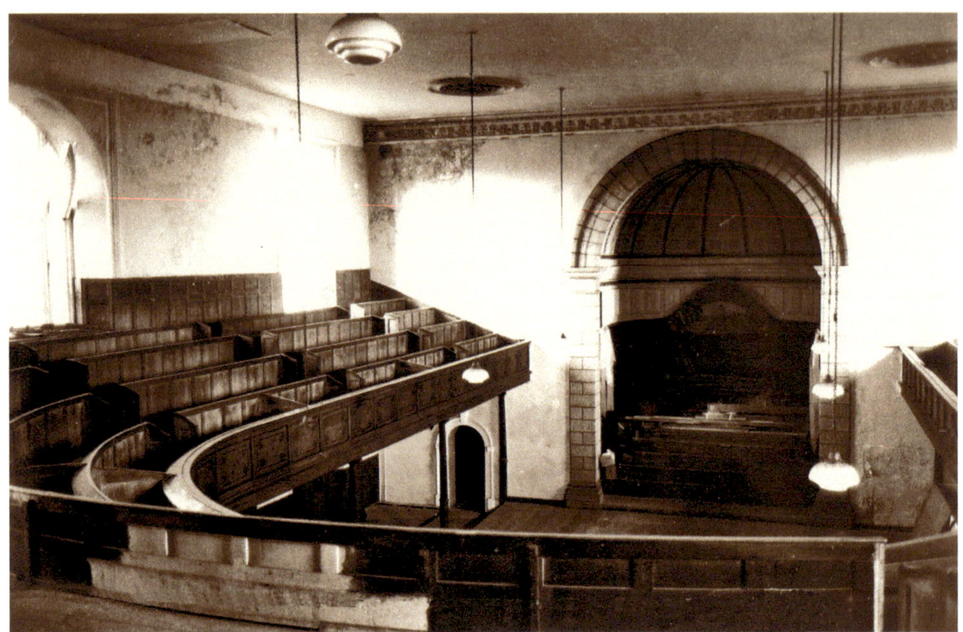

### Inside St James the Less

St James the Less is a beautiful neo-classical church built in 1818 and designed by John Wilson, architect of many iconic Guernsey buildings. Built to hold Anglican services in English instead of French, primarily for the English garrisoned soldiers on the island, it thrived as a church for over a century. By the 1970s, it had fallen into such disrepair that it was threatened with demolition. The Friends of St James Association was formed in 1981 to raise funds to rescue and restore the church, and today it is a successful concert and assembly hall.

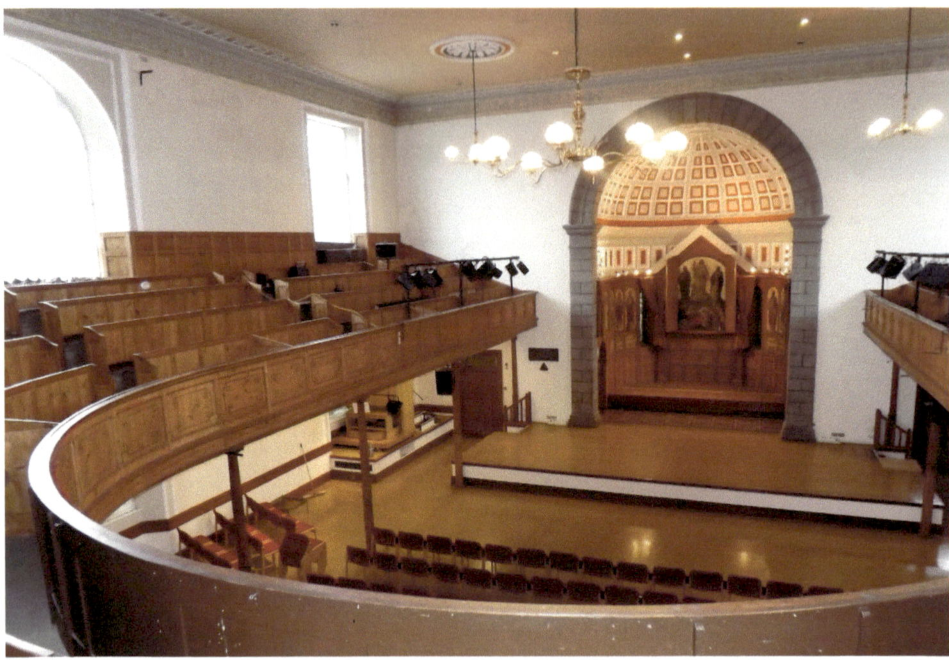

## Victoria Tower

The visit of Queen Victoria to the island in August 1846 was a significant event and, to commemorate it, the tower was commissioned at a cost of £2,000, paid for by public subscription. The architect was William Bunn Colling, an associate of George Gilbert Scott, and Victoria Tower is probably his most important work. Built on the site of a windmill, it is visible from nearly every part of St Peter Port, but most particularly, and pleasingly, from the sea. To climb up the tower today, the key must first be obtained from the Guernsey Museum.

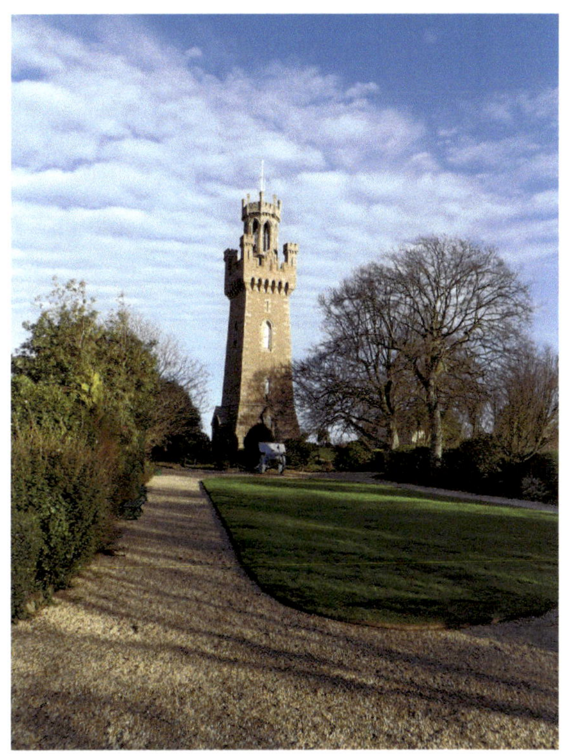

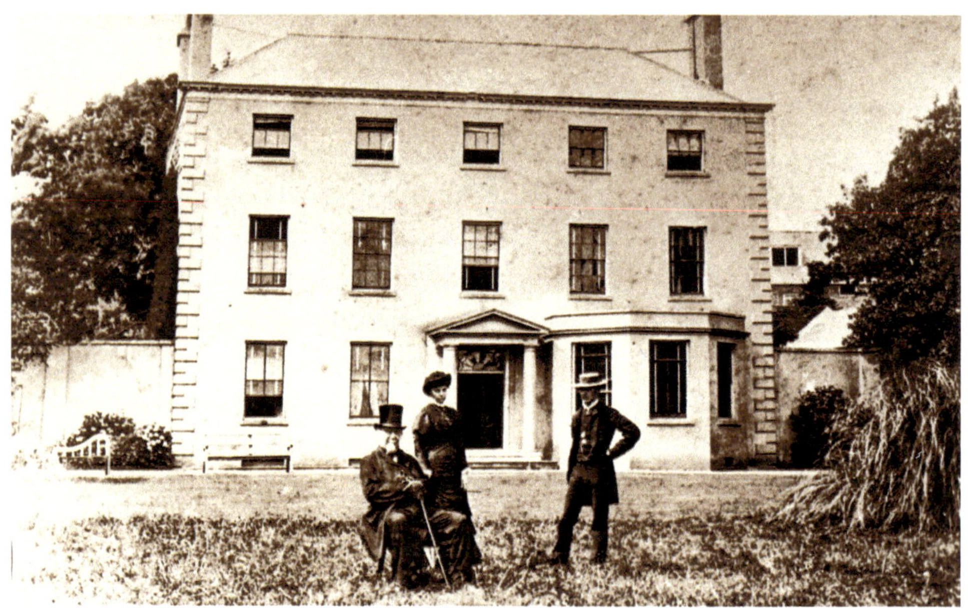

## The Priaulx Library – Candie House

Perched on a hill above St Peter Port, Candie House, built in the 1780s, commands marvellous views over the harbour and other islands. In the 1830s, it was bought by Osmond de Beauvoir Priaulx, who rented the house to the Bailiff of Guernsey, Sir Peter Stafford Carey, pictured on the lawn with his family. Osmond gave the house to the States of Guernsey, along with his vast book collection. After Sir Peter's death in 1886, Candie was converted to Guernsey's first free library in 1889. The library, pictured with members of staff, specialises in local studies.

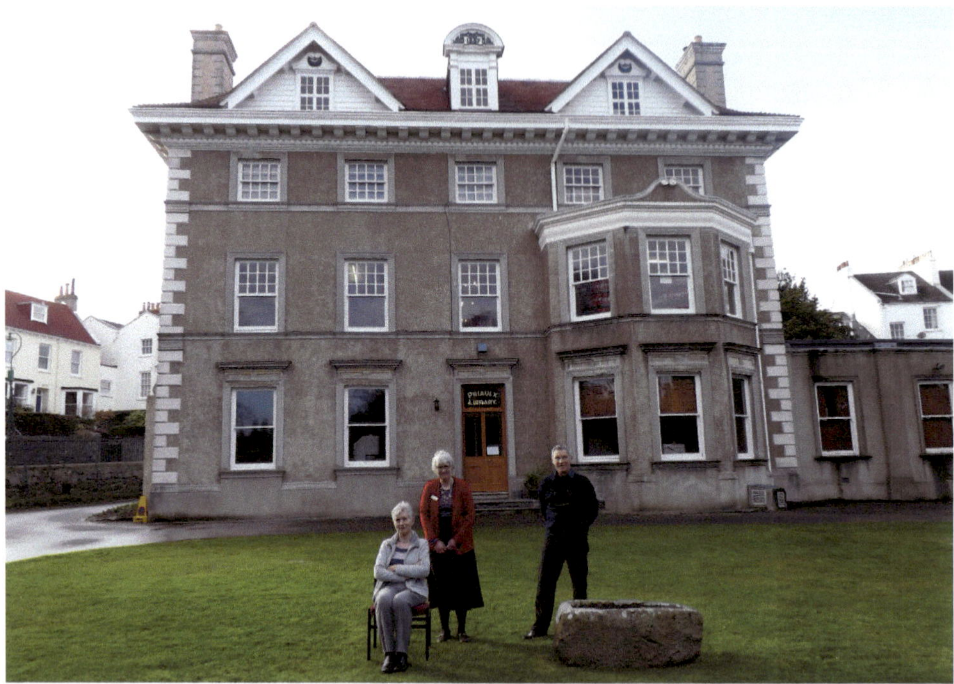

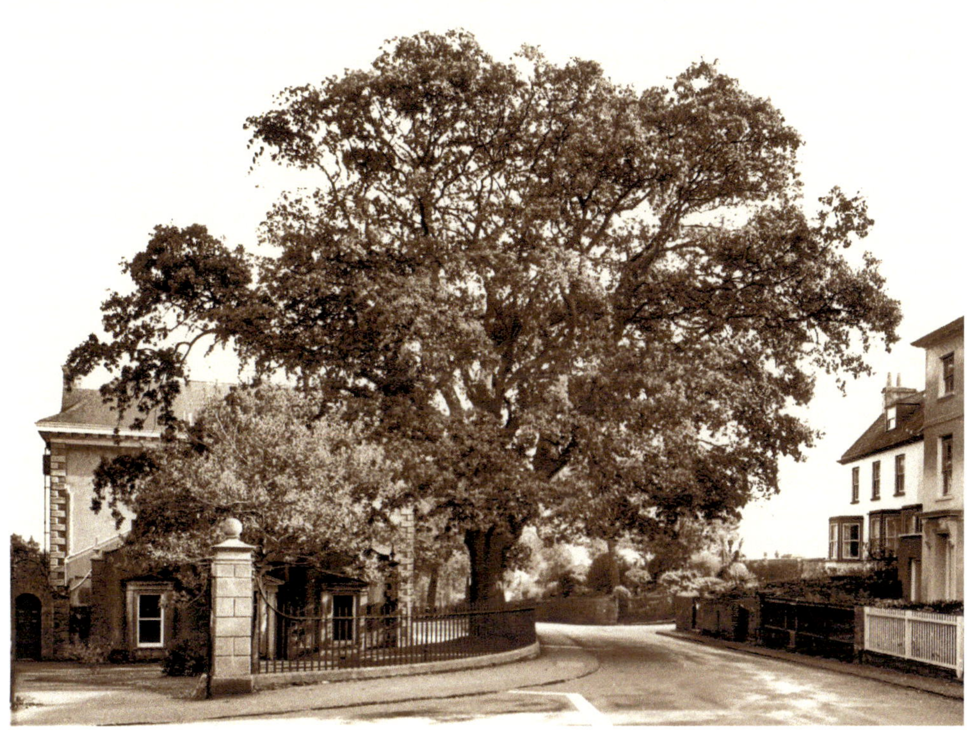

### The Priaulx Library Oak Tree

A magnificent Turkey oak dominates the photograph of the back of the Priaulx Library. It was thought to be at least 150 years old, but unfortunately, in 2007, it was found to be riddled with honey fungus and was condemned. It was replaced by another Turkey oak, planted by the bailiff, Sir Geoffrey Rowland, in November 2007, but the new tree has many years of growing before it will rival its predecessor in size.

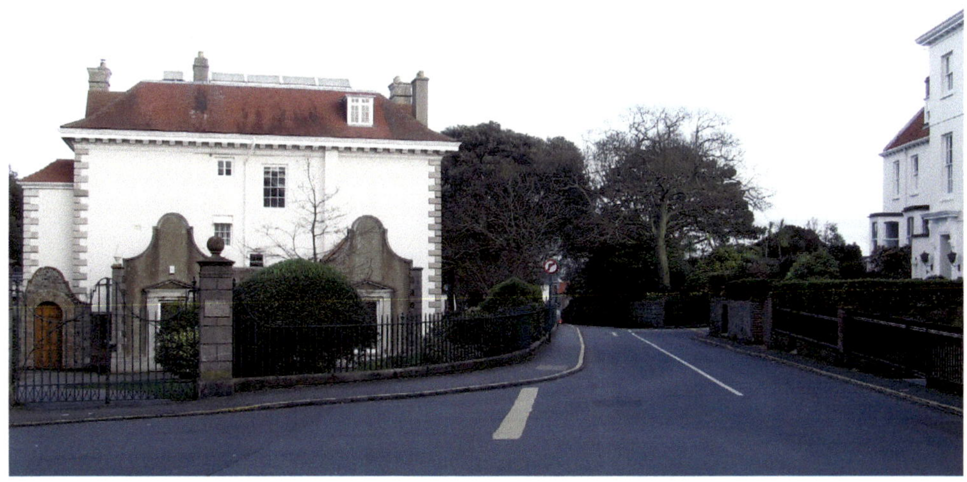

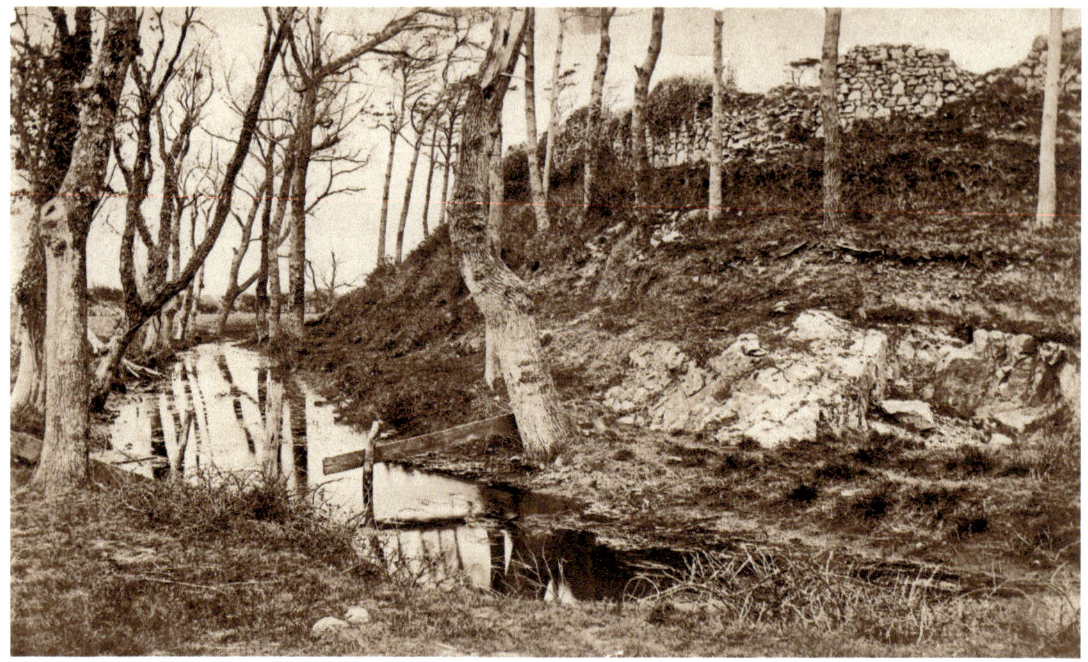

### Le Chateau des Marais

On the northern boundary of St Peter Port, tucked away down a lane in one of the most densely populated parts of the island, is a hidden treasure – a moated medieval castle. It is known that a castle existed on the spot as early as the twelfth century but, as a fortification, it was of minor importance once Castle Cornet was built in the thirteenth century. The castle was refortified in the Napoleonic era. Today, little can be seen of the walls from the outside as it lives up to its more popular local name of 'Ivy Castle'.

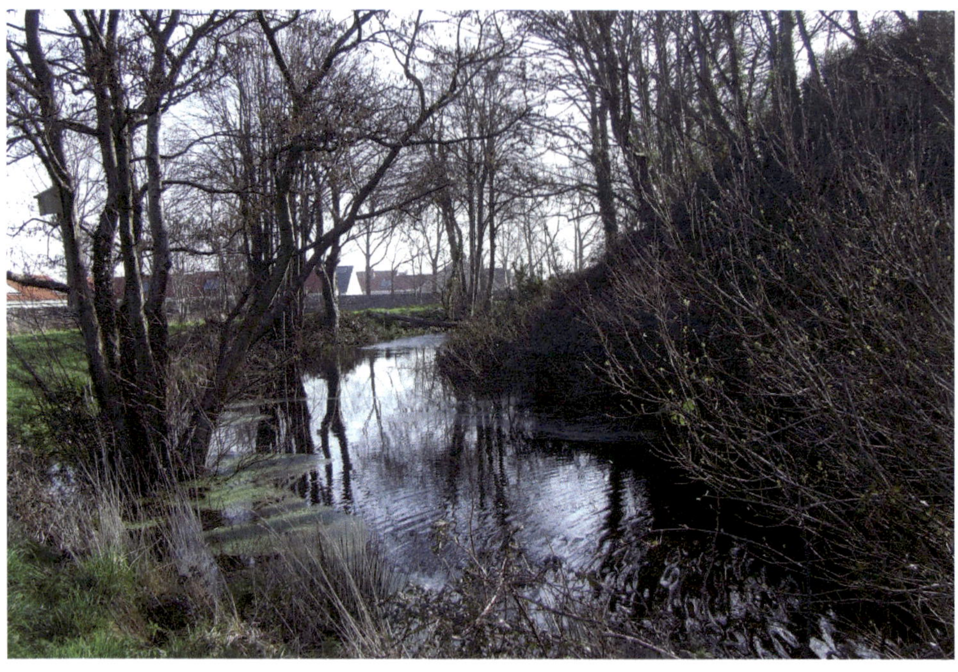

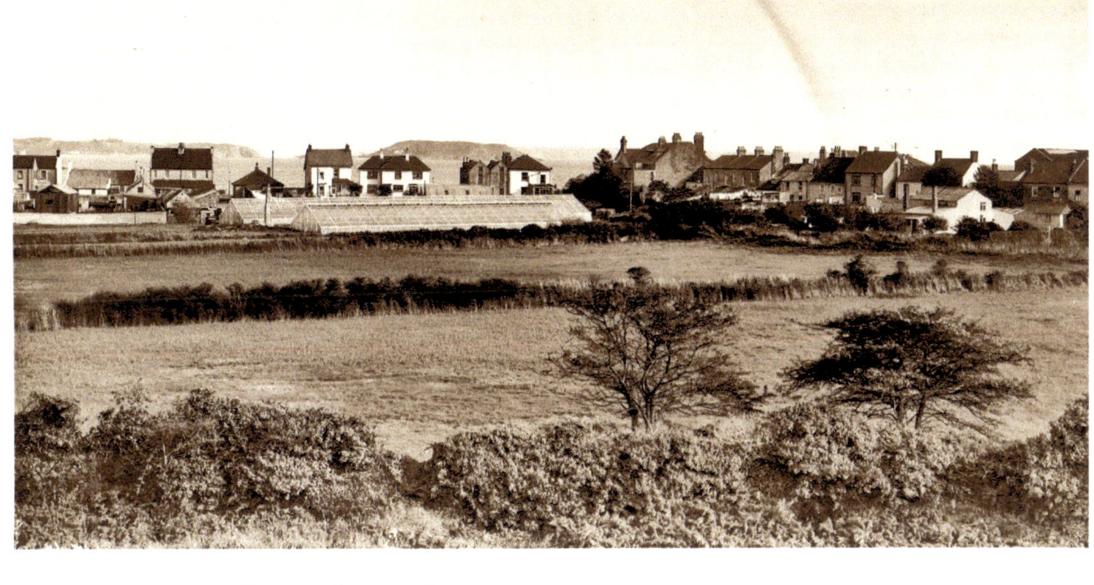

### View from Le Chateau des Marais

The view east towards the sea from the highest point of the inner bailey of Chateau des Marais in the 1960s shows that the hillock the castle is built upon is really very small; the few houses along the coast road almost block the sea from view. The building development in the intervening years has hidden the sea altogether. However, the lush grass of the encircling water meadow between the outer walls and the moat shows what a pleasant spot the 'Ivy Castle' is, even among the sprawl of modern development.

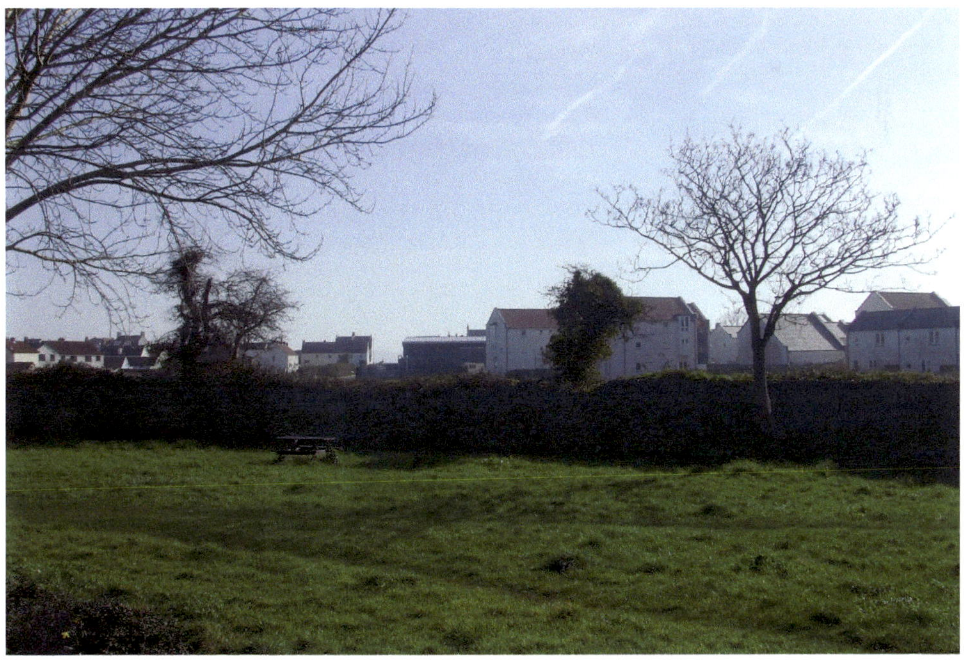

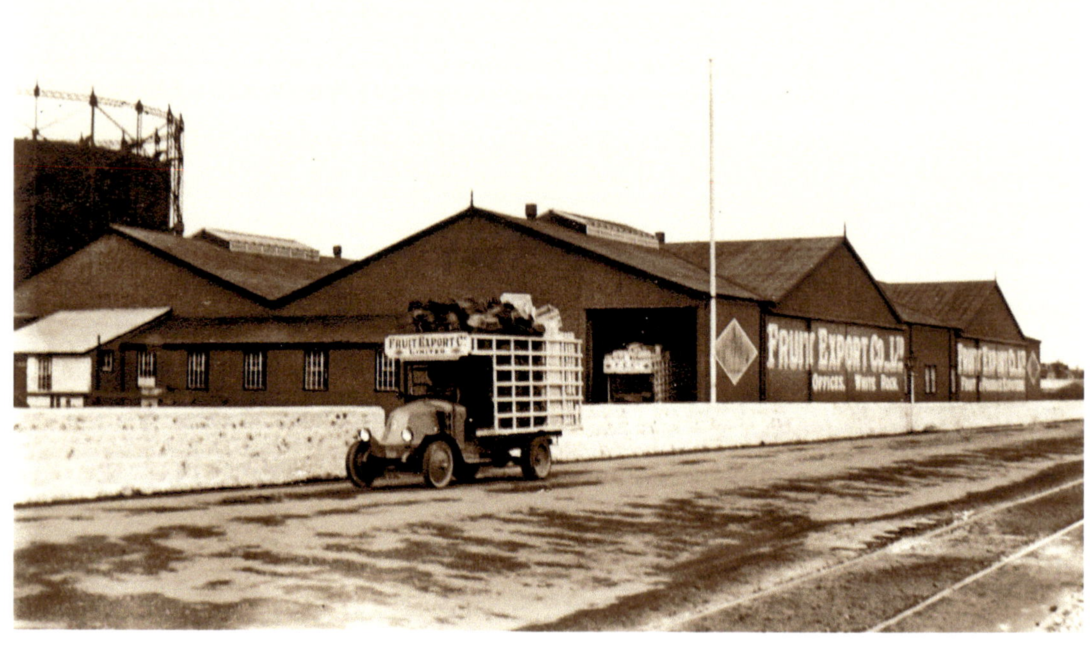


### Fruit Export Ltd, Les Banques

Fruit Export was founded in 1904 as a partnership of fruit commission agents and growers. For the next century, it was at the forefront of Guernsey's horticultural heyday, exporting tomatoes and other produce to the UK and around the world. Their warehouse at Les Banques in St Peter Port was a familiar – although not particularly beautiful – sight. Adapting to the times, the company moved out of St Peter Port and the warehouse was demolished; this rather handsome development of apartments took its place, with fine views over the other islands.

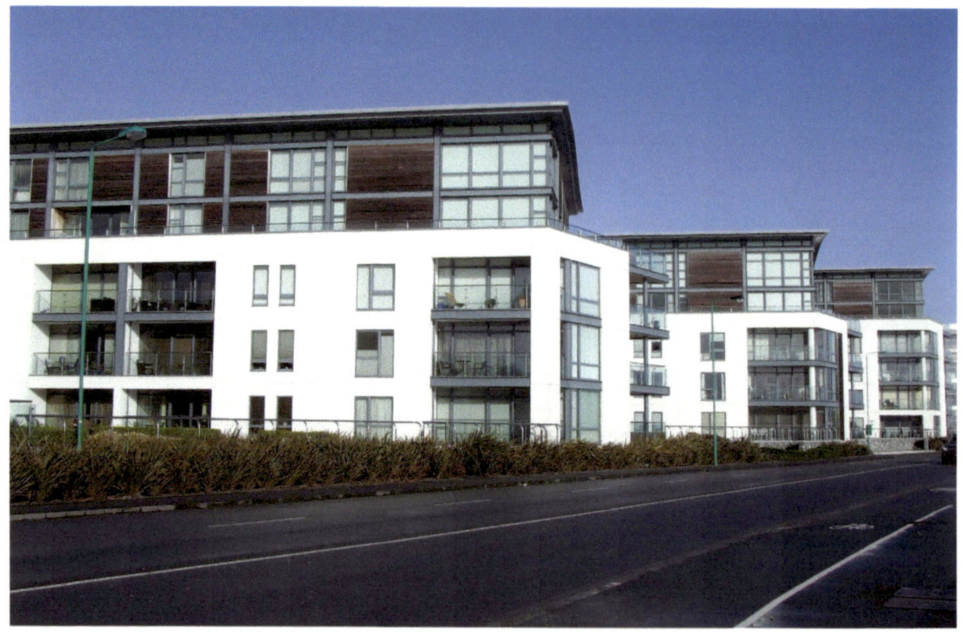

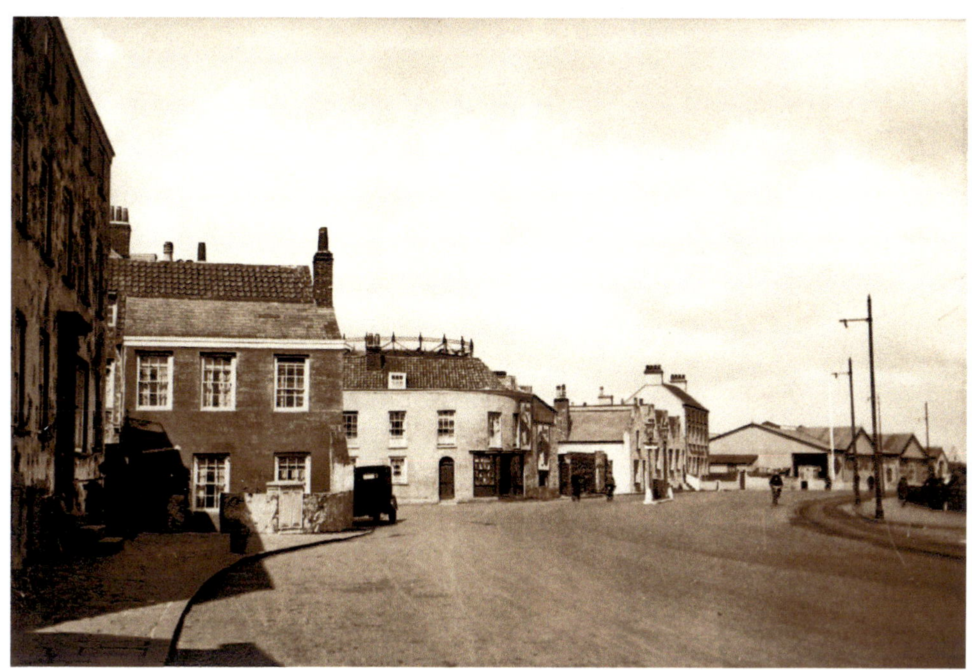

## Longstore, St Peter Port

The Longstore, an area along St Peter Port's east coast that links St George's Esplanade to Les Banques, has always been a bustling area, although it looks rather sleepy in this 1925 photograph. The overhead electricity of the tramline that ran from St Peter Port to St Sampson's can clearly be seen on the right, but the trams are now long gone. The land beyond the pretty, Dutch-fronted cottages has now made way for the ambitious Admiral Park development.

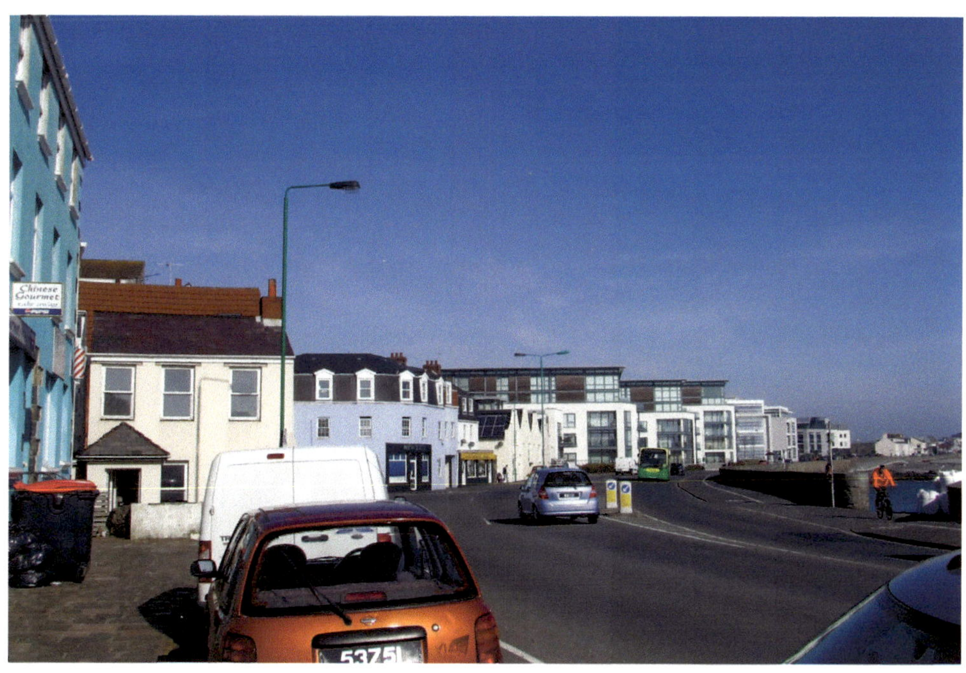

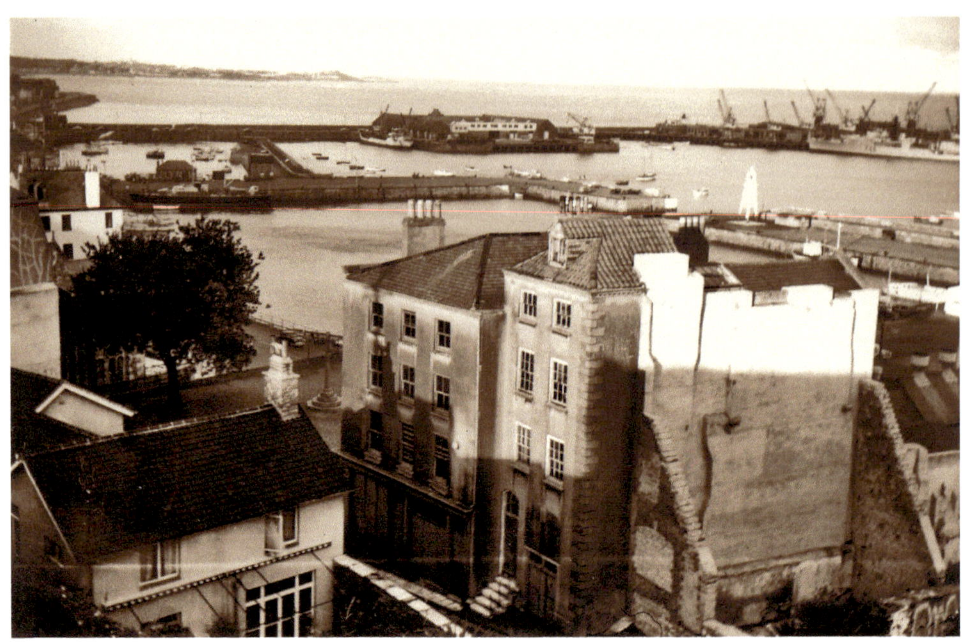

## The Harbour from the Mignot Plateau

The Mignot Plateau can be reached by walking up Cornet Street and the view from the top shows how quickly and steeply the land rises out of St Peter Port. The tranquillity of the inner harbour is in contrast to the proliferation of pontoons and pleasure craft today in the Victoria Marina, and the Elizabeth Marina beyond the Cambridge Berth. The commercial area of the harbour, however, with the cranes ready to lift goods on and off the Lift-on/Lift-off ramps, has changed little over the years.

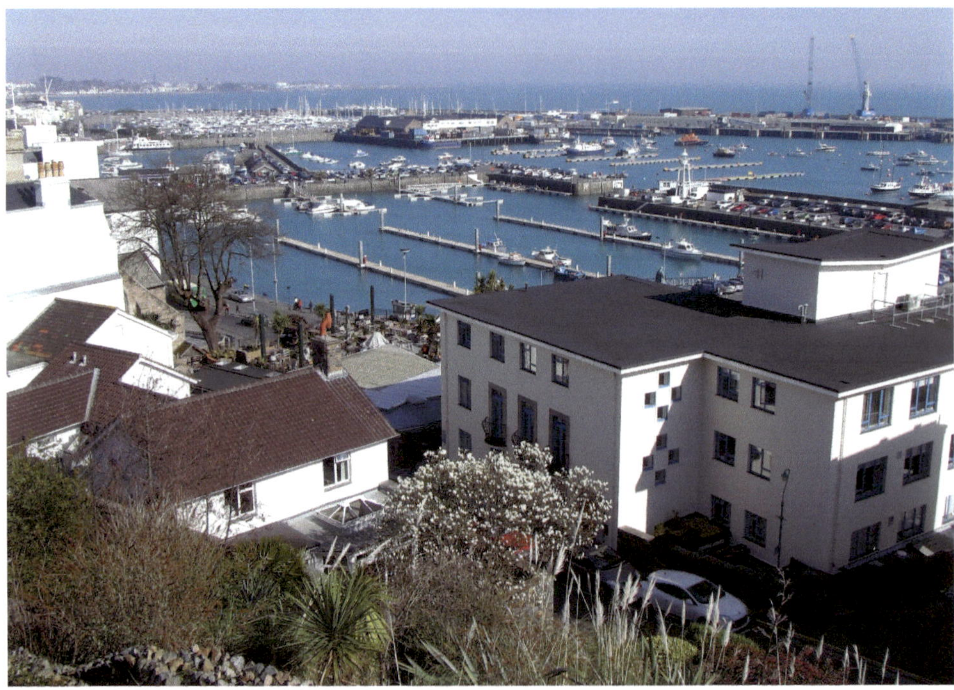

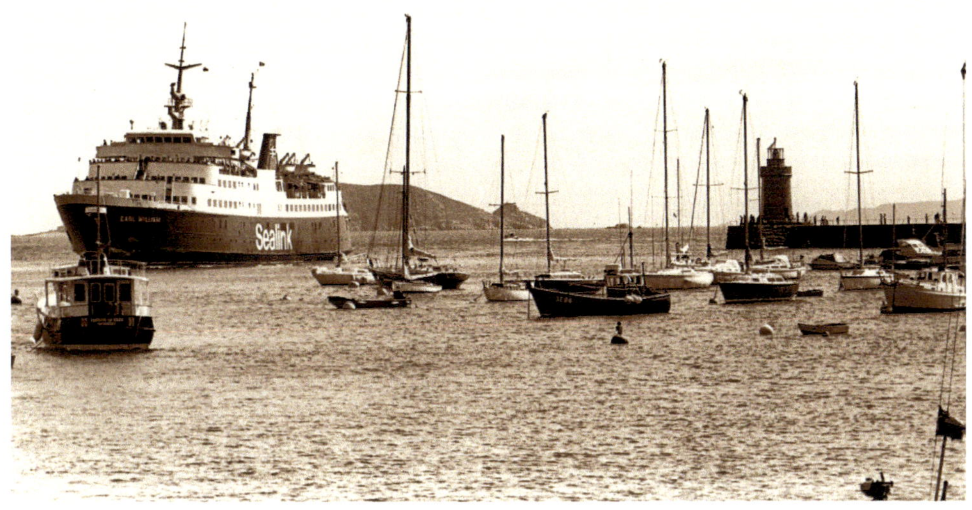

## Passenger Ferry Arriving, St Peter Port Harbour

The Guernsey economy depends heavily on the boats that carry freight and passengers between the islands and the UK or France. Over the years, many different companies have come and gone, but the scene remains the same. Forty years ago, it was Sealink that ferried back and forth. Here, the *Earl William*, built in 1964, carries holidaymakers into St Peter Port. Today, the route to Portsmouth is sailed by the *Commodore Clipper*, the conventional ferry run by Condor Ferries, who began the first high-speed ferry link to the Channel Islands in 1993.

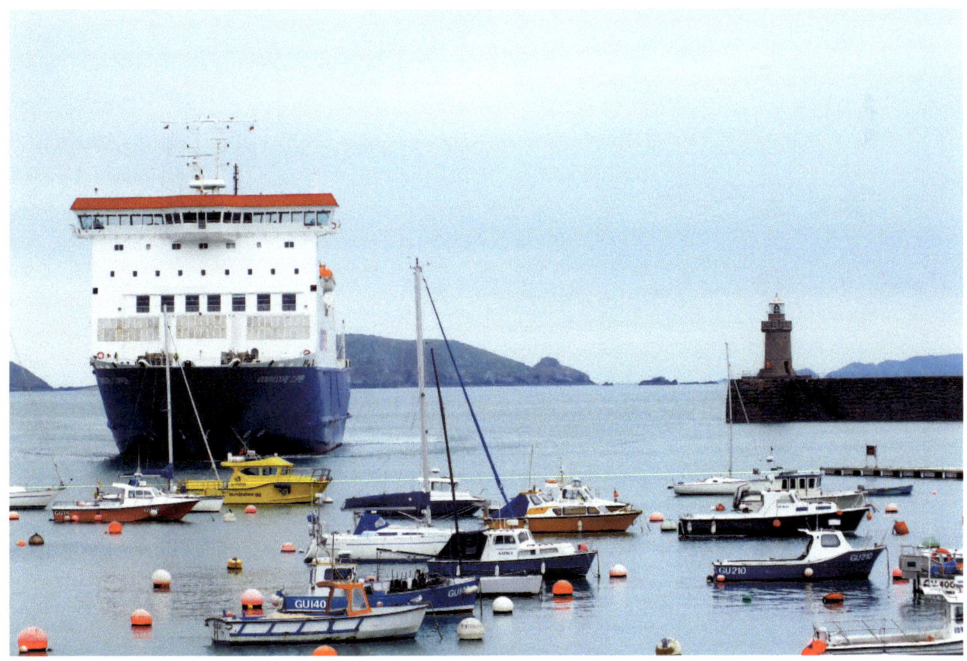

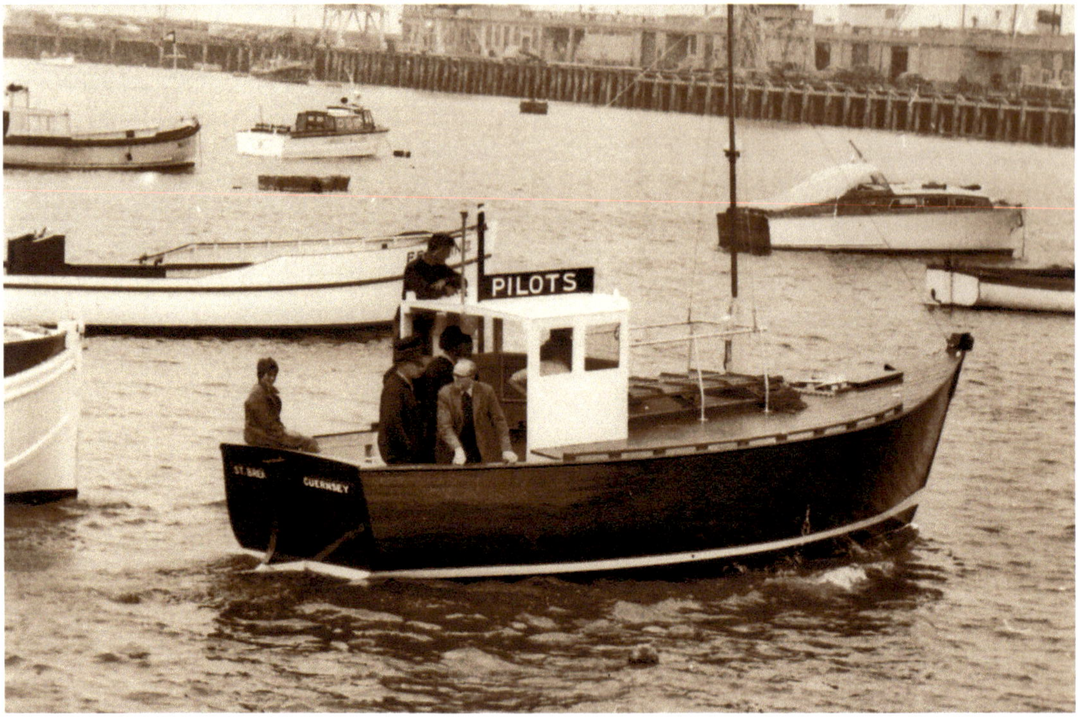

### St Peter Port Pilot Boat

Pilotage is a skilled operation and, in the maritime community of Guernsey, one that is prized, and has been for many centuries. Between the 1960s and the present day, the design of the pilot boats may have changed a little, but the skills remain the same. Today, there are six general pilots who work out of St Peter Port and St Sampson's Harbour, providing a twenty-four-hour service.

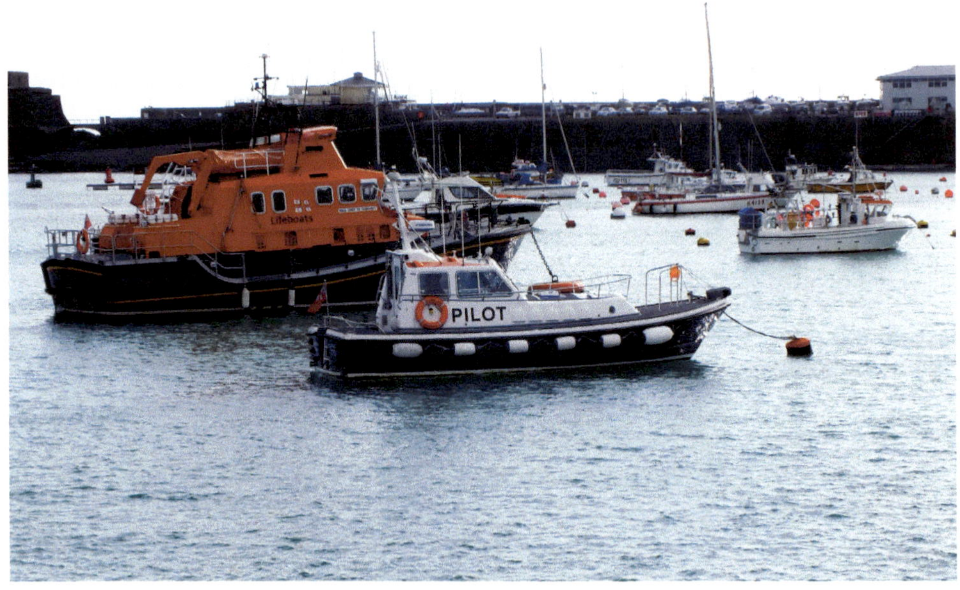

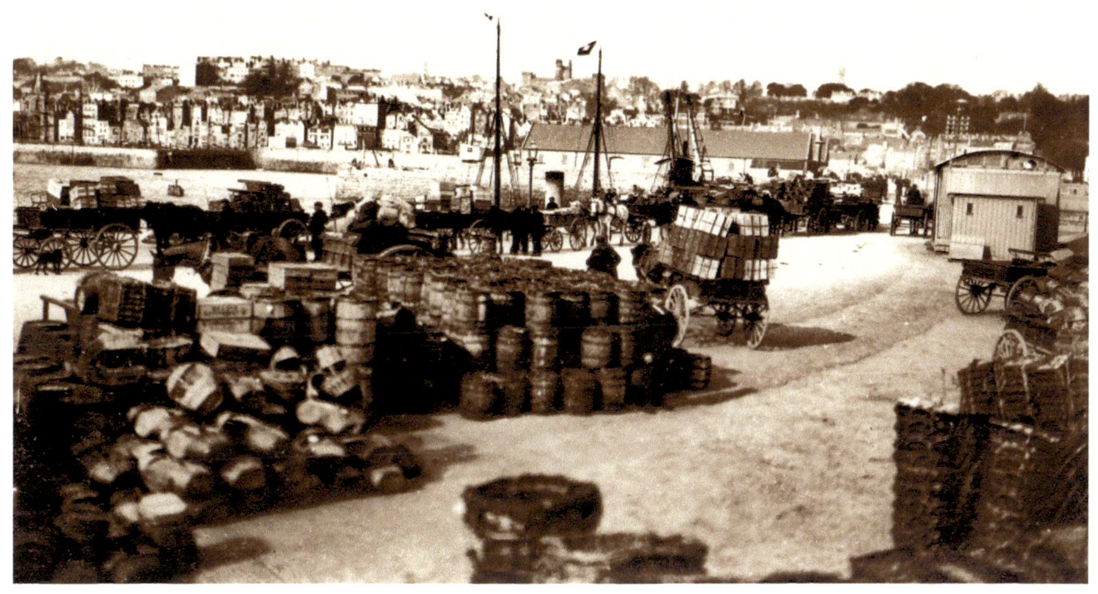

## The White Rock and Cambridge Berth

In the 1920s, Guernsey's biggest industry was horticulture, and a large freight of tomatoes, flowers and fruit awaits loading at the White Rock pier. Tomatoes dominated; they were packed into wicker baskets, and around 22,000 tons were exported in 1925 alone. Since the 1980s, other industries have taken the place of the humble Guernsey Tom – finance being one of them. With the advent of Roll-on/Roll-off ramps at the harbour, the commercial operations have been squeezed into a smaller space. The White Rock and the Victorian Cambridge Berth are rather quieter today.

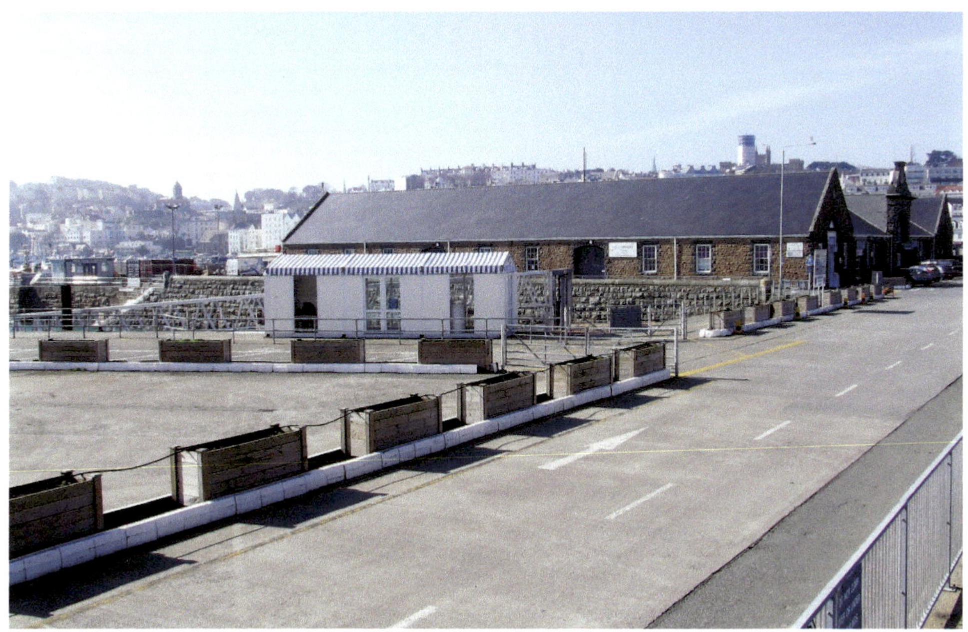

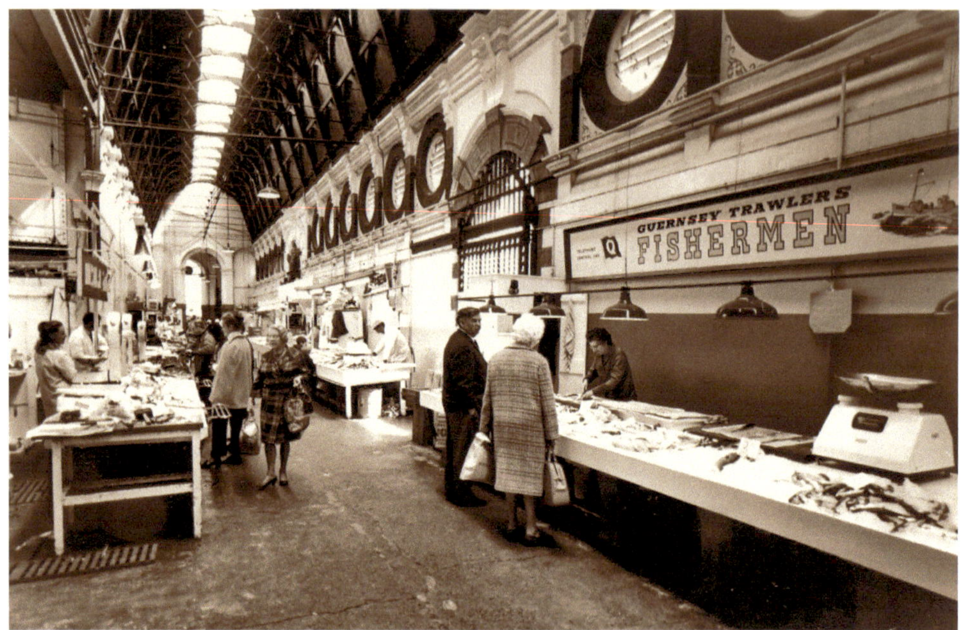

### Fresh from the Sea

Guernsey's 170 commercial fishing vessels catch about 1,500 tons of fish each year. Most of the catch is exported, with only a small fraction remaining on the island for the domestic market. It was a different picture two generations ago, when the fish market in St Peter Port was heaving with fishmongers selling the catch. Today, they are all gone, but Seafresh, an independent fishmonger situated a mere 200 metres from the Fish Quay, maintains the tradition. Here, Bernie Le Gallais shows off freshly cooked spider and 'cancre' crabs.

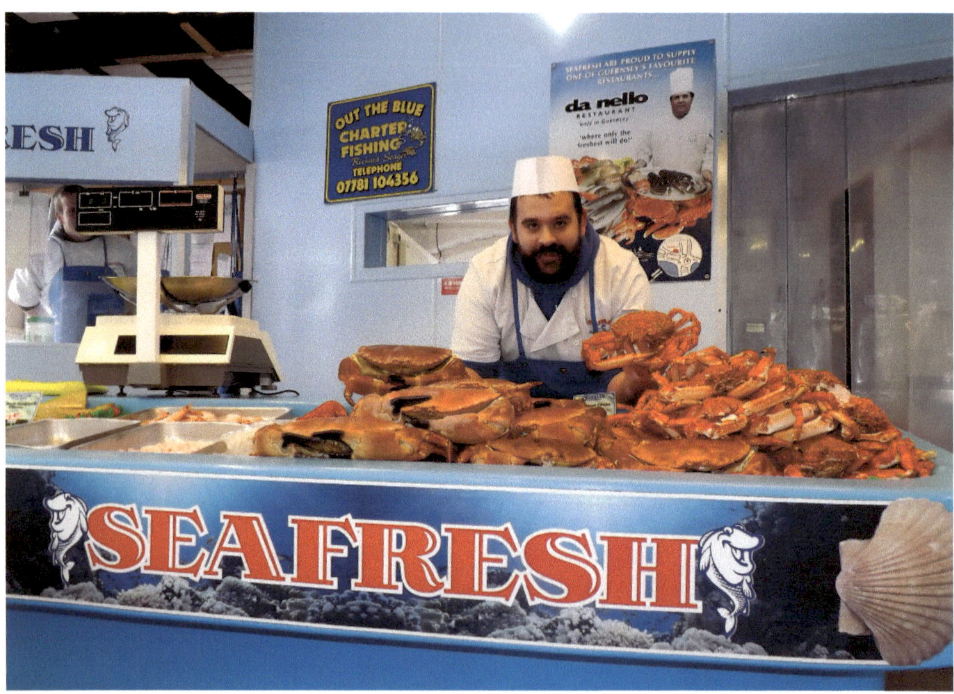

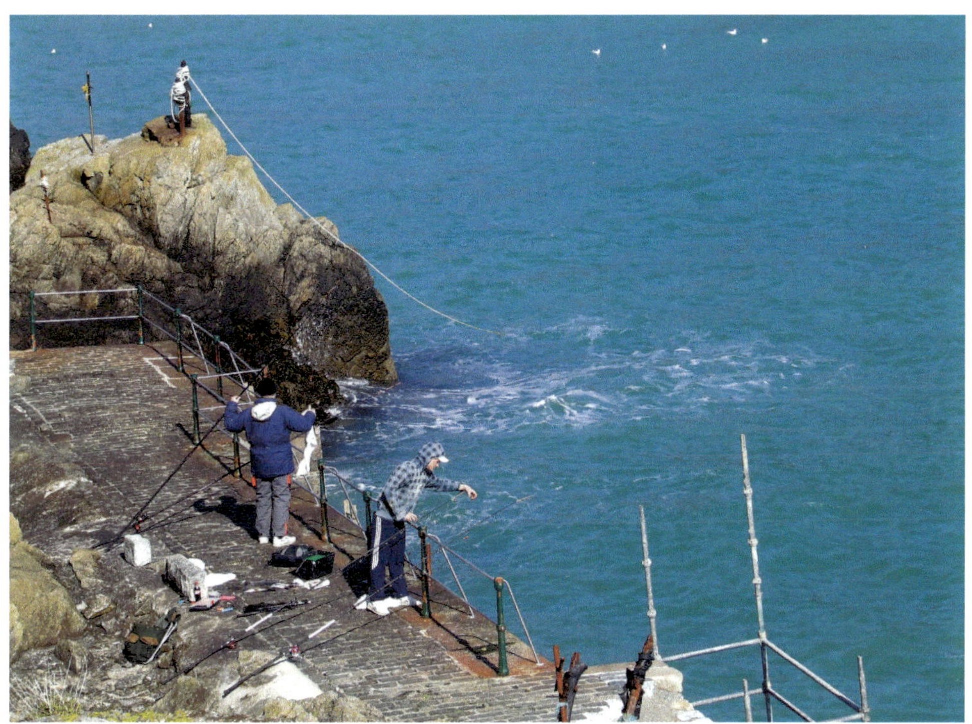

## Fishermen at Saints Harbour

Fishing is naturally a popular pursuit in Guernsey – the water is clean, the species varied and the views spectacular. A favourite spot is Saints Harbour, particularly on a sunny day, but in the nineteenth century, fishing was not quite as easy from this spot. Although Saints had a substantial number of commercial fishermen, they had few facilities and no quay, and it was not until 1909 that the parish paid £750 to build the small stone quay that can be seen today. Below, the fishermen scramble up the rocks to display their catch to the camera.

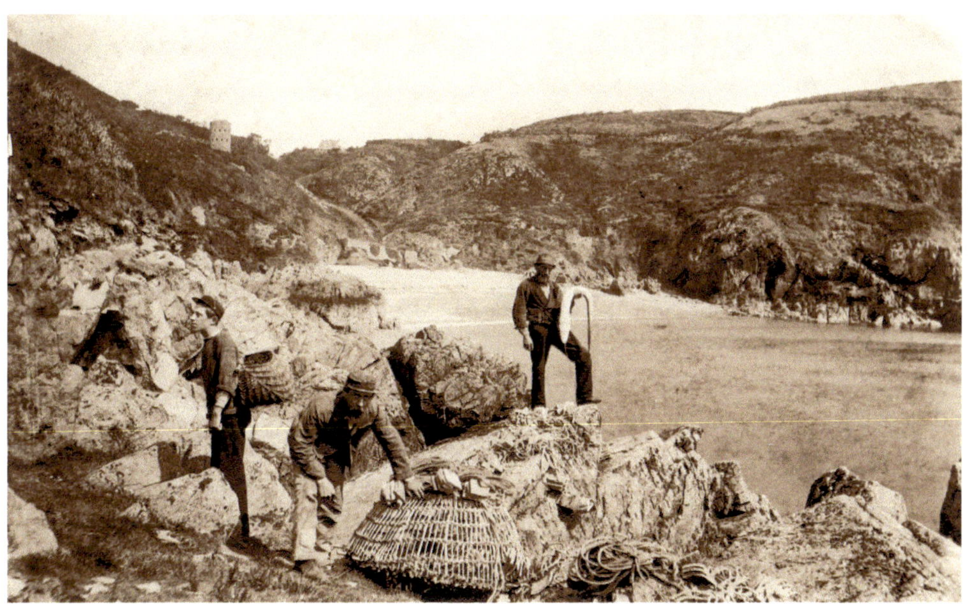

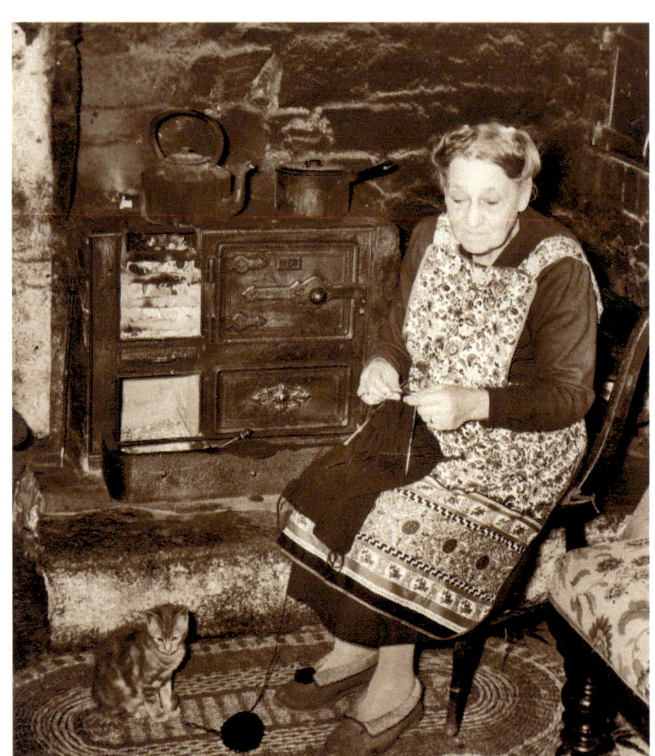



### Knitting a Guernsey

The traditional Guernsey is a design classic and has been knitted by hand for many generations. Originally worn by fishermen, it is knitted with worsted wool in fine stocking stitch, making it virtually weatherproof, and it has been supplied to both the RNLI and the Armed Forces. Today, at factory shop Le Tricoteur, the front, back and sleeves of the Guernsey are knitted on a six-gauge flatbed knitting machine. The shoulder seams, underarm gusset and the neckband are then finished by hand in the traditional method. Here, Jan from Le Tricoteur joins the front and back pieces of a Guernsey with a linking machine.

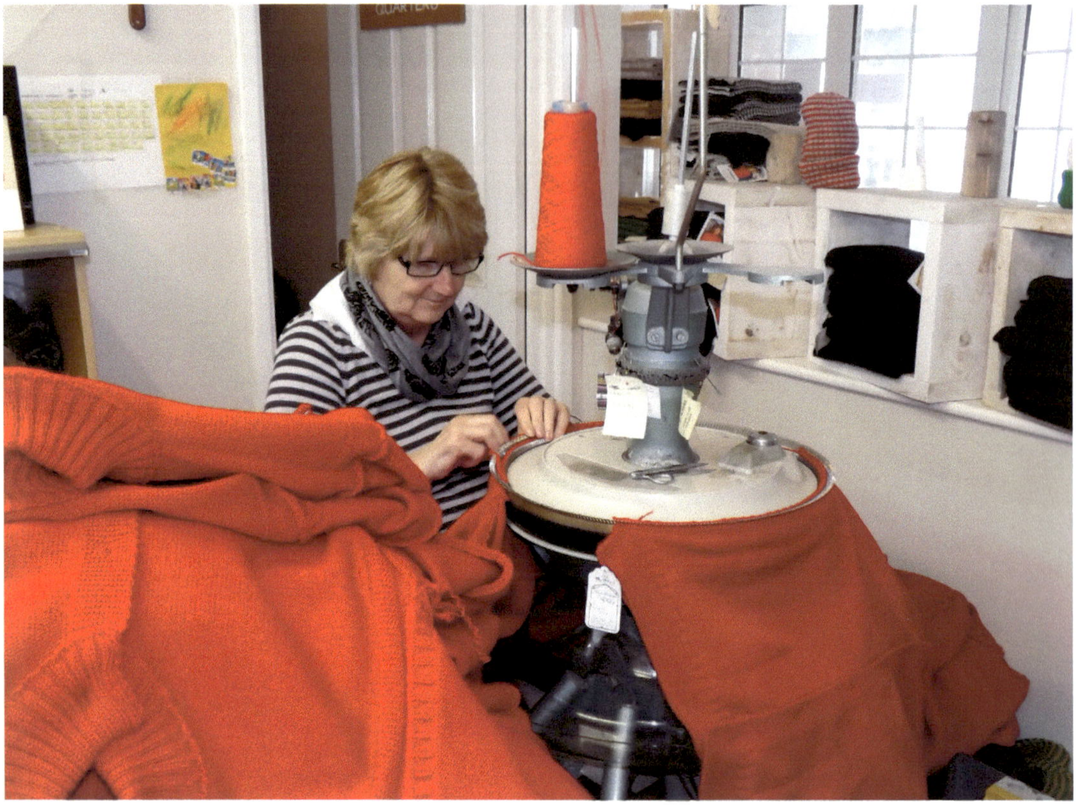

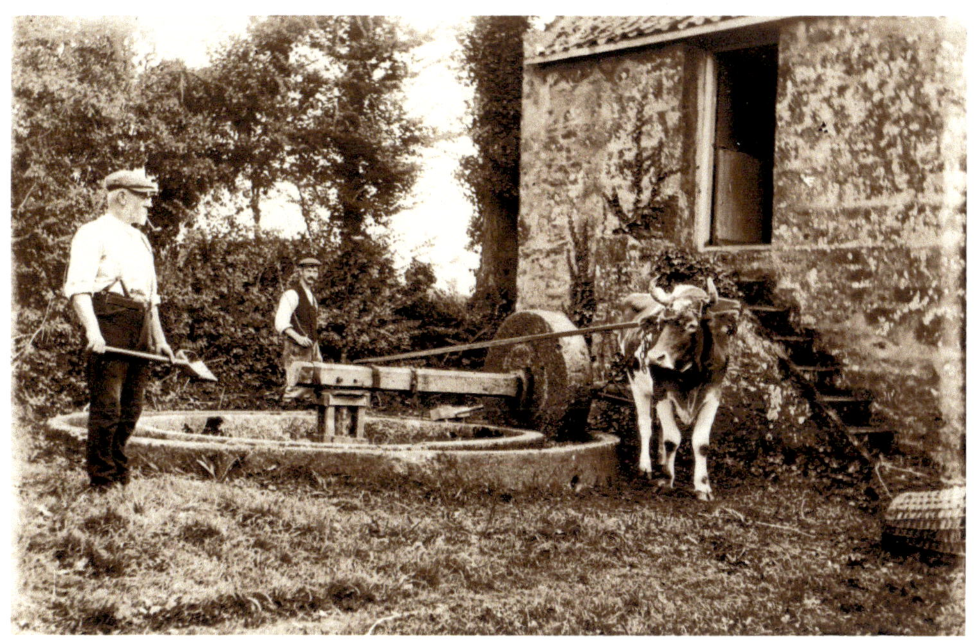

## Le Tour – Crushing the Cider Apples

For several centuries, no farm in Guernsey was complete without an apple orchard and Le Tour, the wheel and stone trough used to crush the apples before pressing. Wooden wheels were more common than stone – it was felt that the wood, impregnated with juice after years of crushing, added flavour to the cider. However, it is the stone wheels that have survived, and a few can be found around the island, used as decoration, or as a quaint reminder of traditions now lost. This one can be found in the old Le Couteur property at Rocquaine.

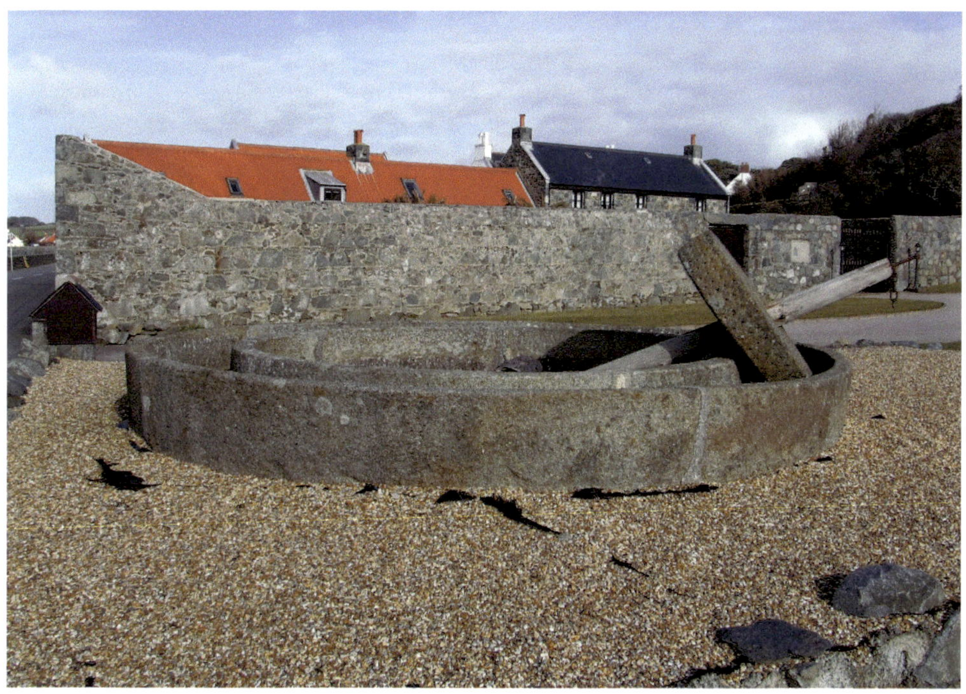

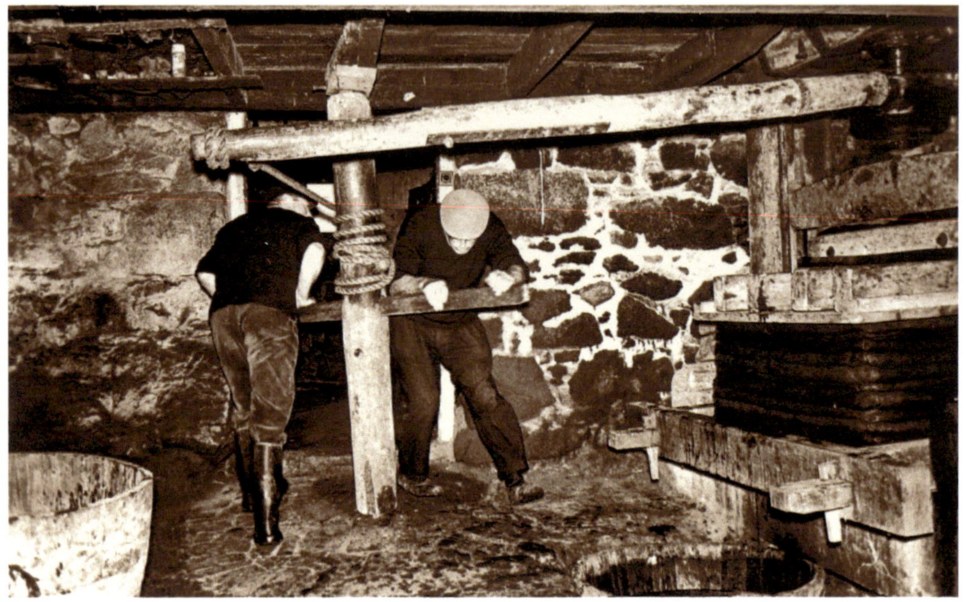

## Cider Making, a Guernsey Tradition

Cider has been made in Guernsey for hundreds of years, both for private consumption and commercially. In 1960, traditional cider production was photographed at Les Fauxquets de Haut, a farmhouse owned by the de Garis family. Mr J. M. de Garis helps to work the massive apple press, and the juice is collected in a tub below ground level. In 1998, Guernsey commercial cider-making was restored to Les Fauxquets de Haut by the Rocquette Cider Company, who have embraced traditional values while employing modern methods. Here Miguel Gomes pushes a pallet of freshly kegged cider.

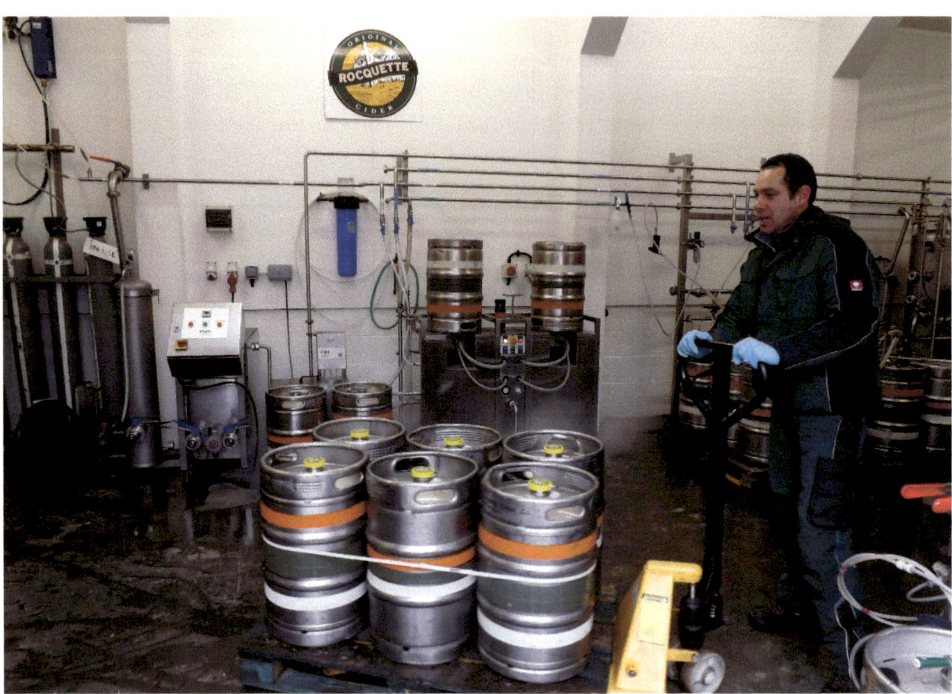

## Cider-Making at Les Fauxquets de Haut

Apple juice was fermented in huge casks with an open bunghole at the top, through which the impurities could escape. The casks had to be constantly topped up, a task requiring skill and experience. At the Rocquette Cider Company, the cider has been through the fermentation, maturation and blending process, and is ready for carbonation. It is cooled in large stainless steel vats to 2 °C before $CO_2$ gas is passed through it. It is then put in kegs under pressure. When the kegs are opened, the bubbles are released.

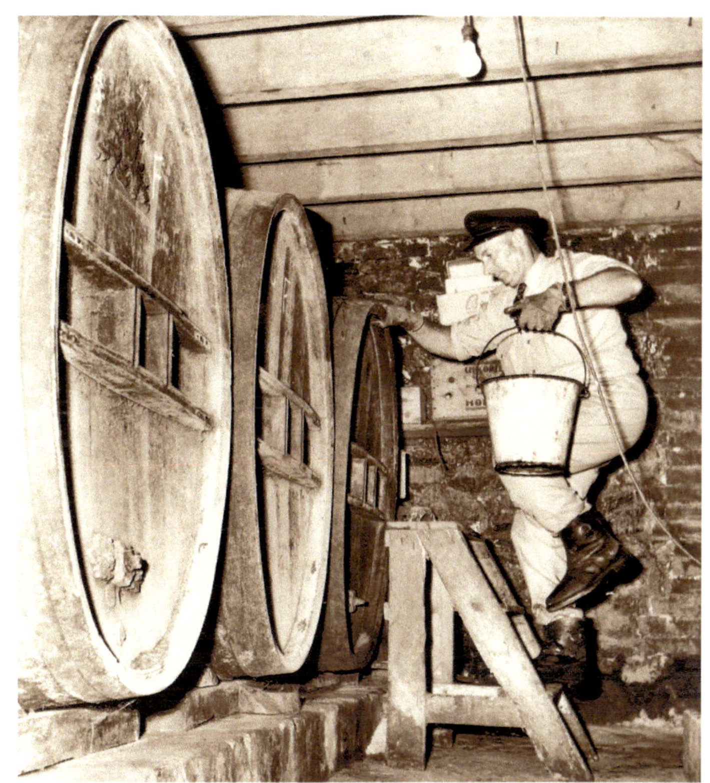

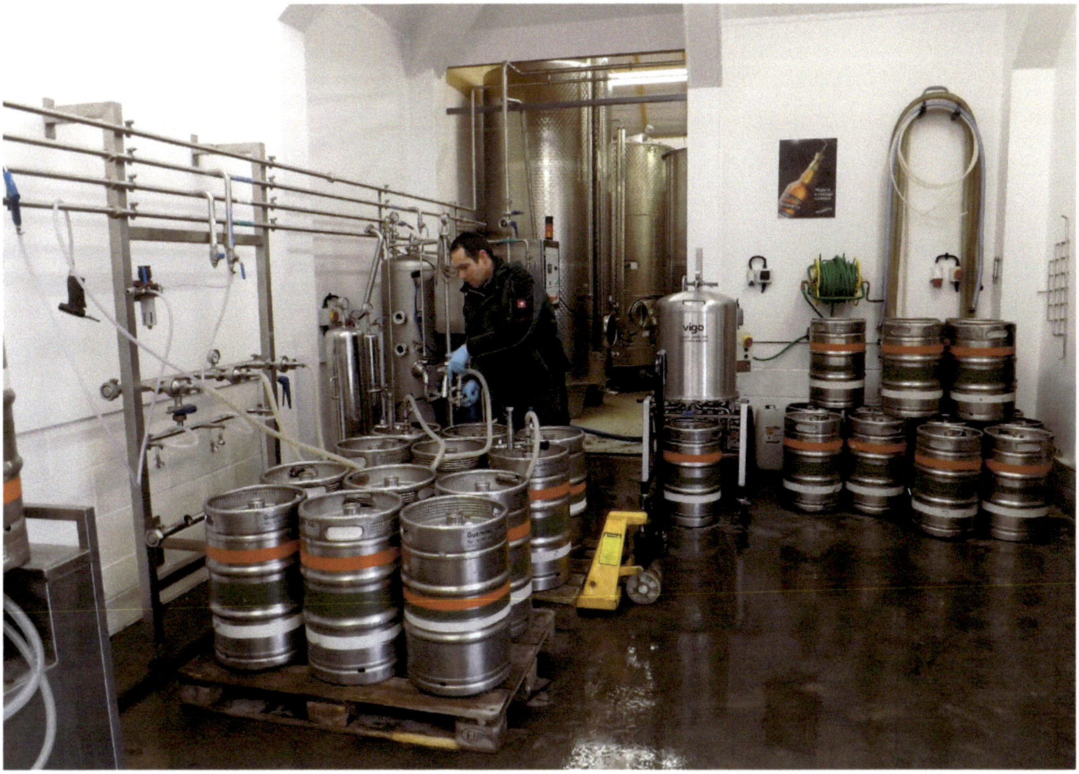

43

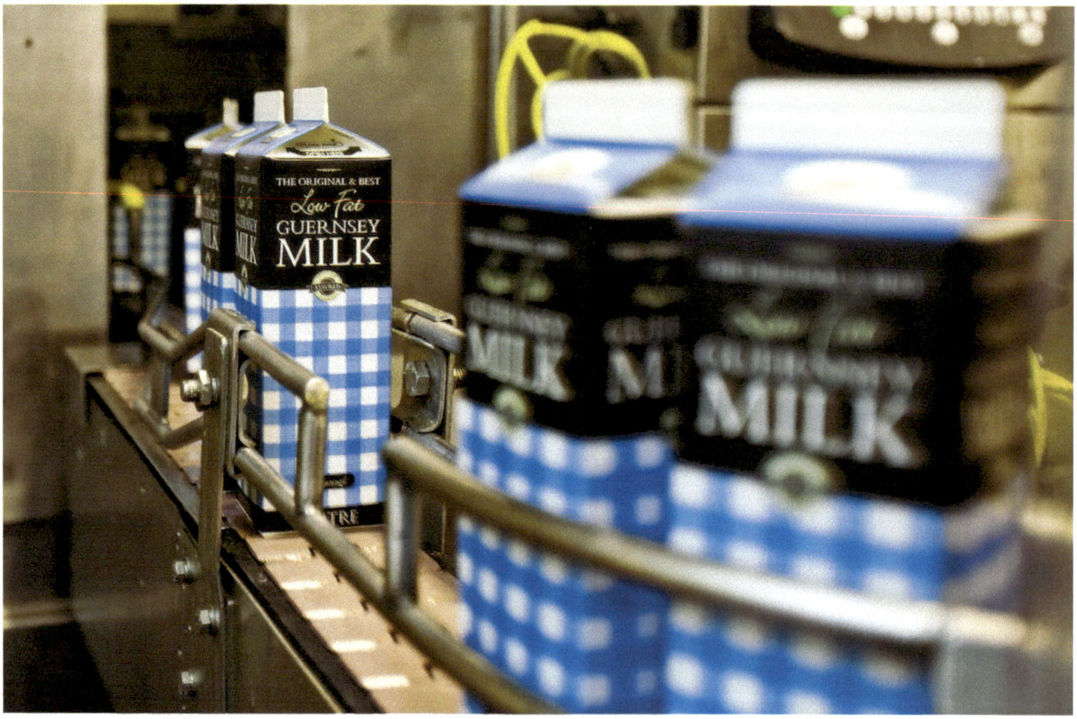

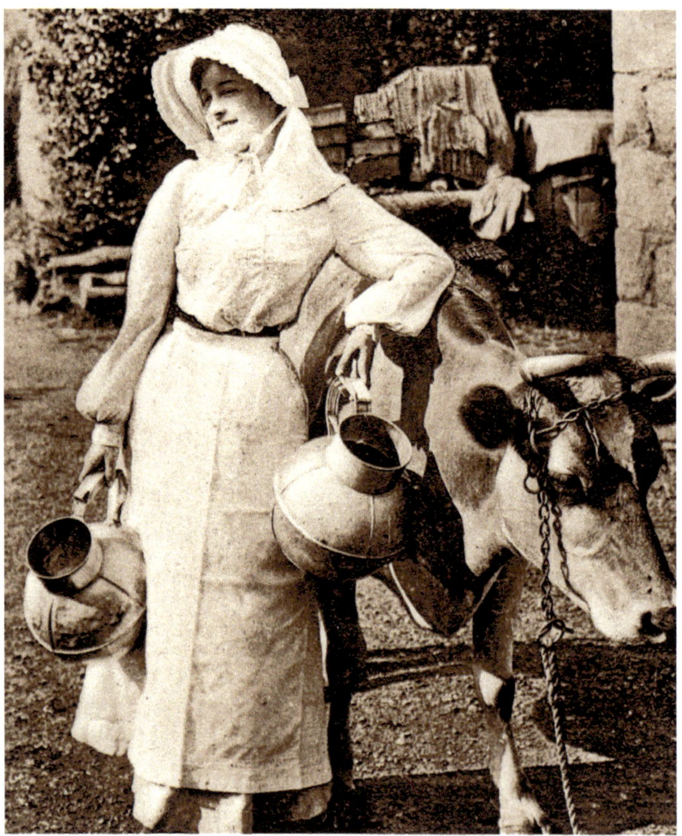

### Going a Milking

Guernsey is home to the world-famous Golden Guernsey cow – a breed recognised for its docile temperament and high yield of rich, creamy milk. Since 1951, from its base in the heart of St Andrews, the Guernsey Dairy has collected and processed milk from local herds to satisfy the island's demand for milk. In the past, there were over 400 farms on the island and milk was supplied to the dairy by these small herds on an ad hoc basis – hence the postcard of the pretty milkmaid with her cow and her Guernsey milk cans. Today, the dairy processes and packages 6.5 million litres of milk annually from the fifteen registered local dairy farms, with every drop coming from a pedigree Golden Guernsey cow.

## Guernsey Butter-Making

Guernsey butter is unique. A genetic quirk in the Guernsey breed means that the cow cannot fully digest beta-Carotene, which means the milk assumes a rich golden colour. This is further enhanced when the liquid cream is churned into butter. Nineteenth-century butter churning by hand at Duvaux Farm would have been a familiar sight at the time, and every farm had its own hand-carved wooden butter mould to identify its origins. Today, butter-making at the Guernsey Dairy is highly mechanised, but the principles, natural ingredients and the delicious product remain the same.

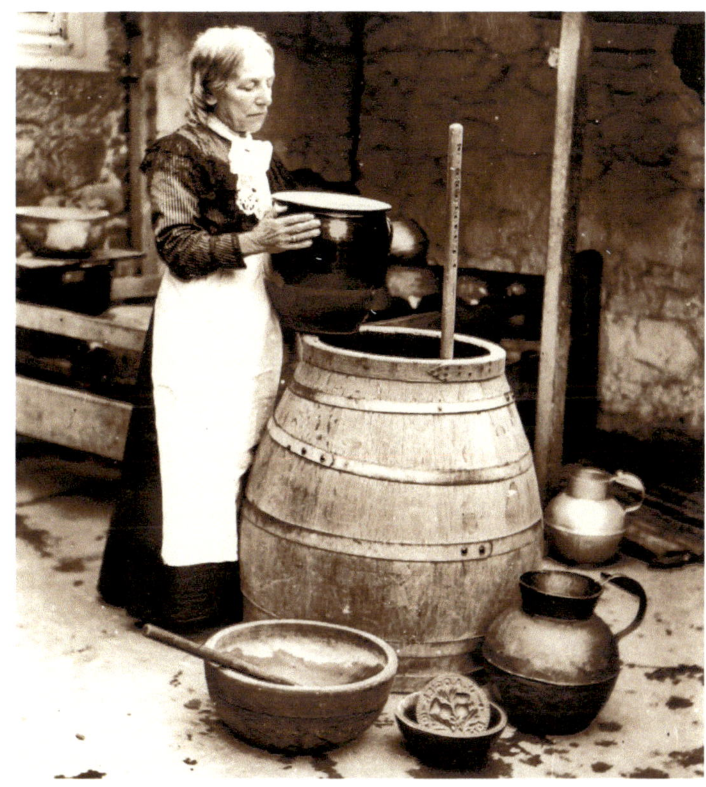

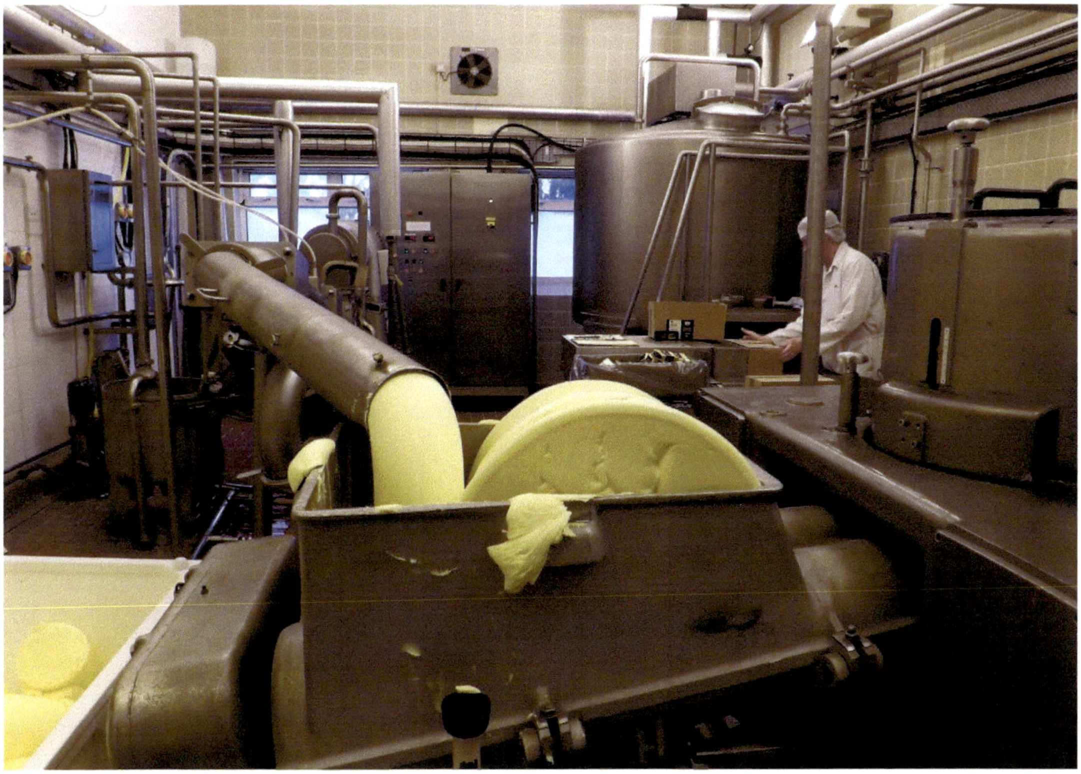

45

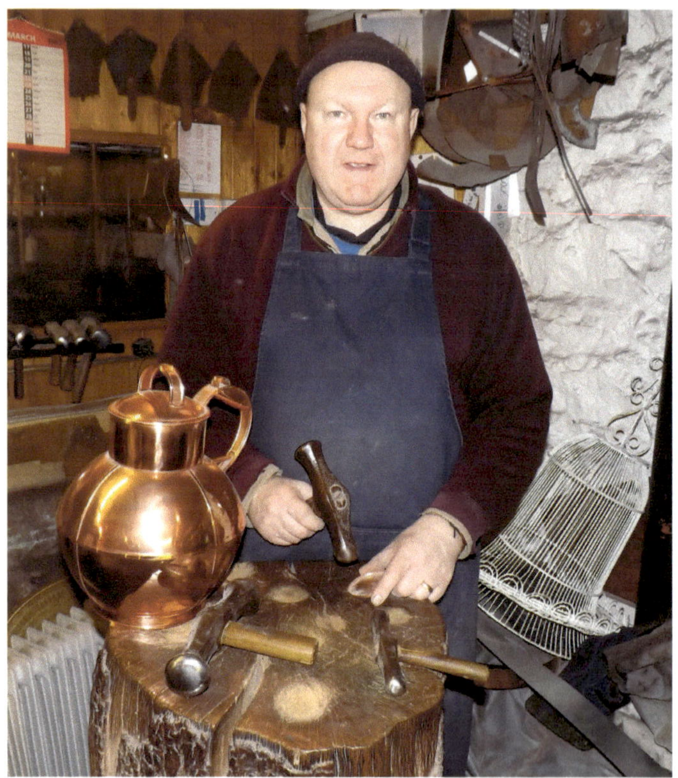

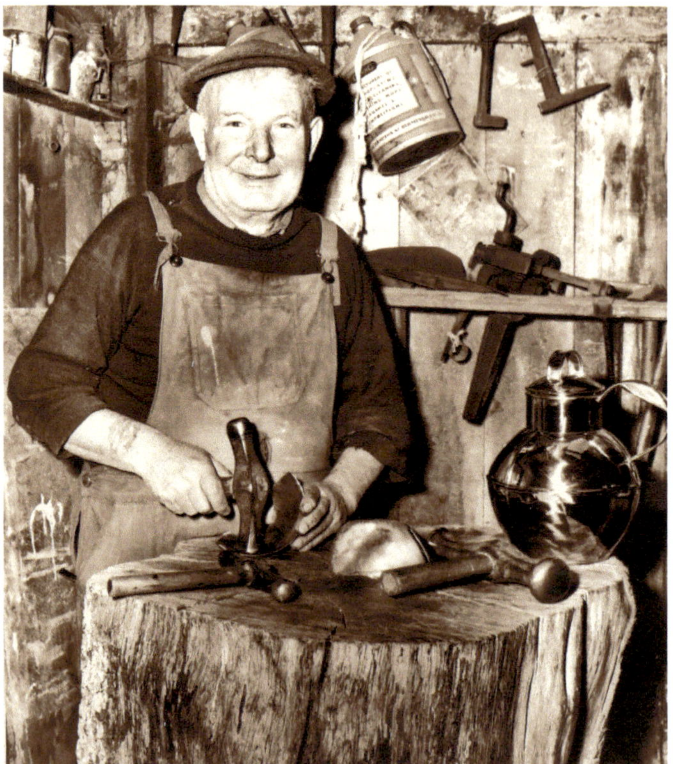

### The Last Coppersmith

Trevor Rogers-Davis is Guernsey's last working coppersmith, and represents an unbroken line going back to 1709. He was apprenticed to Arthur Russell, son of Morley Russell, pictured below in 1947. Morley himself was taught by De La Rue Copper and Tin Smiths of Fountain Street, whose business was founded in 1709. The link is physical as well as intellectual – both Trevor and Morley are using the same hammer, which was inherited from the De La Rues. They are both making a Guernsey can – a traditional milk carrier, which developed its characteristic shape over many centuries.

## Brick Kilns at Oatlands Farm, St Sampson's

Oatlands Farm was one of many island brickfields in the nineteenth century. Guernsey bricks were very 'friable' (soft) and were not used to any great extent for building houses, especially as granite was so readily available, but they were invaluable to local growers for building the chimney stacks and boiler pits needed to heat their greenhouses. The surviving brick kilns at Oatlands were built in 1892 and are a scheduled ancient monument. The farm was sold in 1982 and the kilns and barns were restored. It is now used as a craft and retail centre.

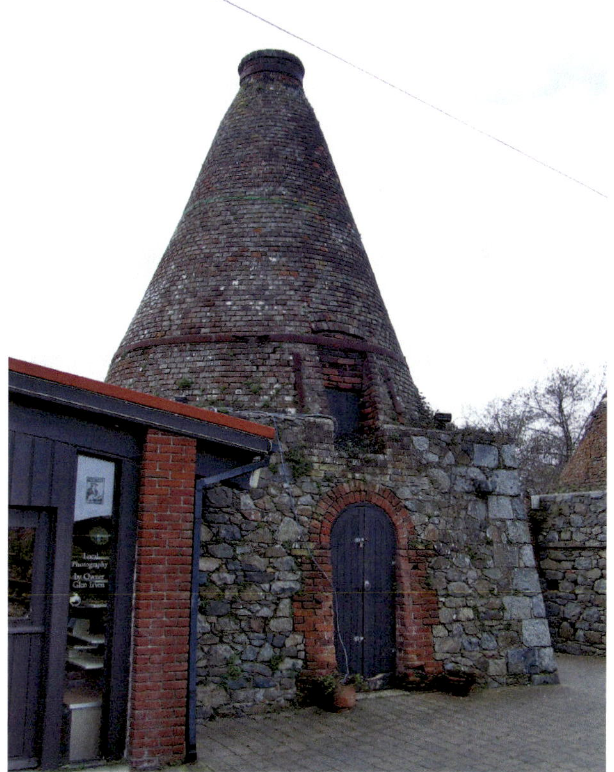

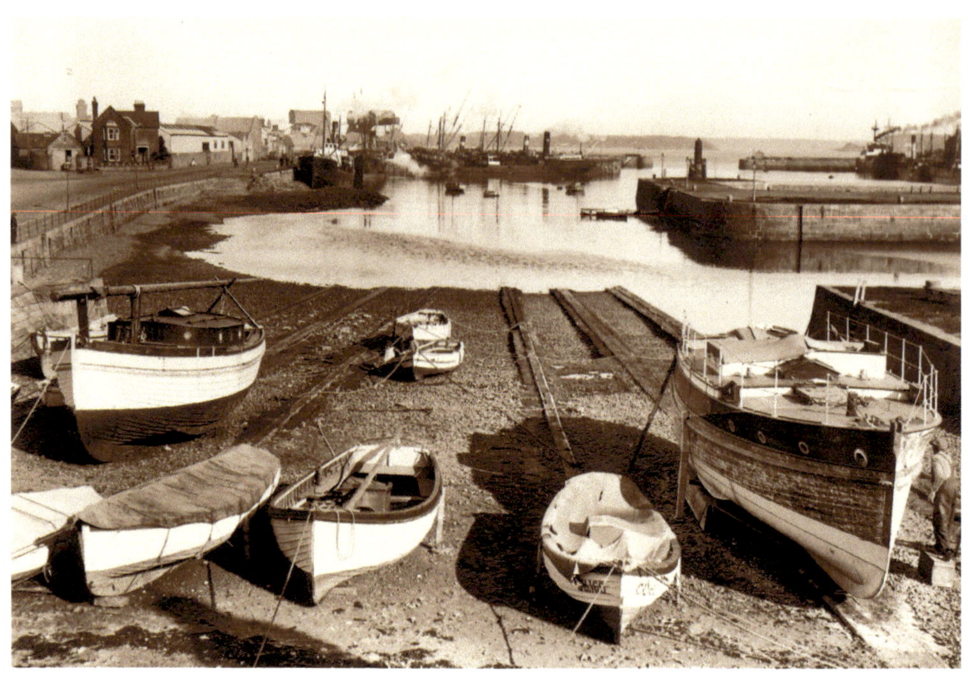

## St Sampson's Careening Hard

In the nineteenth century, St Sampson's Harbour was a very large bulk cargo port, moving quarried stone, timber and coal. The older photograph shows a number of steam cargo ships docked at the North Quay, while in the foreground, pulled up on the Careening Hard, are number of small fishing vessels and dinghies, showing that it was a working harbour for locals and families as well as for heavy industry. Today, the area is used by Marine & General who are continuing the island's shipbuilding tradition.

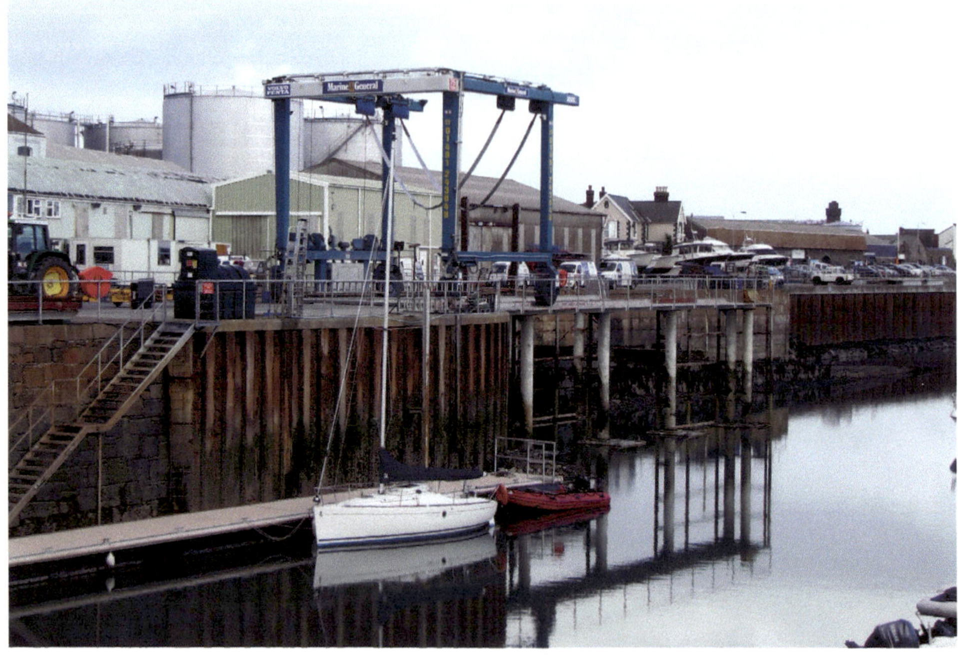

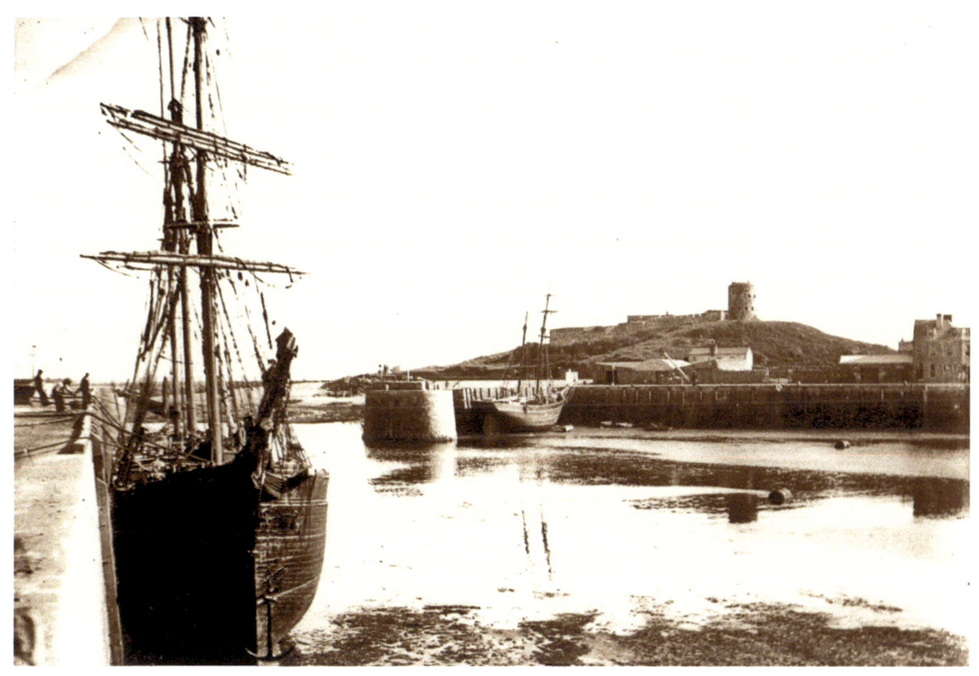

## Mont Crevelt from the North Quay

A view across St Sampson's Harbour to Mont Crevelt at the far south end of the harbour mouth. The pre-Martello tower, erected in the 1779 during the War of American Independence, sits upon a prominent hill that had probably been fortified in one way or another since the Middle Ages. In holds a commanding defensive position and it is not surprising that the German Army fortified it further during the Second World War. The modern photograph shows the encroachment of industrialisation, but the fort itself remains largely unchanged.

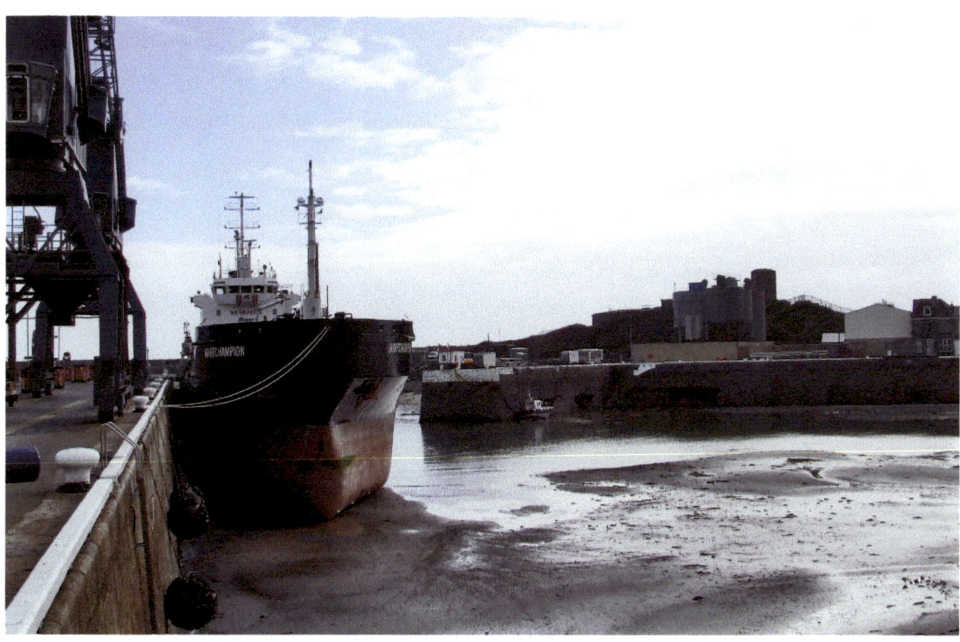

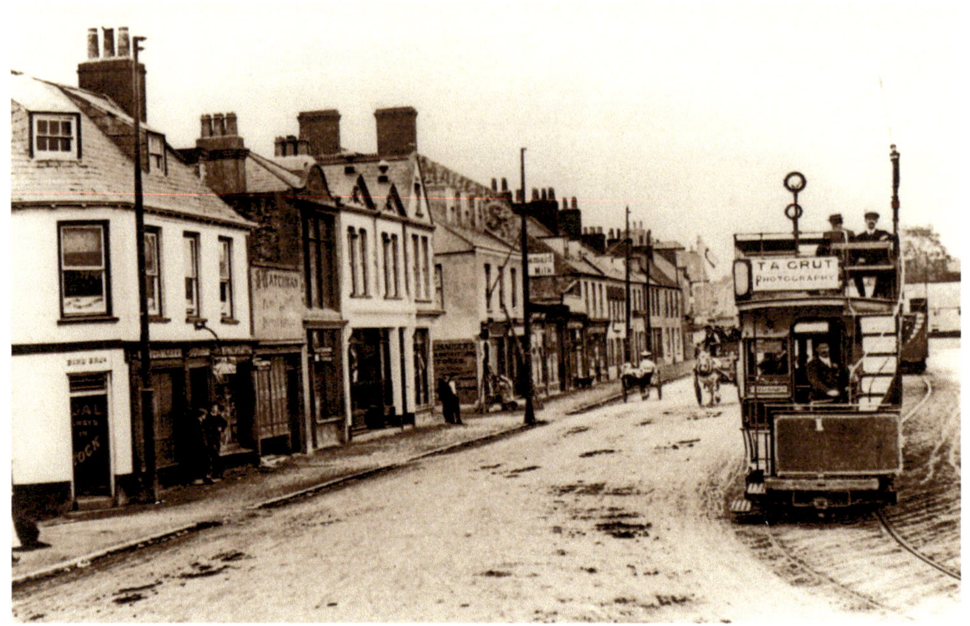


### The Bridge, St Sampson's

Guernsey was once two islands, divided by a channel of water called the Braye du Valle, which ran from Grand Havre Bay in the west to Sampson Creek in the east. When the Braye was reclaimed from the sea between 1806 and 1808, the north and south sides of St Sampson's Harbour were joined by the Pont de Valle – known ever since as the 'Bridge'. This late nineteenth-century postcard shows the bustle of traffic and shops on the Bridge. The shops are little changed, but the mode of transport is somewhat different.

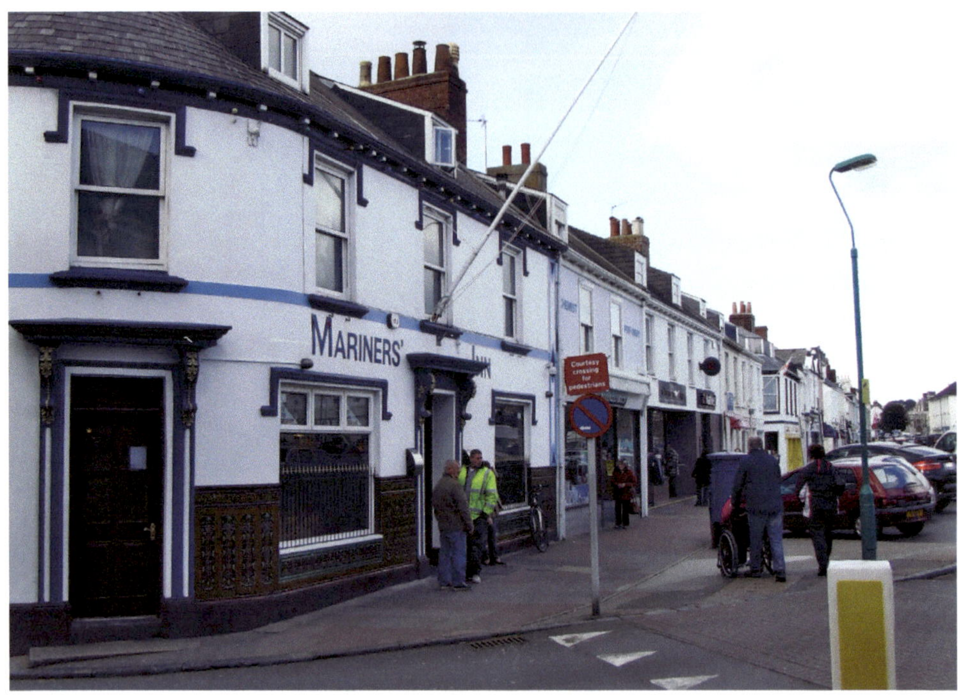

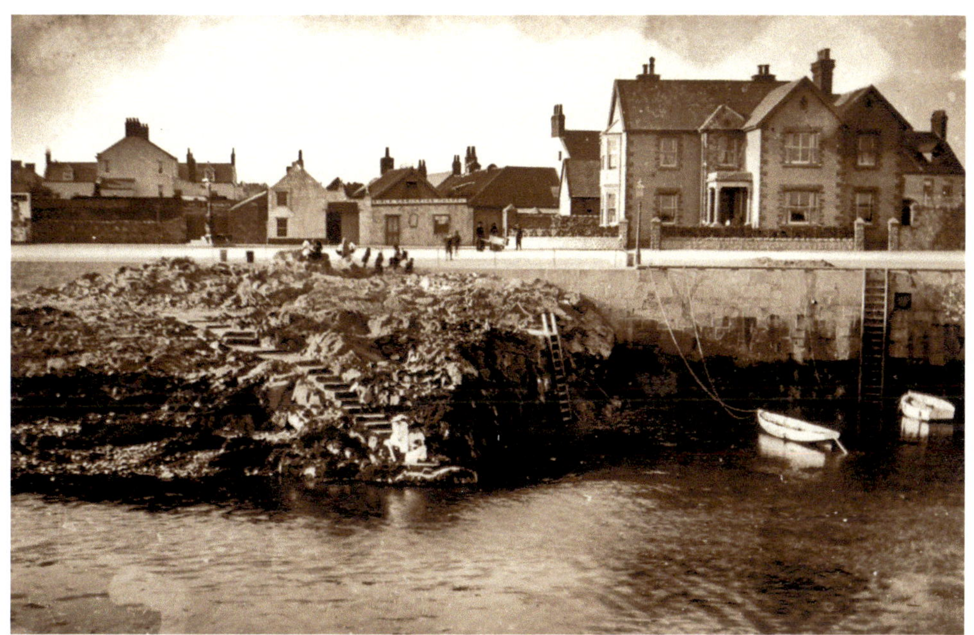

## North Side, Vale

Guernsey Electricity oil storage tanks completely dominate this scene on the north side of St Sampson's Harbour, and the rocky reef of La Maisonette is almost swallowed by the Trafalgar Quay. The photograph of the 1890s, by contrast, shows children playing on the stone-cut landing steps of the reef, and it was a favourite spot for fishing. On the quayside, Durlston House has barely changed; now the offices of an advertising agency, is was home to a number of different families in the late nineteenth century – mainly carters and stonecrackers.

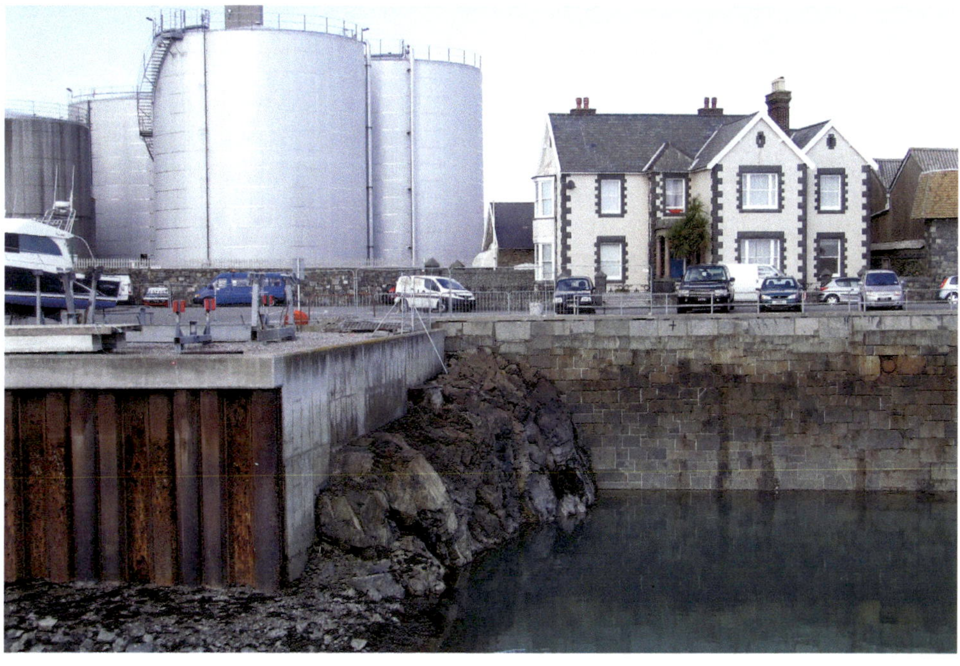

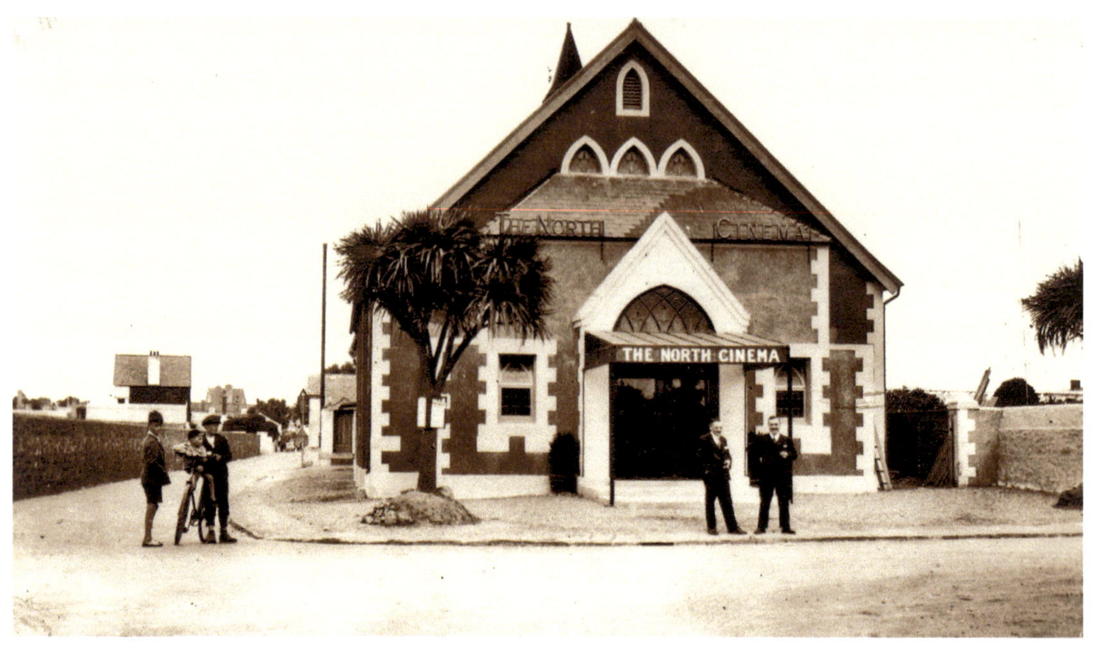

## The North Cinema, Vale Avenue

Cinema arrived in Guernsey at St Julian's Theatre in 1896, and many picture houses followed: The Lyric in New Street, The Empire at Mont Crevelt and the North Cinema in Vale Avenue, among others. The North Cinema started life in 1909 as the Vale Avenue Wesleyan Methodist chapel; the chapel closed in 1928 and was quickly converted to a cinema – entertaining the inhabitants of the north side until it reached its natural end in 1957. The building was converted to a garage in 1960.

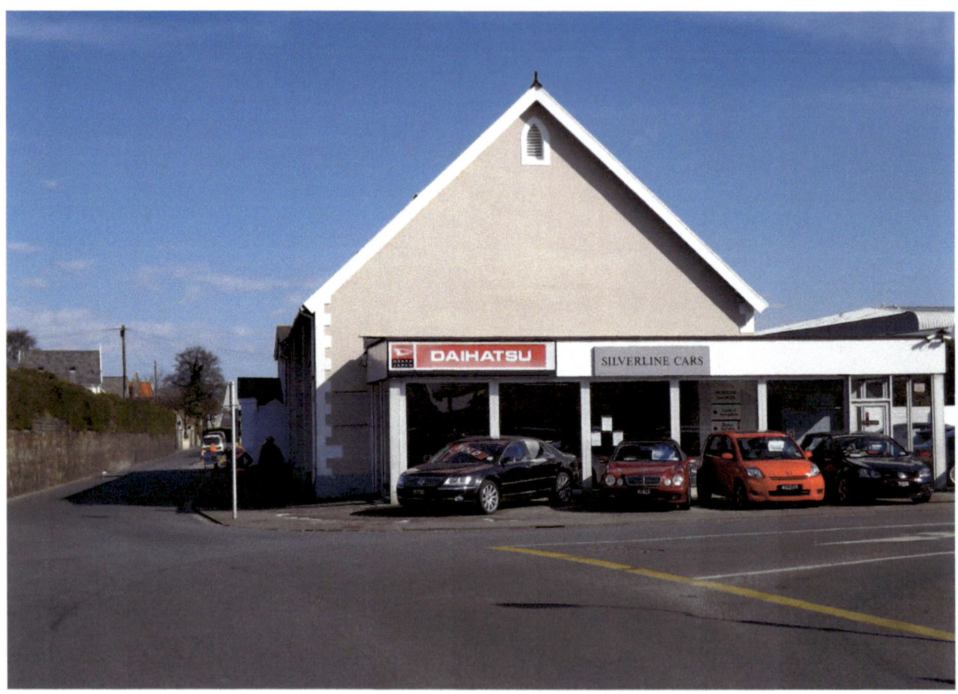

## Vale Mill

Vale Mill was situated in the Clos du Valle, an area of the Vale parish that, 200 years ago, was separated from the rest of Guernsey by a channel of water. The mill was built so that the inhabitants of the Clos du Valle would not have to take their corn over to the mainland to be ground. During the Second World War, the German occupying forces added several concrete levels so the mill could be used as an observation tower. The mill, with the German additions, was restored in 2006 and is now a private residence.

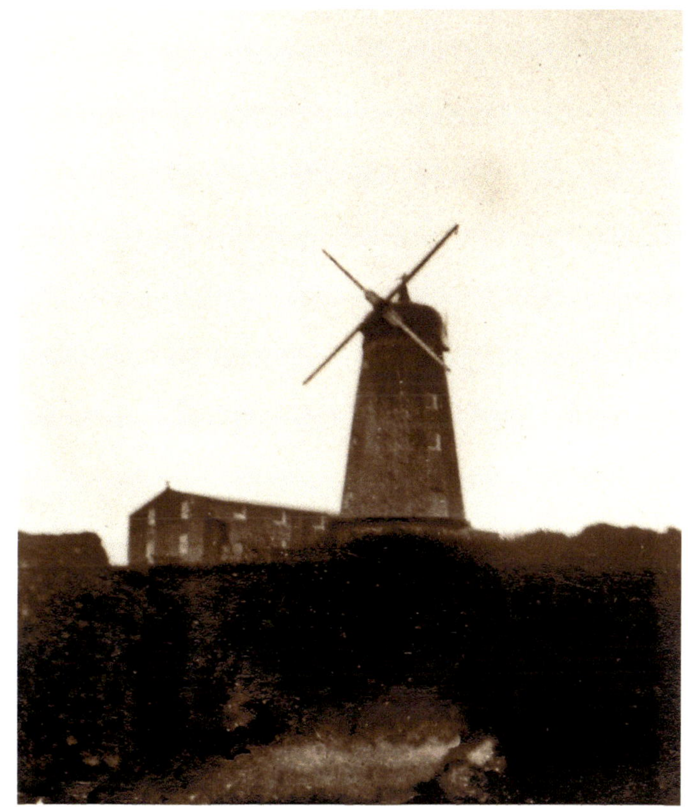

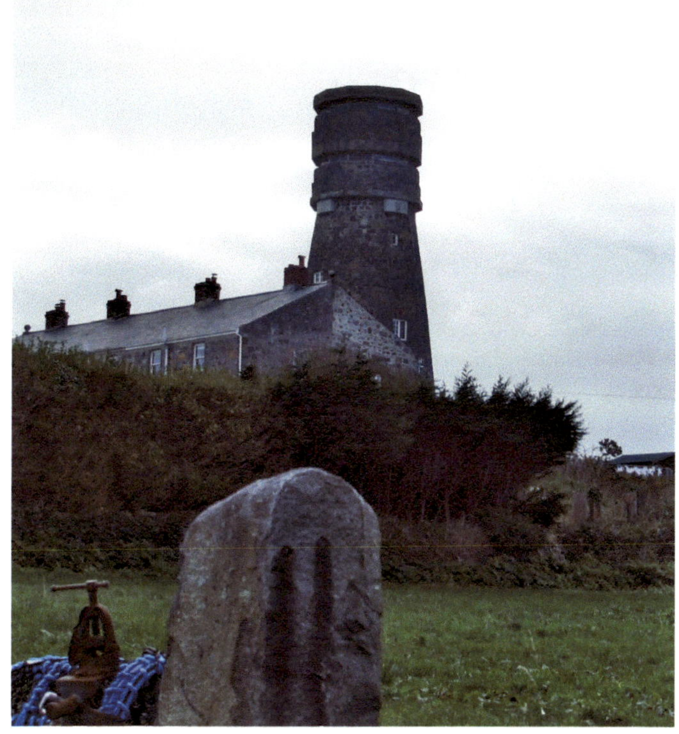

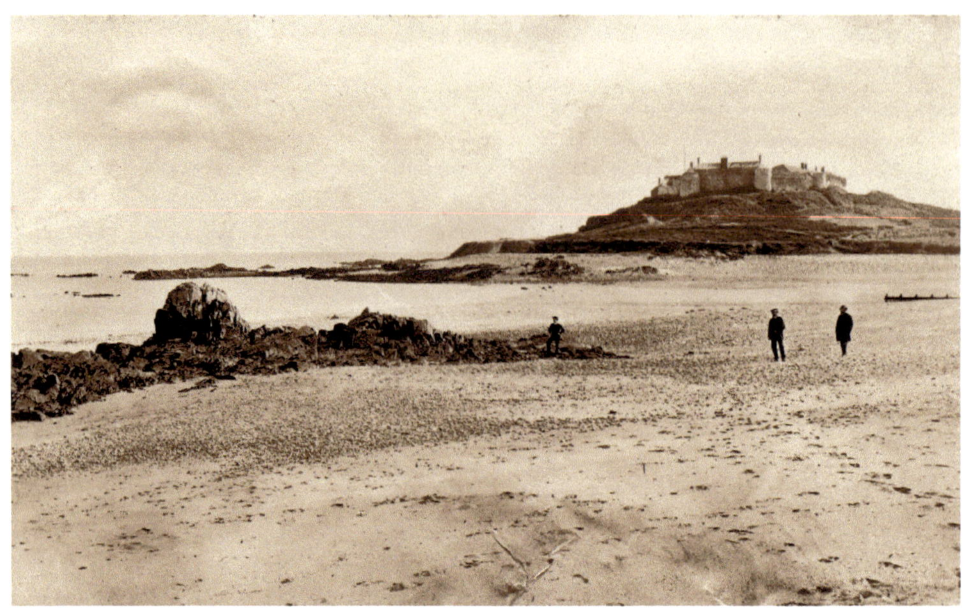

## Vale Castle from Bordeaux

The origins of Vale Castle are uncertain; it certainly dates to the medieval period, but the first official record of it does not appear until the early sixteenth century. It was considerably refortified during the War of American Independence and became an important garrison for English soldiers. With fine views to the east and south, it dominates the south end of Bordeaux Bay and now holds an important place in the island's cultural calendar. As well as being a venue for open-air theatre, every August it hosts a popular music festival – the Vale Earth Fair.

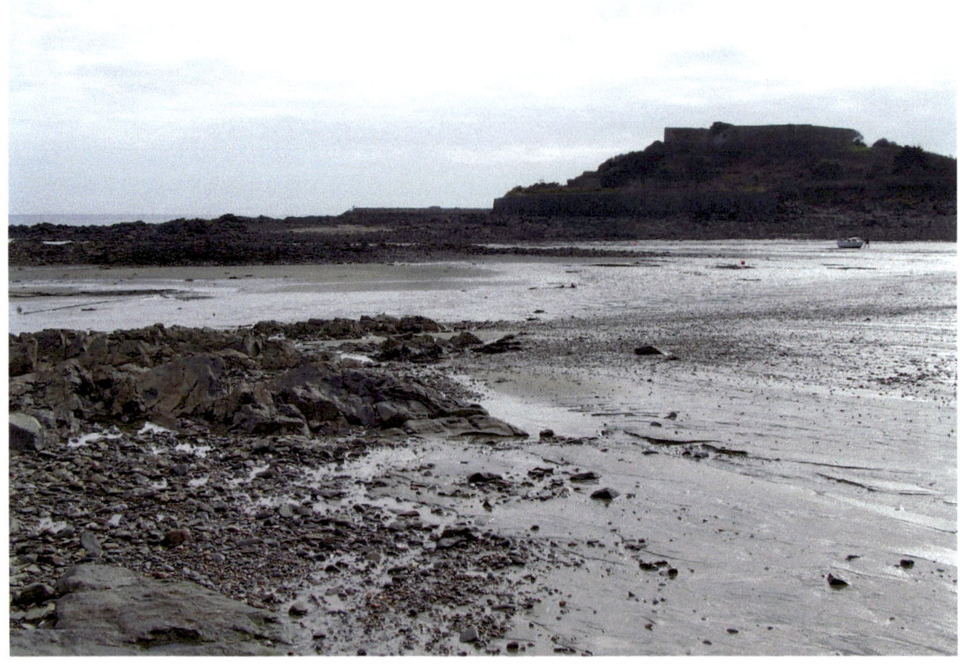

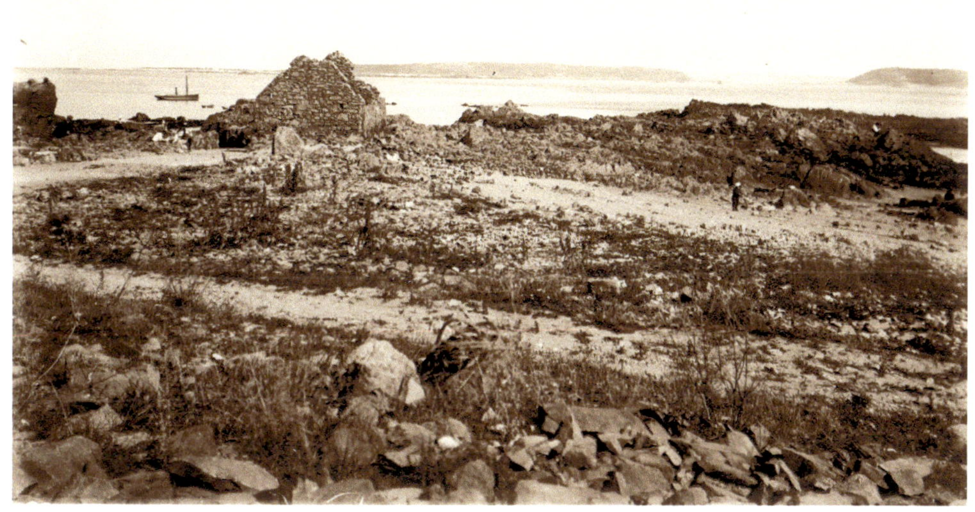

## Fisherman's Hut at Bordeaux Harbour

The name of Bordeaux is of French origin, meaning 'on the water's edge', and the fisherman's hut pictured in this 1872 photograph is demonstrating the literal definition! Behind the hut is a small granite quay, built in 1862, and the hut was probably built very soon after this as a convenient place for storing nets, pots and ropes. Only ten years later, it was falling into ruin. Today, the only trace that remains is a flattened rock on the reef, into which a foundation trench had been laboriously cut.

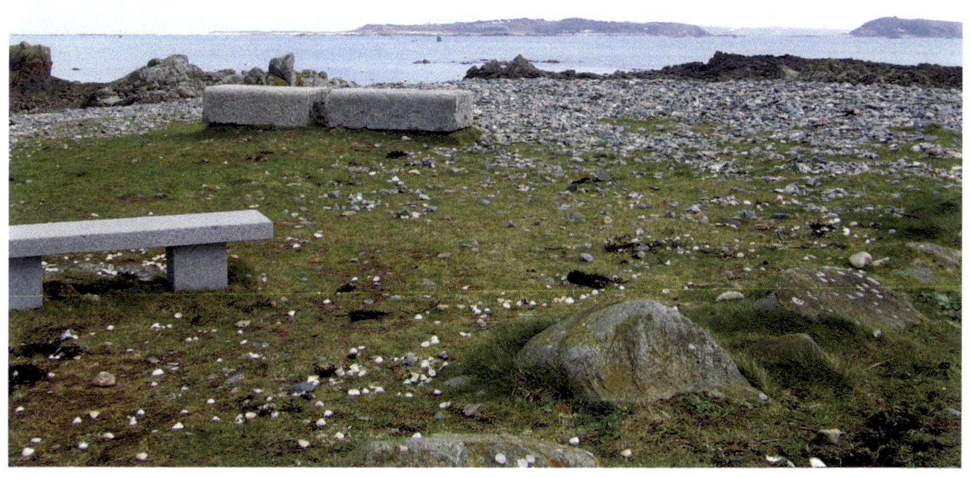

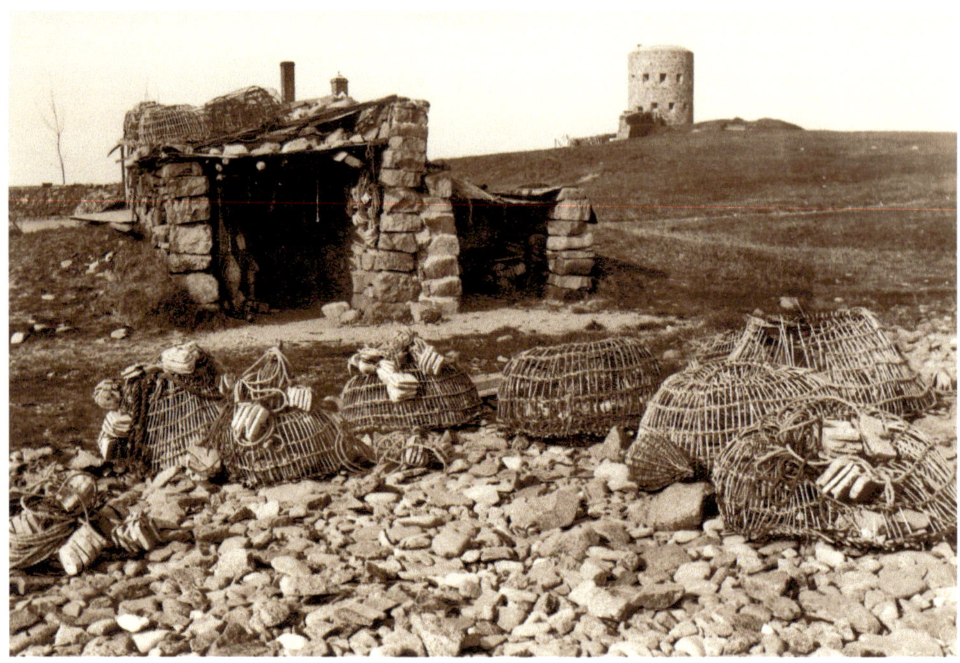

## Fishermen's Huts at Rousse

The small harbour at Rousse sits on the south-west side of Grand Havre Bay and is overlooked by a Martello tower, built in 1804 to guard against French attack. Dinghies are moored by ropes anchored in the shingle bank below the small fishermen's huts, which were built to store ropes, nets and pots. In 1934, there were two huts on the shore, but today, the smaller one has disappeared.

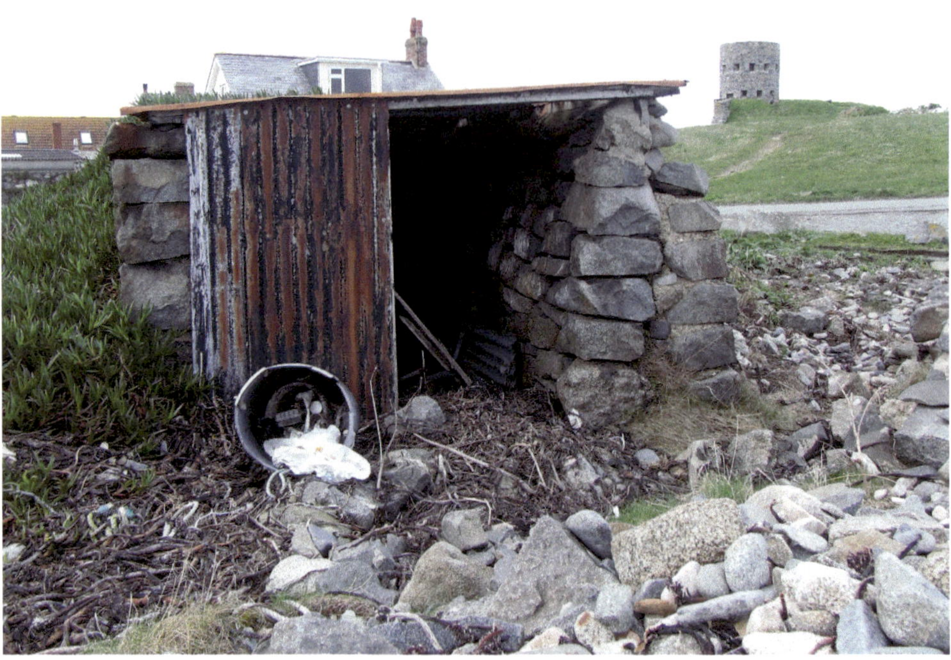

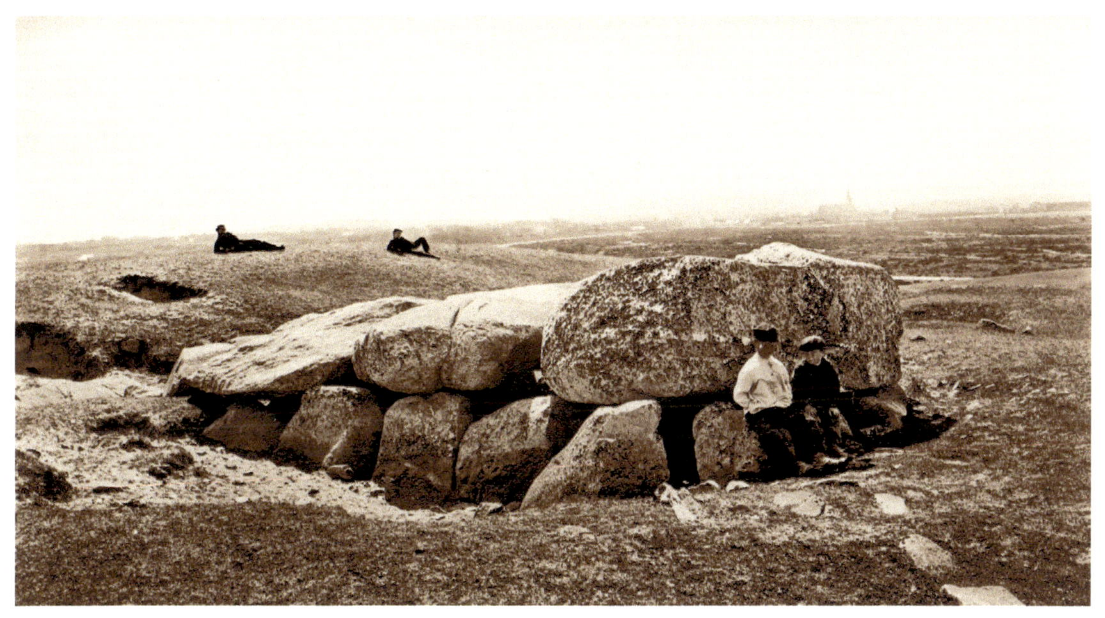

### La Varde Dolmen, L'Ancresse

Perched on a hill above L'Ancresse Common, it is difficult to believe that this large passage grave – 11 metres in length – was only revealed to the modern era in 1811, when it was uncovered by soldiers of the 103rd regiment. It is not only the largest megalithic structure on Guernsey, but one of the oldest, being at least 4,000 years old. Today, in accordance with modern practice, the ground has been allowed to swallow the tomb so that only the top of the largest capstone can be seen; however, the interior of the tomb is still accessible.

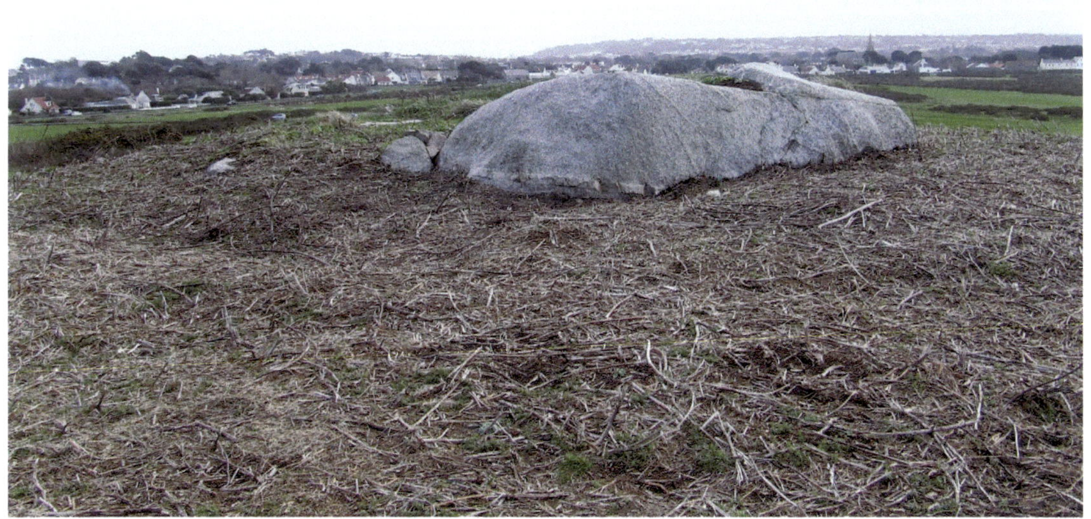

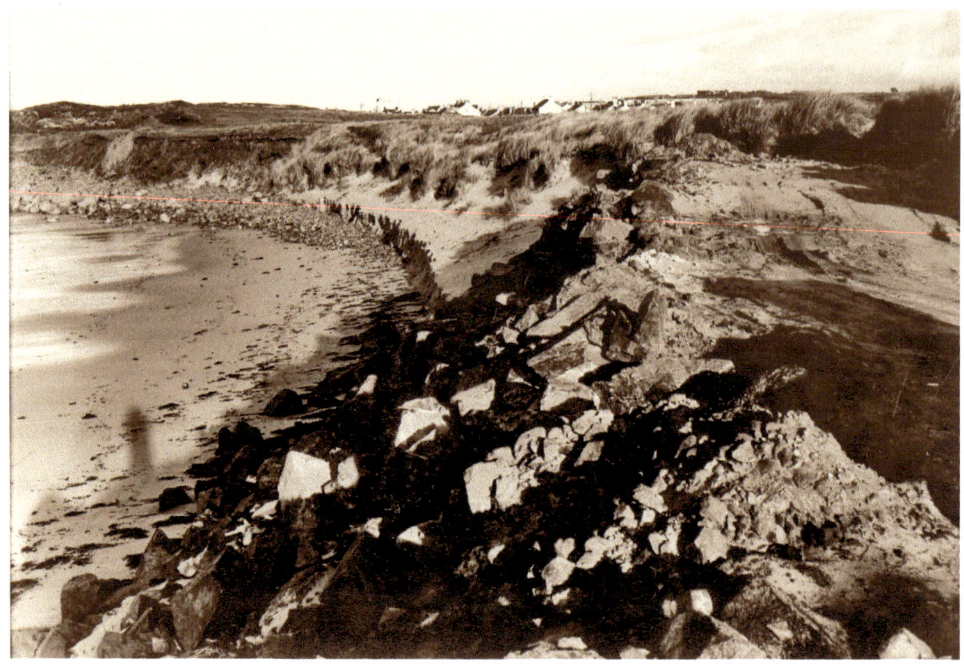

## Port Soif

A small but beautiful sandy bay on Guernsey's north-west coast, Port Soif has remained pristine and unspoilt. It is also one of the rarest habitats on the island – a mobile sand dune, in which areas of bare sand are moved around by the wind. In 1986, the Environment Department took action to prevent the erosion of this important feature, and strategic fences were installed and sand couch planted to stabilise the dune. The success of this venture is evident in the comparison of the photograph from fifty years ago.

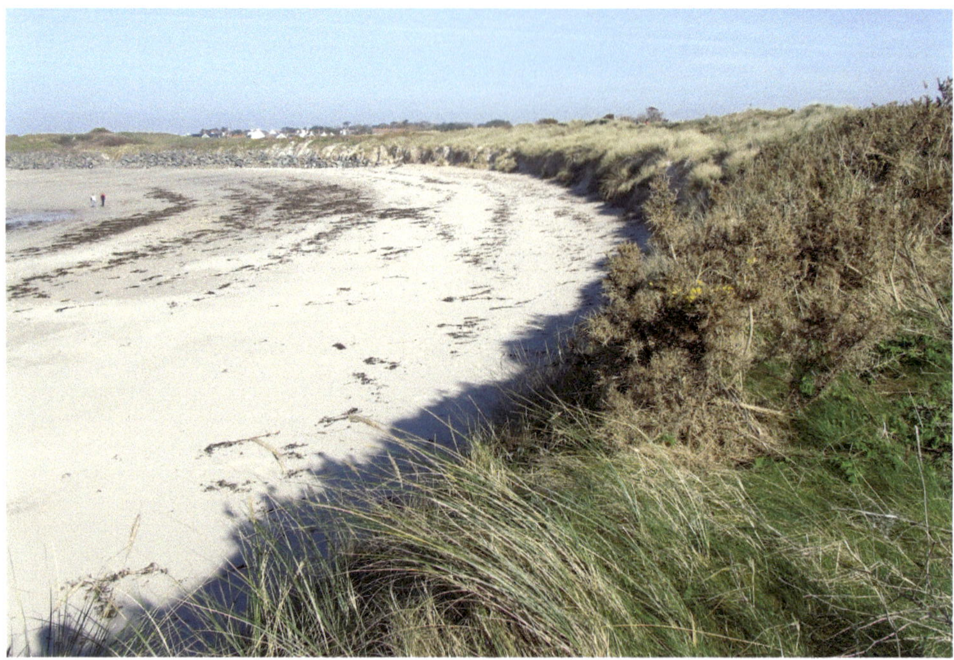

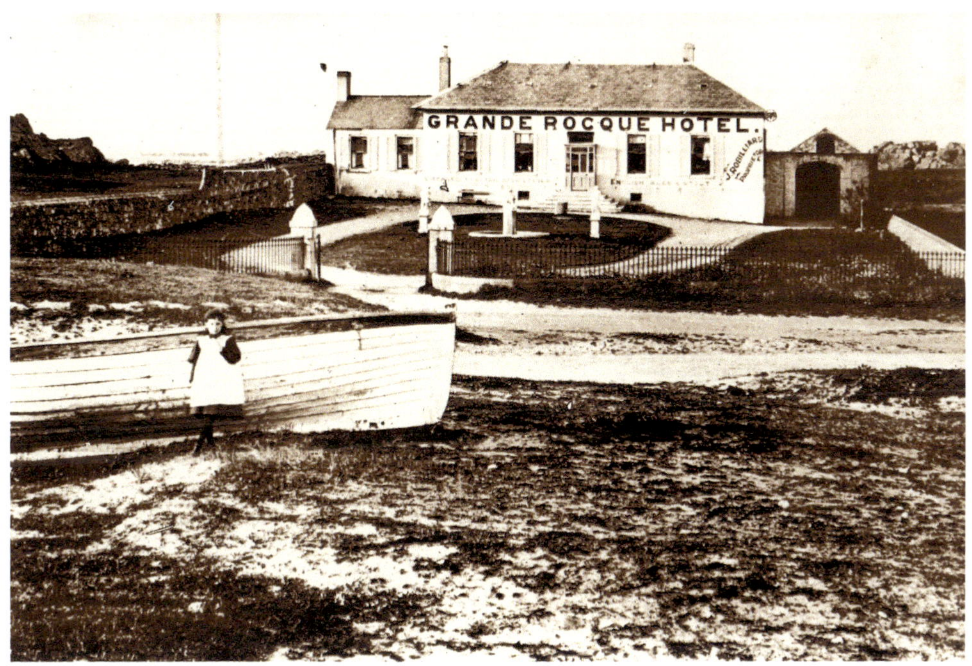


## Grande Rocque Hotel

There has been a hotel on the Grande Rocque peninsular for nearly 200 years. In the 1880s, the proprietor was John Robilliard, and his name can be seen painted on the hotel frontage. Its transformation from a modest establishment into a mock-Gothic edifice took place in 1892, when the building was purchased by Lord De Saumarez, who converted it into a school for his asthmatic son. The school eventually moved to England in 1902 and the building became a hotel again. It closed its doors in 1988, but is now undergoing yet another transformation.

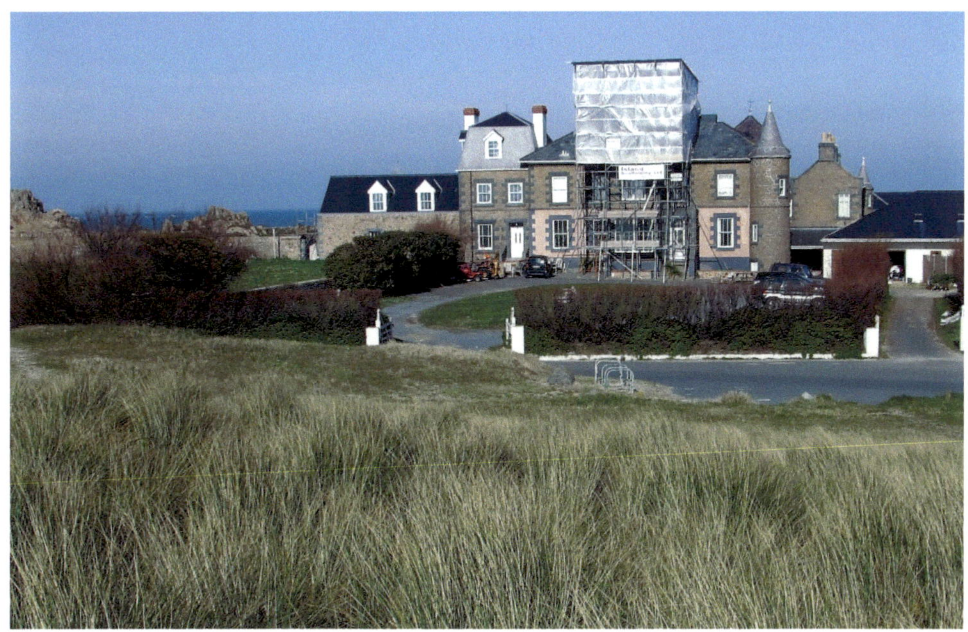

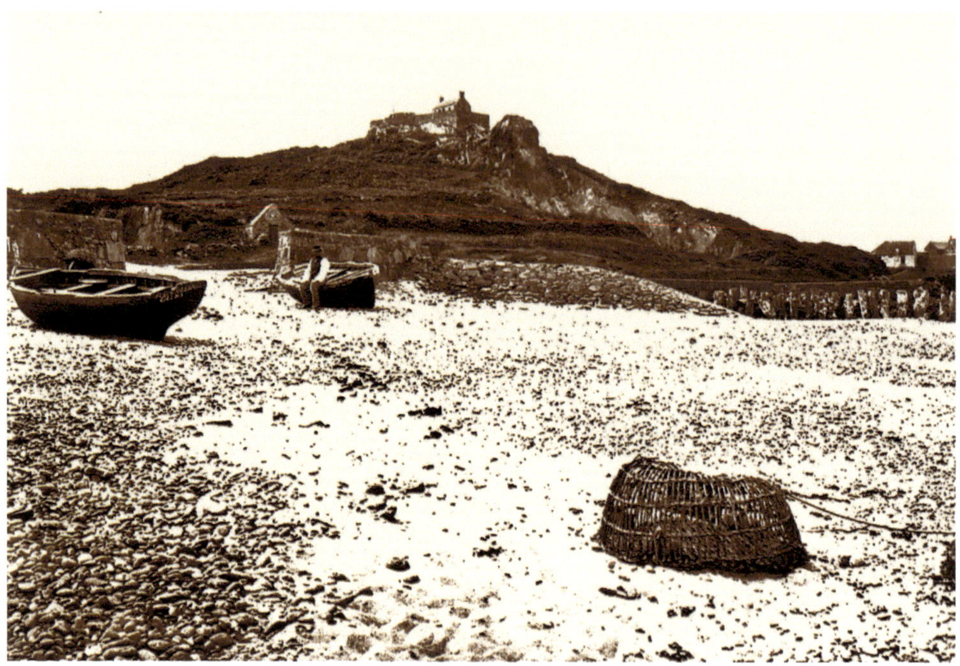

## Le Guet, Cobo

A 'Guet' is a lookout and it is likely that this rocky outcrop overlooking Cobo Bay, known as La Banquette, has been fortified for many centuries. The current watch house was constructed in 1780 at a cost of £1,600 to the parish. It served its purpose throughout the Napoleonic Wars, and was used by the Germans during the occupation, who also installed a battery next to it. The 4th Lord De Saumarez planted Monterey Pines at Le Guet in 1937, completely changing the character of the hill and hiding the watch house from view.

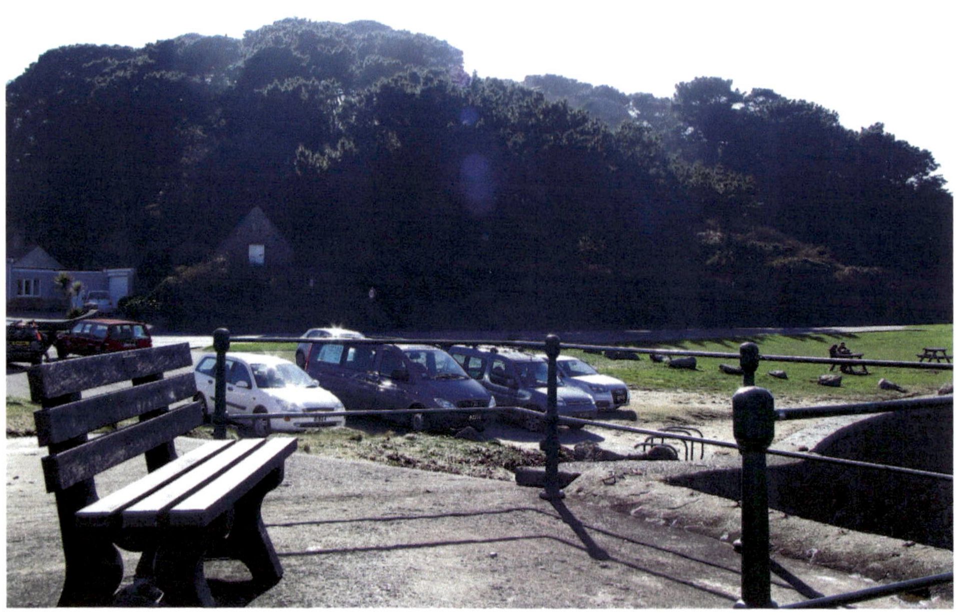

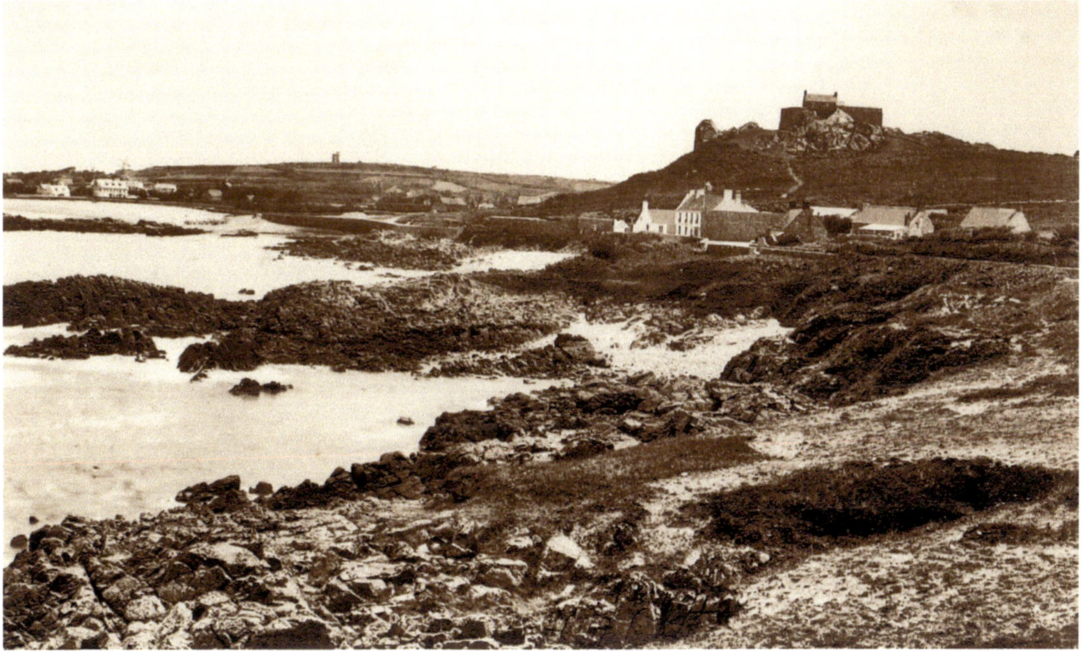

## Cobo Bay

A view of Le Guet from the south, taking in the sweep of Cobo Bay. At the foot of Le Guet is the Cobo Hotel, which, from 1870 to 1880 (the date of the photograph), was owned by Mr Aldridge and advertised as having 'the best wines and spirits' and 'a good skittle alley'. On the horizon can be seen the Ozanne Tower, a nineteenth-century folly built by a family of the same name. The tower can scarcely be seen among the trees today, and the coast road is crowded, full of little cottages and bungalows.

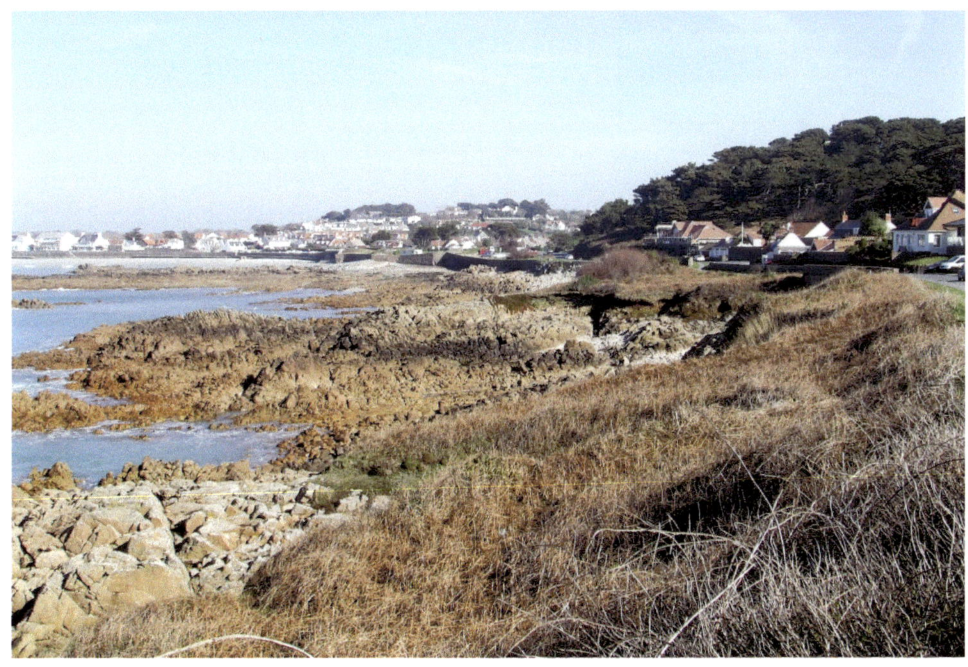

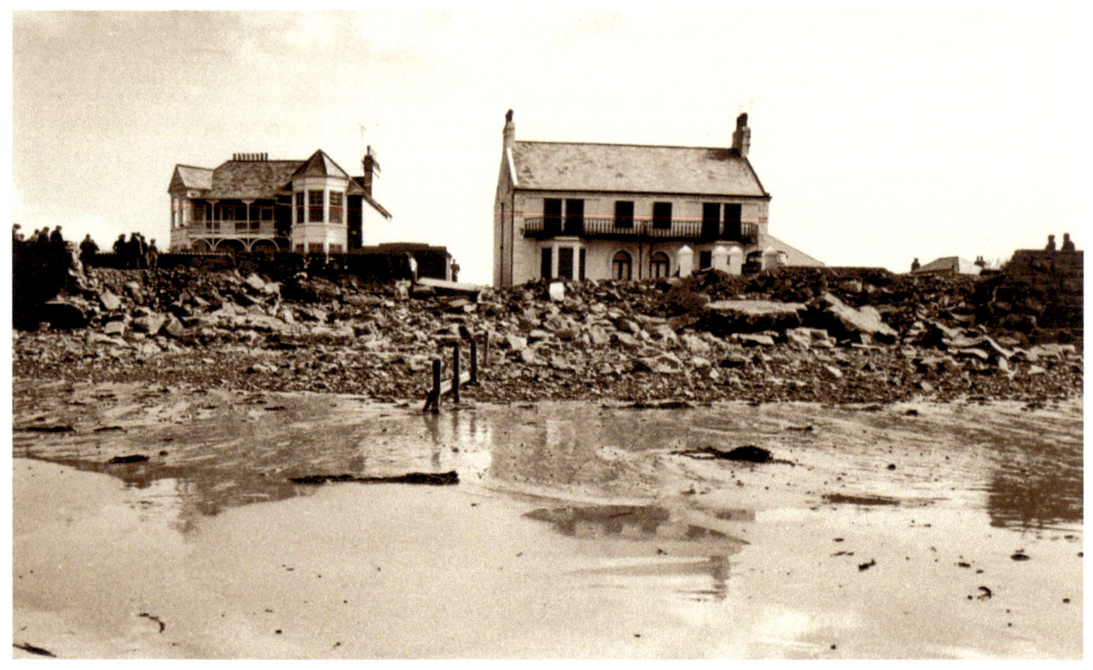

## Cobo Bay After the Storms, 1962

The awesome power of the sea is made plain by the devastated sea wall at Guernsey's Cobo Bay after a storm in April 1962. The westerly gale hit Guernsey's west coast hard, and the sea wall and part of the road at Cobo were destroyed. Such events are a daily part of life on the island, and although the modern photograph shows a tranquil scene, the storms of 2014 caused severe damage to sea defences on other parts of the coast.

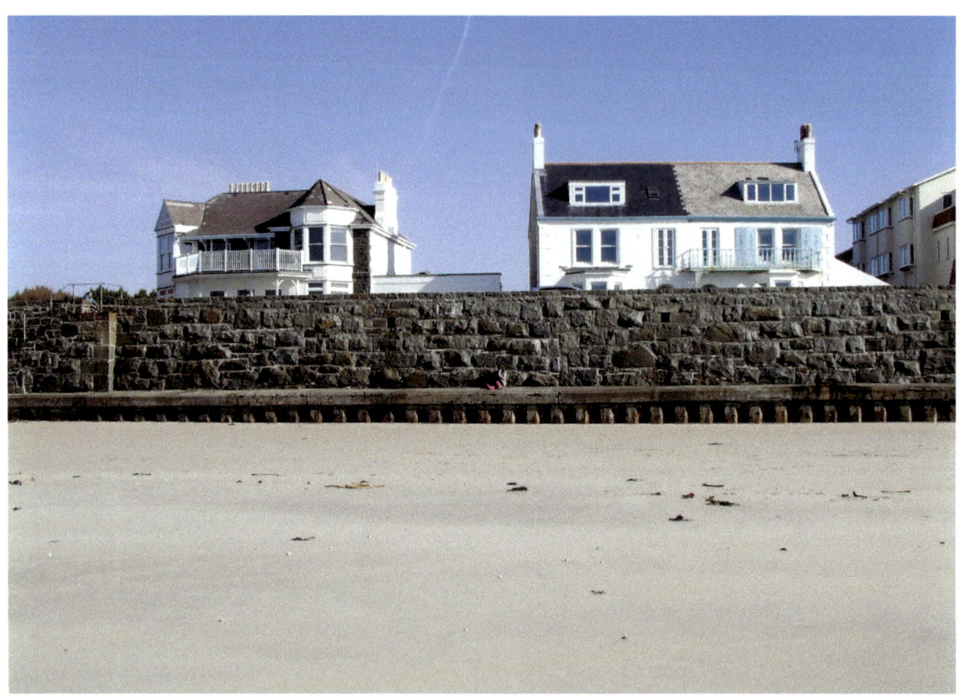

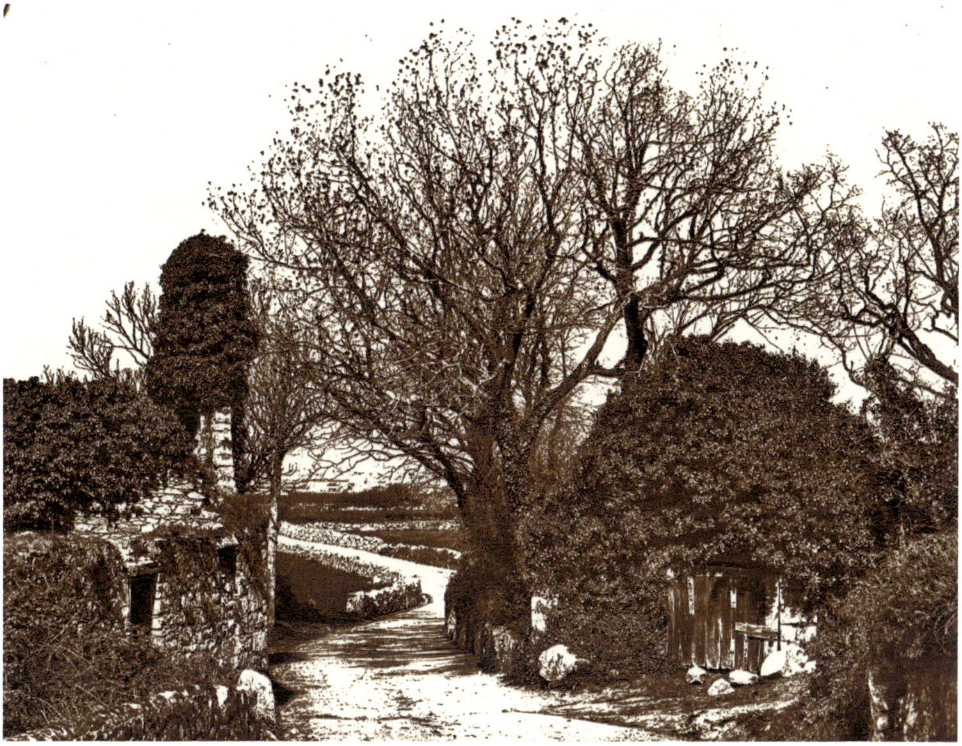

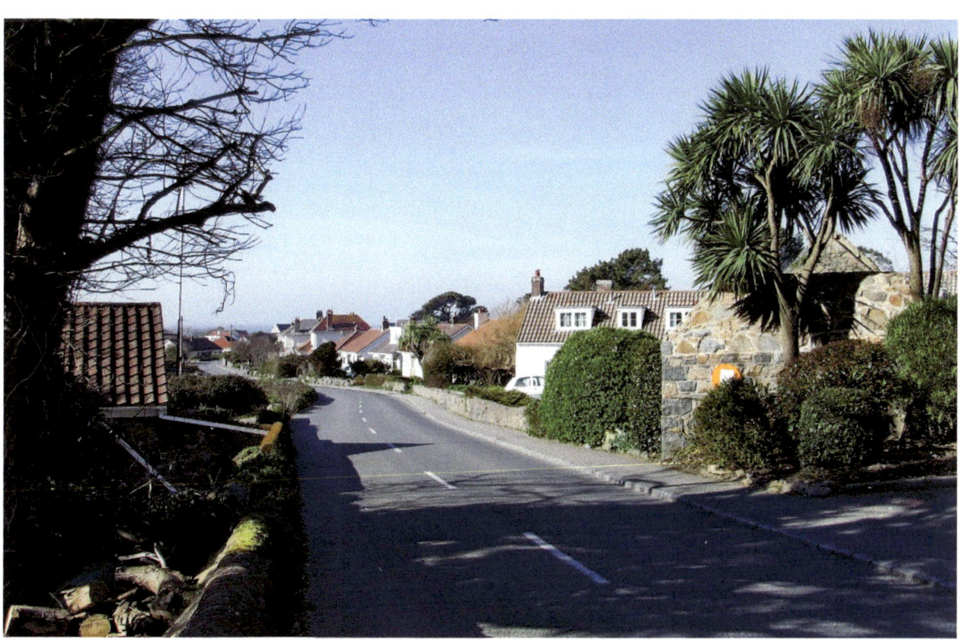

## Les Pins, Route de Cobo

A picturesque photograph from the late nineteenth century, showing the undulating Route de Cobo leading down to Cobo Bay and the sea beyond. Very evident are the granite walls bounding the road, which today has been widened so that some of the original walls have disappeared. On the left was once an old farmhouse called Les Pins.

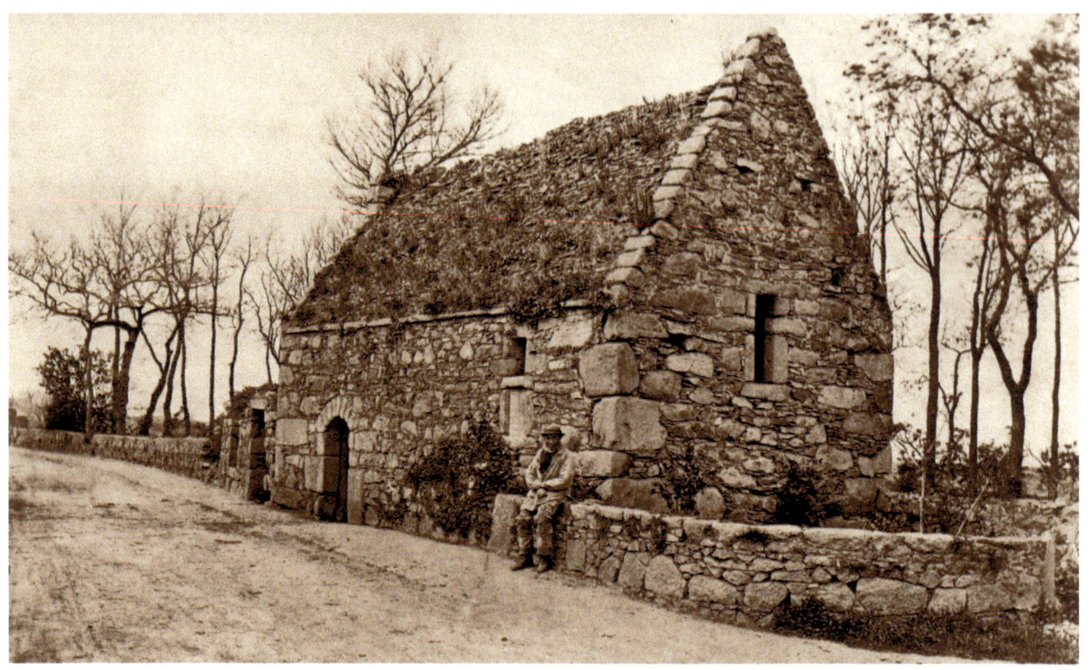

## St Appoline's Chapel, St Saviour's

This tiny medieval chapel was built from pink Cobo granite by Nicholas Henry in 1392 in thanksgiving for his survival after service in the English Navy. It remained in use until the Reformation, but afterwards was used as a stable, and this photograph of 1870 demonstrates what a sorry state it had fallen into. Despite this, the remarkable medieval frescos painted on the walls remained largely intact. The chapel was bought by the States of Guernsey in the 1873 for £120 and was carefully restored over many decades, most recently by Wessex Archaeology in 2003.

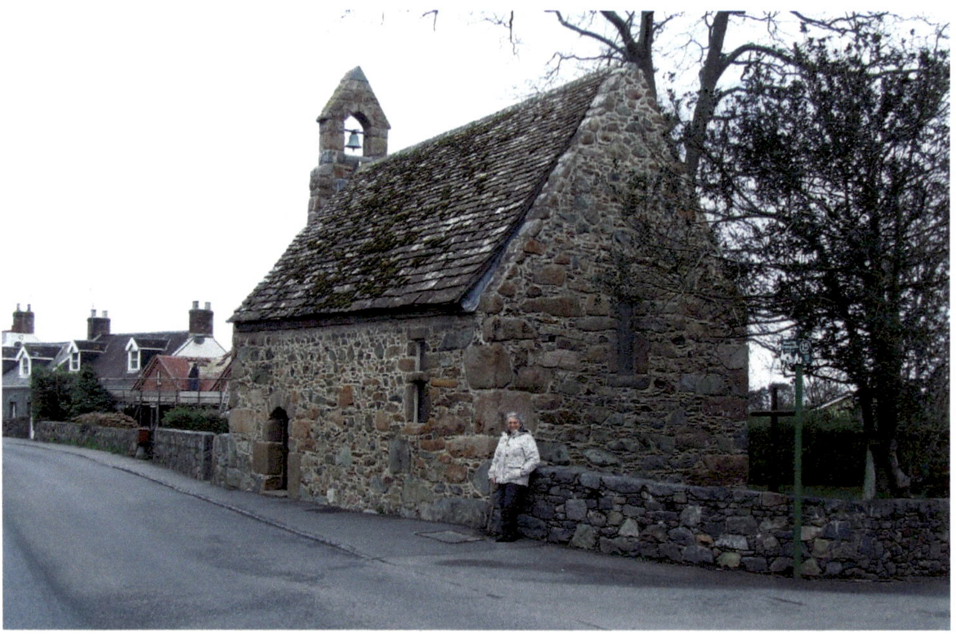

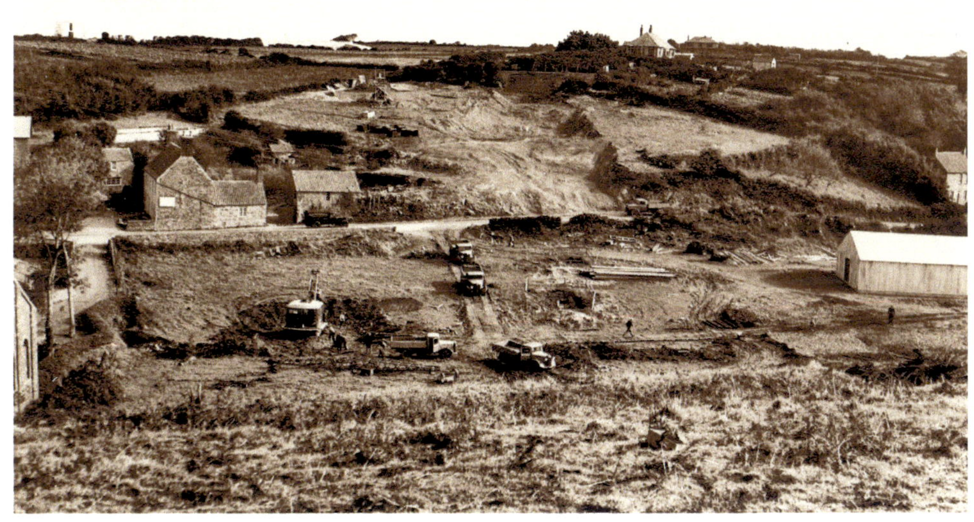

## The Reservoir Takes Shape

In 1938, work began on one of the largest engineering projects the island had ever seen – a new reservoir in St Saviours. Excavation had begun and the site of the dam was cleared of trees when this photograph was taken in September of that year. The site today scarcely looks like the same place, but the greenhouses on the horizon still survive. Work on the reservoir had to be abandoned during the German occupation and was not fully completed until January 1947, when the dam was sealed and the filling process could begin.

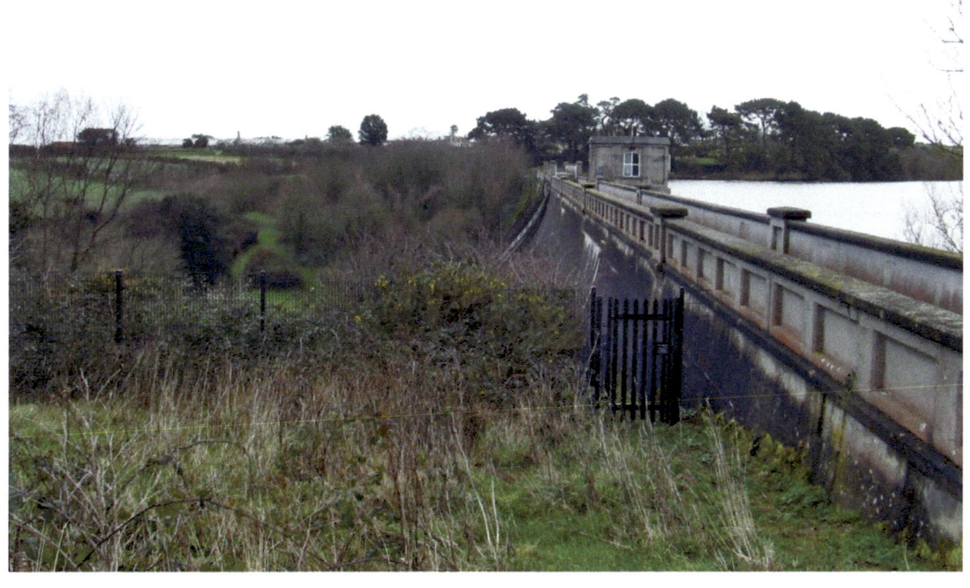

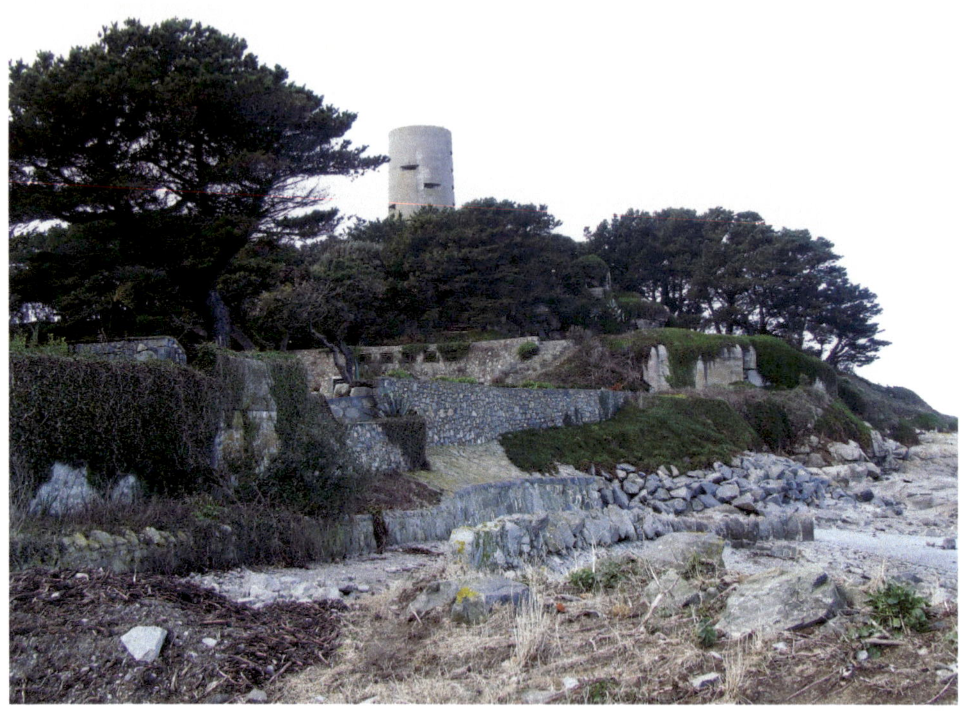

## Fort Saumarez

Of all of the fortifications around Guernsey's coastline, Fort Saumarez was perhaps the most changed by the German occupation. It began life as a true Martello tower, erected on the orders of Sir John Doyle in 1805, and named to honour Guernsey's naval hero, Sir James Saumarez. The stronghold was enclosed in walls and, in 1938, was still an impressive complex. The Germans built a massive concrete observation tower of little aesthetic merit on top of the original tower. However, as the late Nigel Jee remarked, 'although not in itself a thing of beauty, it would be missed...'

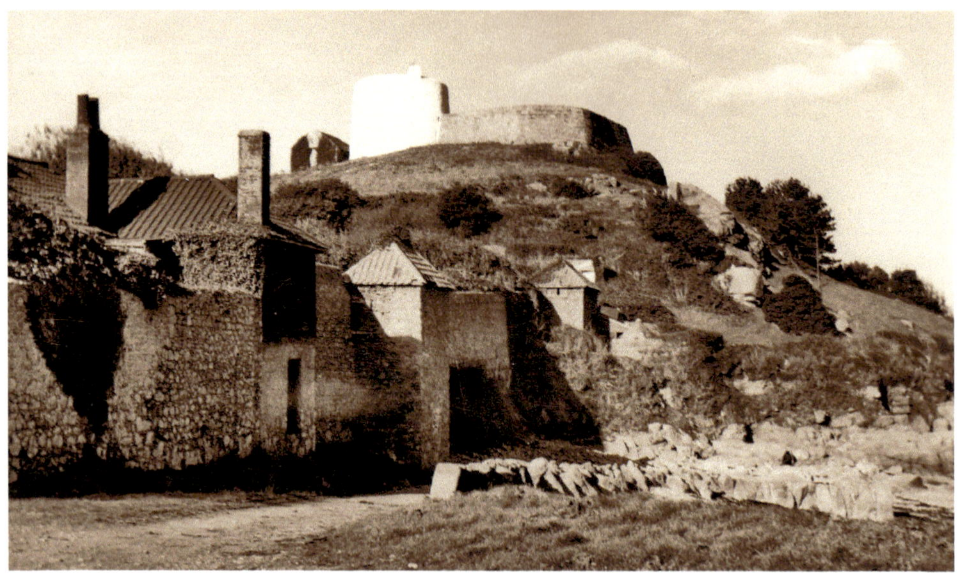

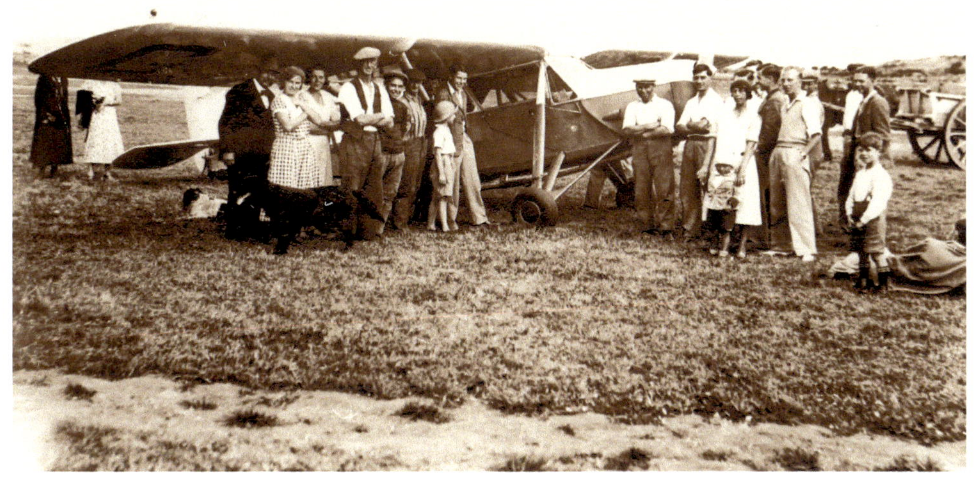

## L'Erée Aerodrome

Commercial air travel to the Channel Islands began in 1923 with Sea Eagle flying boats, and quickly expanded to other amphibious aircraft. In 1934, Guernsey Airlines made an attempt to introduce a landing strip at L'Erée as an alternative. The landing strip remained active only until 1939, when Guernsey Airport was opened, but the name 'L'Erée Aerodrome' has stuck to this day. Officially, it is the Colin Best Nature Reserve and is cared for by La Société Guernesiaise. The land encompasses several natural habitats, including a rare salt marsh, pictured here.

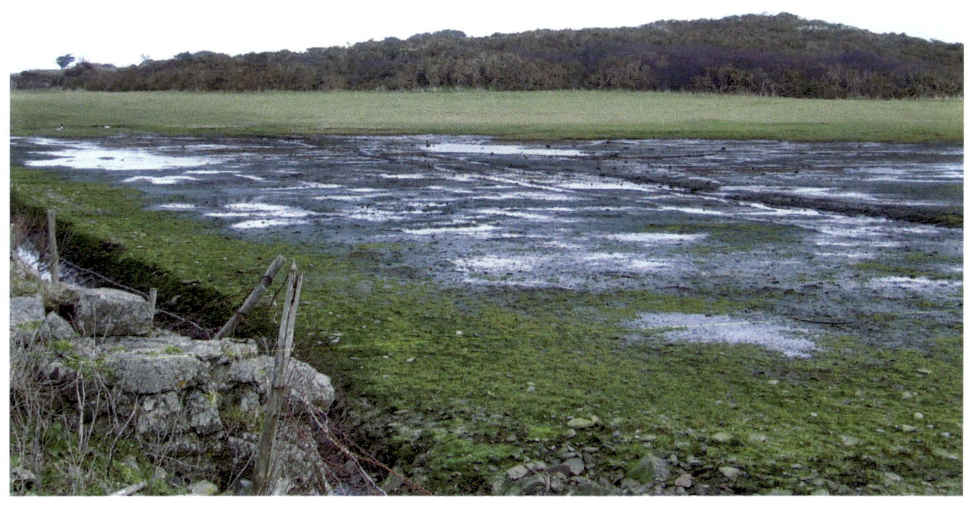

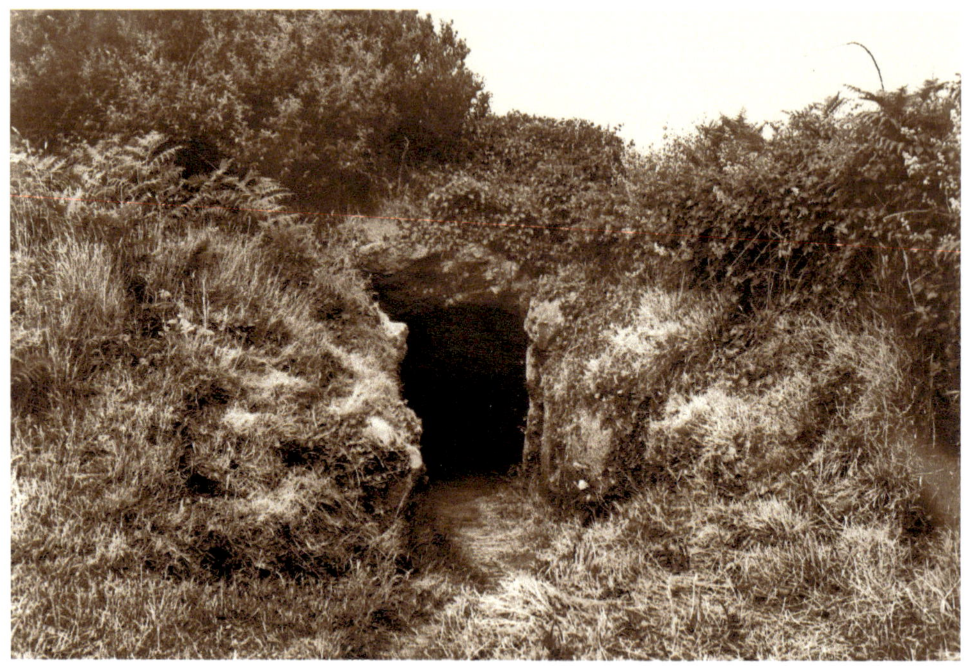

## Le Creux ès Faïes

Literally the 'Cave of the Fairies', this 4,000-year-old passage grave in St Pierre du Bois, is traditionally the entrance to the fairy kingdom. Guernsey Faïes, or Pouques, were not the pretty, benign spirits of fairy stories, but capricious tricksters who were to be avoided or placated with gifts. The short passage of fifty years between these photographs is but a moment in the life of the dolmen, but its mysteries still intrigue; at the very back of the 9-metre-long chamber is a rock shaped like a doorway – where it leads, nobody knows.

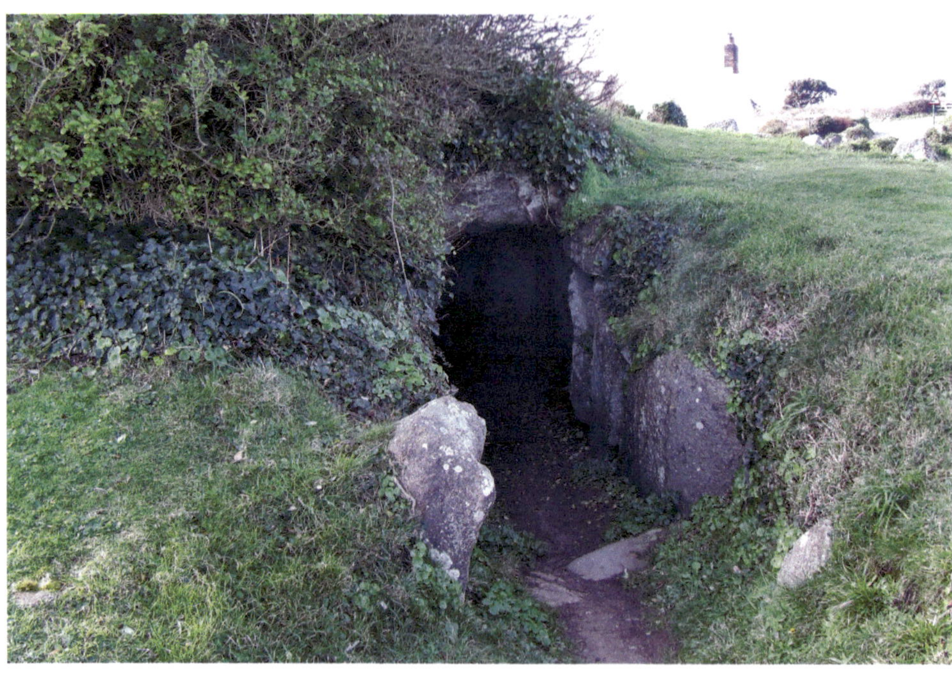

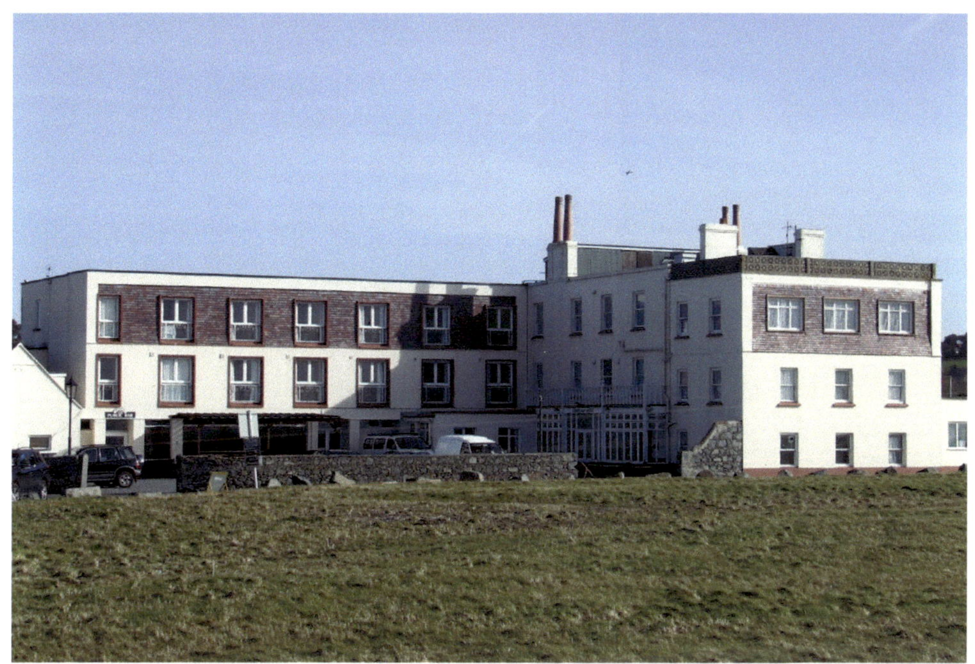

## L'Erée Hotel

L'Erée Hotel can boast of being as close to the seaside as almost anywhere else on Guernsey. L'Erée, the northernmost part of the broad sweep of Rocquaine Bay, is well known for its broad stretch of sand beach and up until the late 1940s, when the sea defences were constructed, the area was actually a large, natural sand dune. There has been a hotel on the site since at least the middle of the nineteenth century and it was a favourite stopping-off place for island tours by omnibus, serving afternoon tea and slices of Guernsey 'Gâche', a rich currant loaf.

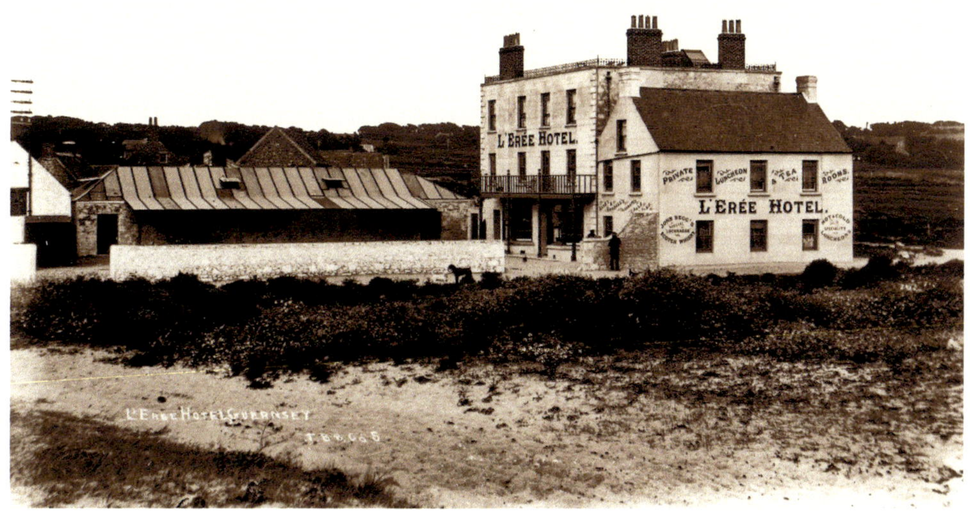

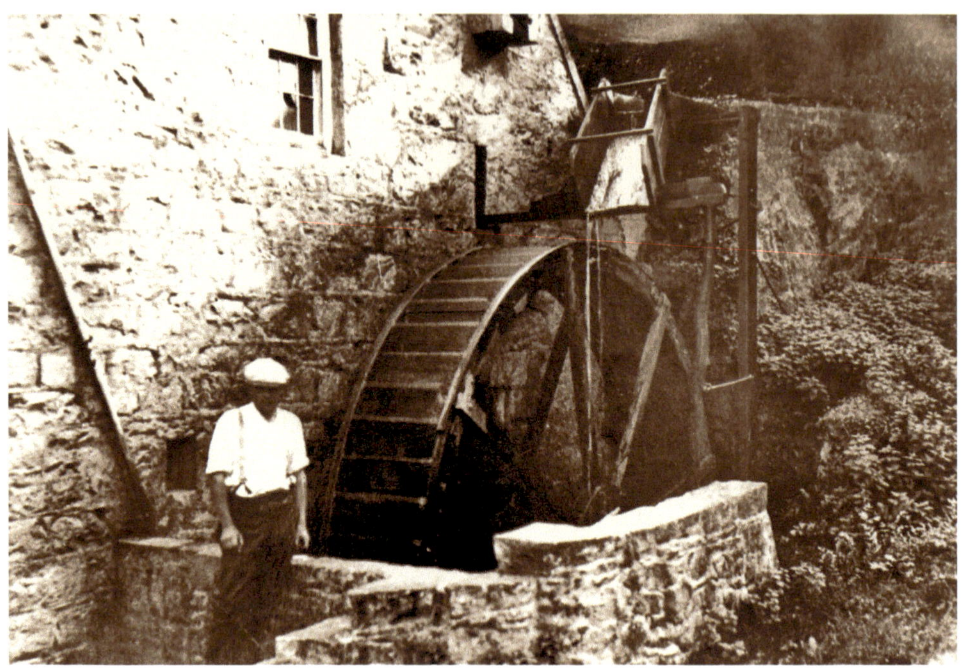

## Le Moulin de Canteraine

Deep in a beautiful valley in St Pierre du Bois is Guernsey's last functional watermill. The waterwheel is attached to a sixteenth-century farm complex called La Quanteraine (or Canteraine) owned for many generations by the de Garis family. Pictured is Mr F. de Garis' farm carpenter W. Le Lacheur in around 1930, shortly before the wheel fell into disuse. The property was given to the National Trust of Guernsey in 1989, and fully restored with the help of students from the College of Further Education.

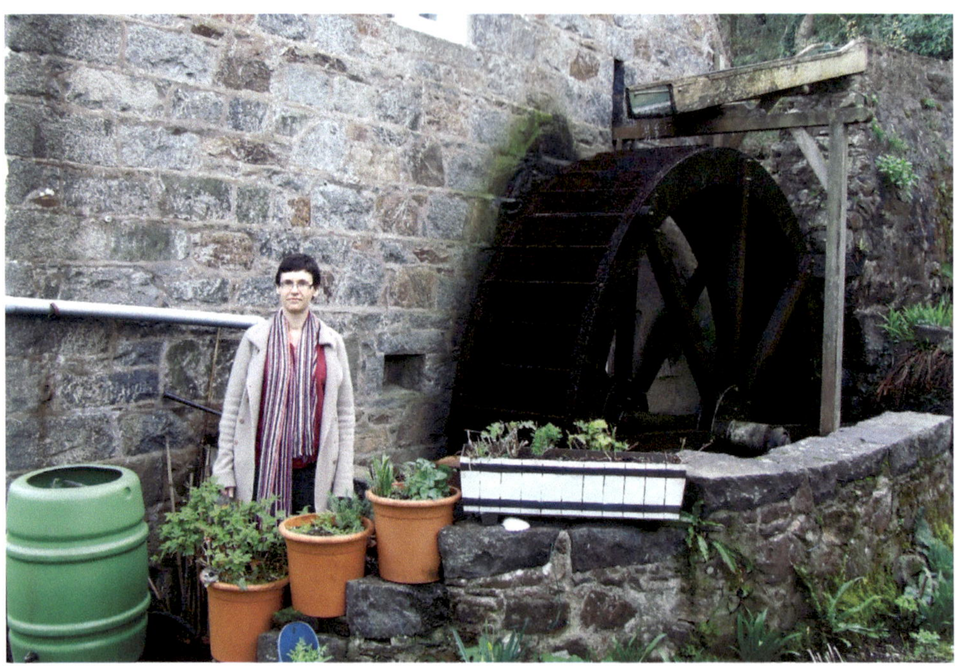

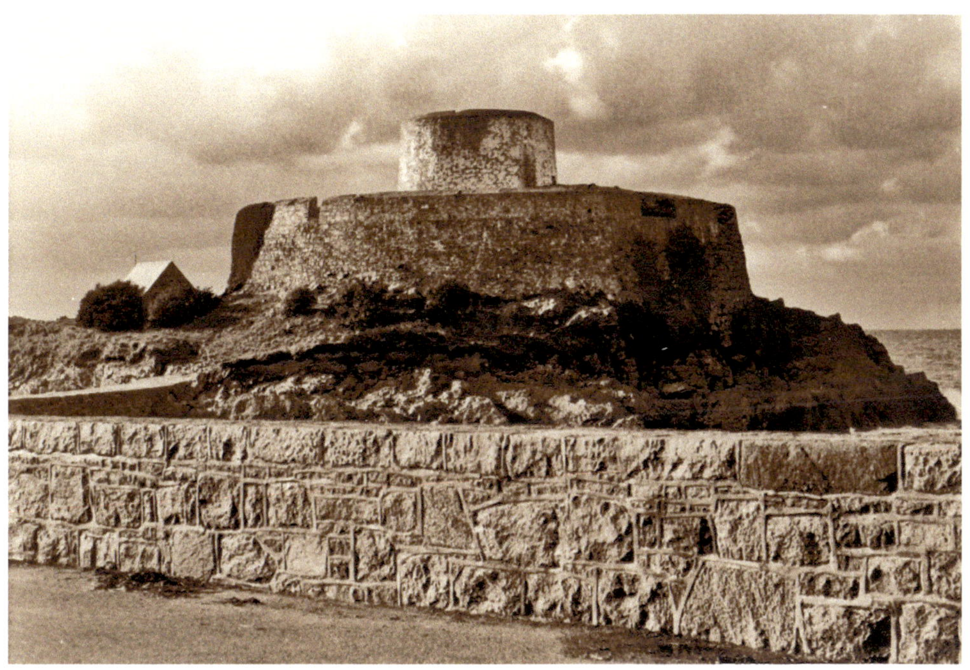

## Fort Grey

A fort with many names. It was originally Chateau de Rocquaine, before being renamed Fort Grey during the Napoleonic era, but this west coast fort is known more familiarly by islanders as 'The Cup and Saucer'. The photographs, taken before and after a major restoration in 1975, show how much work was done to turn the fort into a tourist attraction without detracting from its charm. Originally a small medieval castle, a Martello tower was built in the centre and a curtain wall erected by Sir John Doyle in 1804. Today, the Martello tower houses a fascinating shipwreck museum.

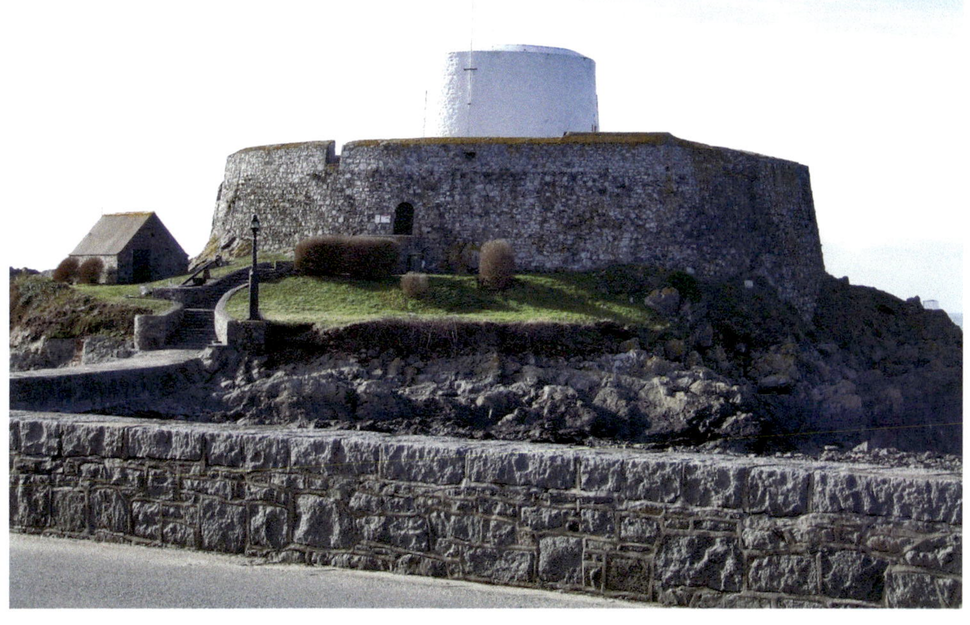

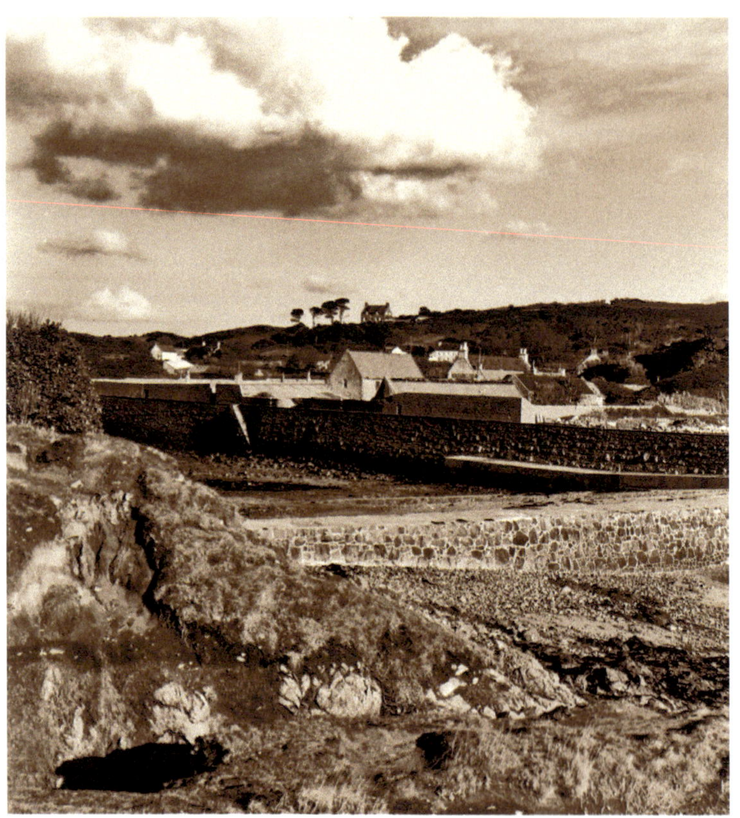

**View from Fort Grey**
Looking back towards the Rocquaine coast road from the foot of Fort Grey, the nineteenth-century causeway remains unchanged over the decades. The fort is built on a tidal islet and would be otherwise inaccessible by foot during the high tide. The cluster of buildings directly opposite comprised the house, workshops and vinery of the Le Couteur family. The house on the hill above, with its distinctive dormer windows, was designed by renowned architect Spencer Carey Curtis. It has since been demolished and replaced by a larger house, now somewhat obscured by trees.

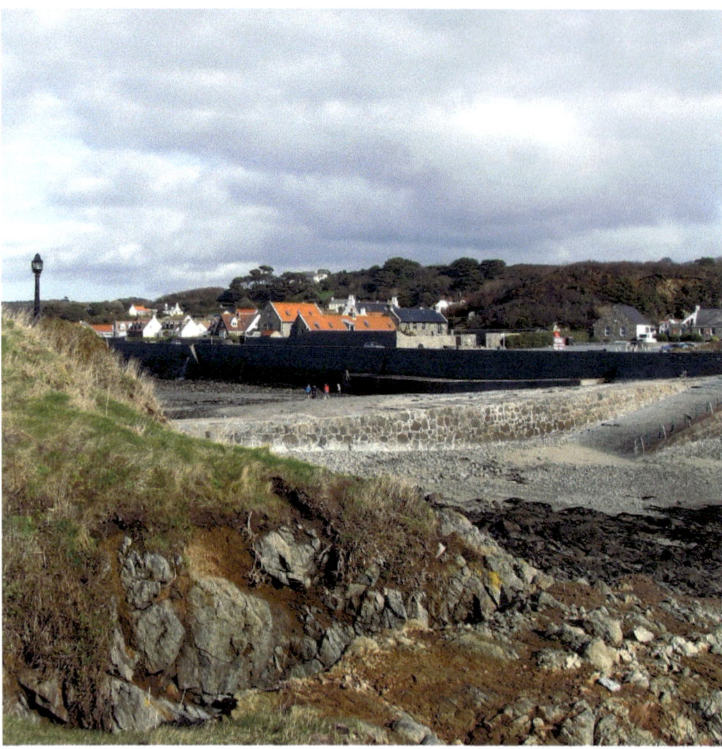

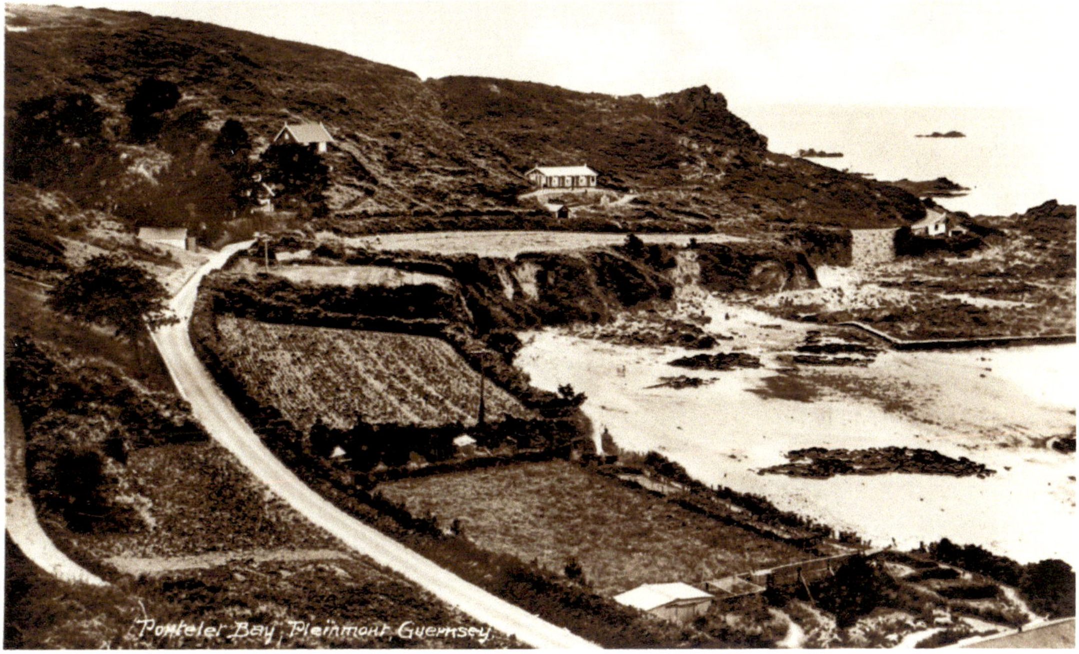

### Portelet Bay, Torteval

This pretty little working harbour with its picturesque piers, mussel and oyster beds and a sandy sweep of beach has always been popular with locals and families. In the 1930s, the road to Pezeries Point that runs behind the bay was in daily use and the land tidily cultivated. Now pine trees dominate the landscape and the road was closed in the late 1980s, as it was becoming unstable.

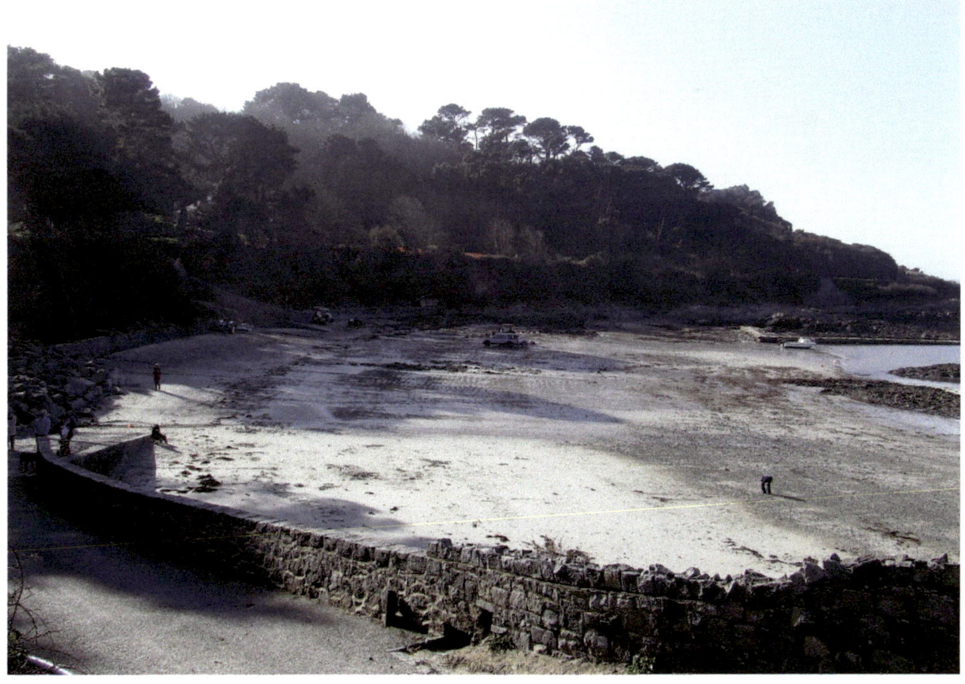

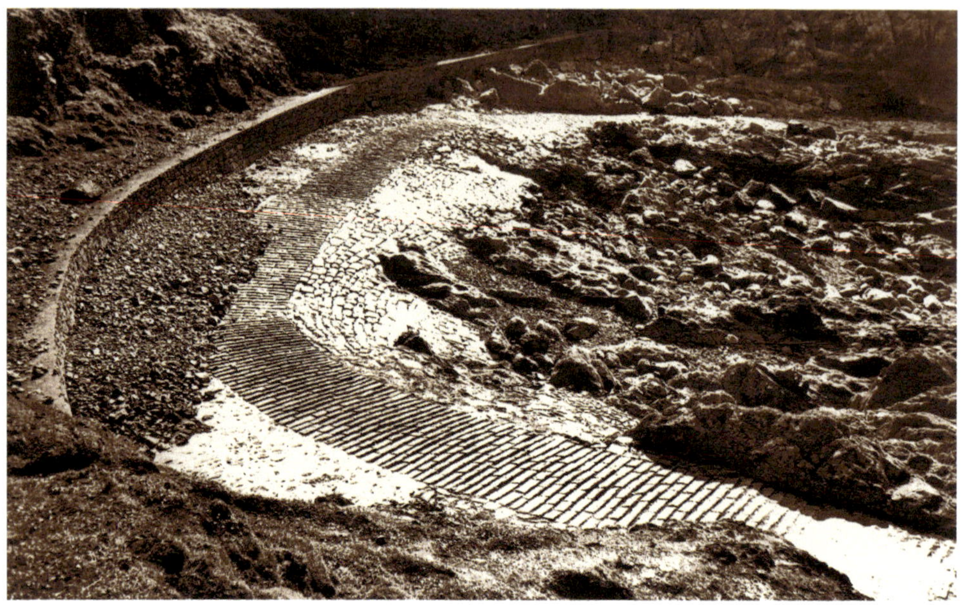

## Vraicing Slipway at Les Pezeries, Torteval

'Vraic' is seaweed (usually bladderwrack), which was collected at certain times of year by cutting (*vraic scié*) or by collecting weed that had washed up on the shore (*vraic venant*). It was used as a fertiliser for the soil as it is rich in potash, but it could also be dried and used as fuel. The collecting of vraic was a common right and a free commodity. This slipway was designed for the horse-drawn carts, laden with vraic, to safely carry their load. The shifting of pebbles is the only observable change over fifty years.

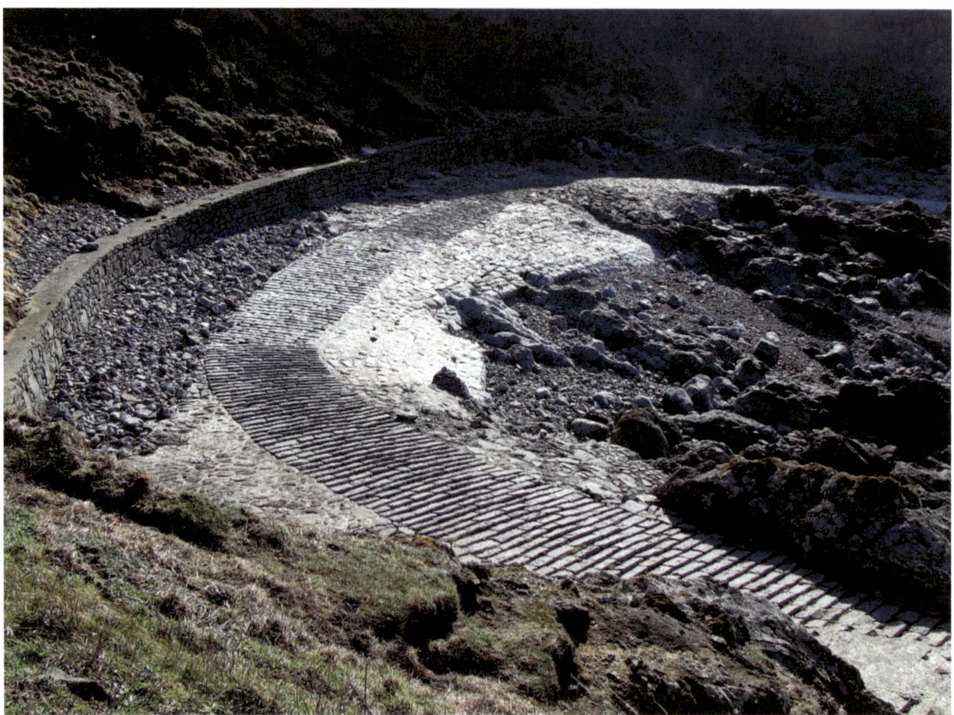

## Victor Hugo's Haunted House

Victor Hugo lived in exile on Guernsey from 1855 to 1870 and during that time wrote some of his most enduring works, including *Les Misérables.* However, it is *Lcs Travailleurs de la Mer,* the novel set in Guernsey, which is best remembered on the island. In the novel, a Napoleonic watch house on the Torteval cliffs becomes a strange and haunted place. He said of the windows, 'they resemble the sockets of the eyes from which the balls have been torn...' Alas, all that remains today are the ruined walls.

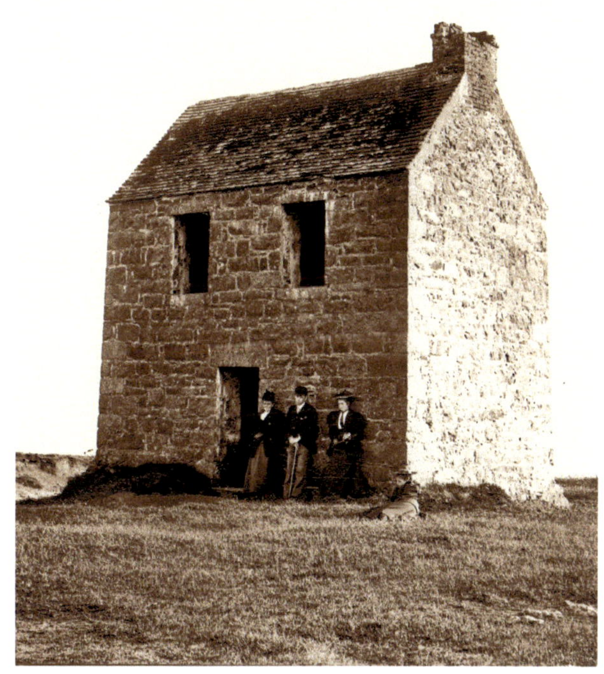

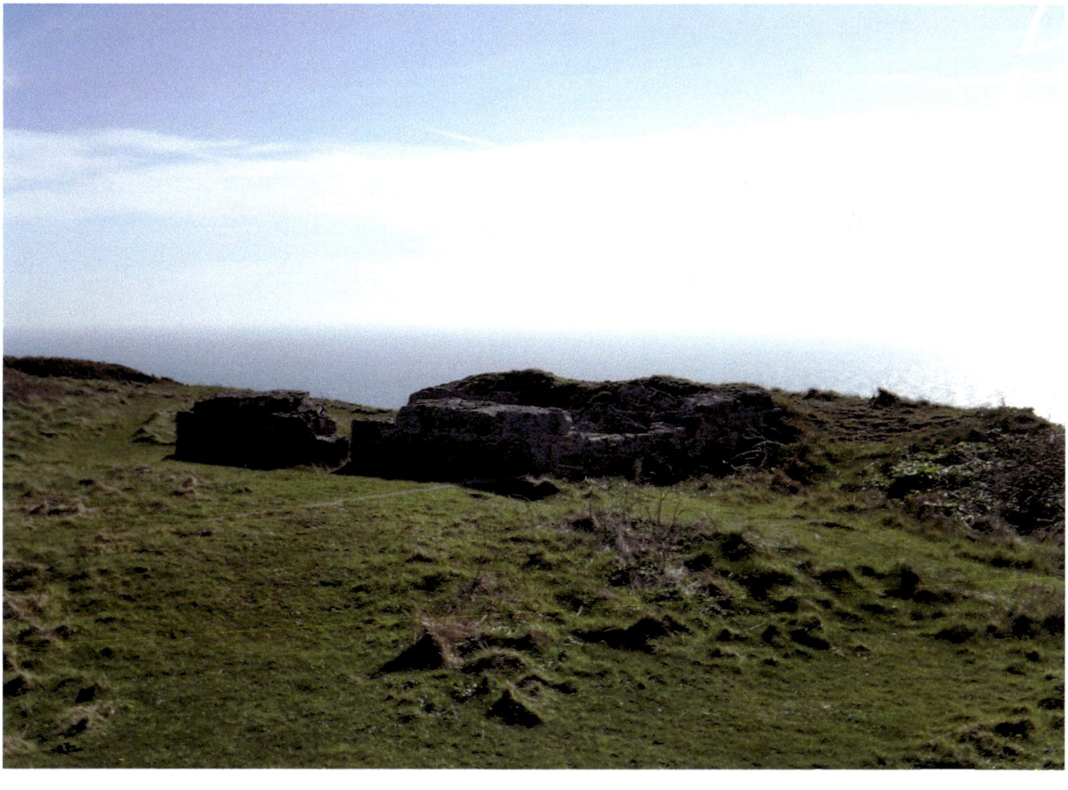

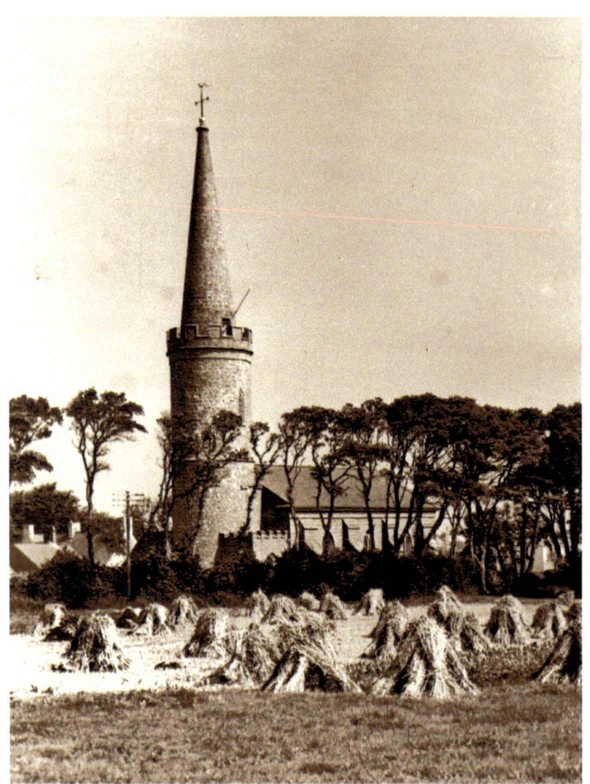

### St Philippe de Torteval

The parish church of St Philippe de Torteval is a study in contrasts: it is the smallest of the ten parish churches, yet has the tallest spire; it was the most recently built, yet boasts the oldest peal of bells; and it is the only church with a round spire. It was built by architect John Wilson in 1816 to replace the old church of St Marie de Torteval, which had fallen into disrepair. Whatever the date, season or weather, it drowses peacefully in its rural setting.

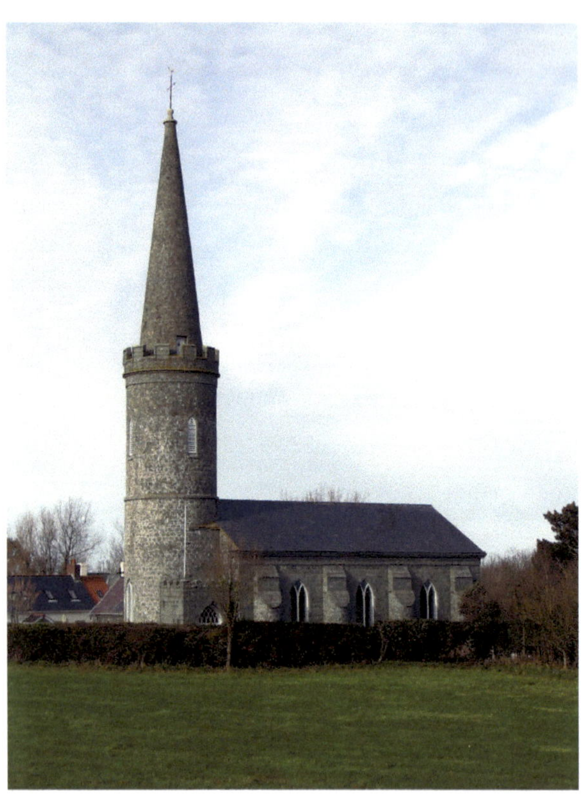

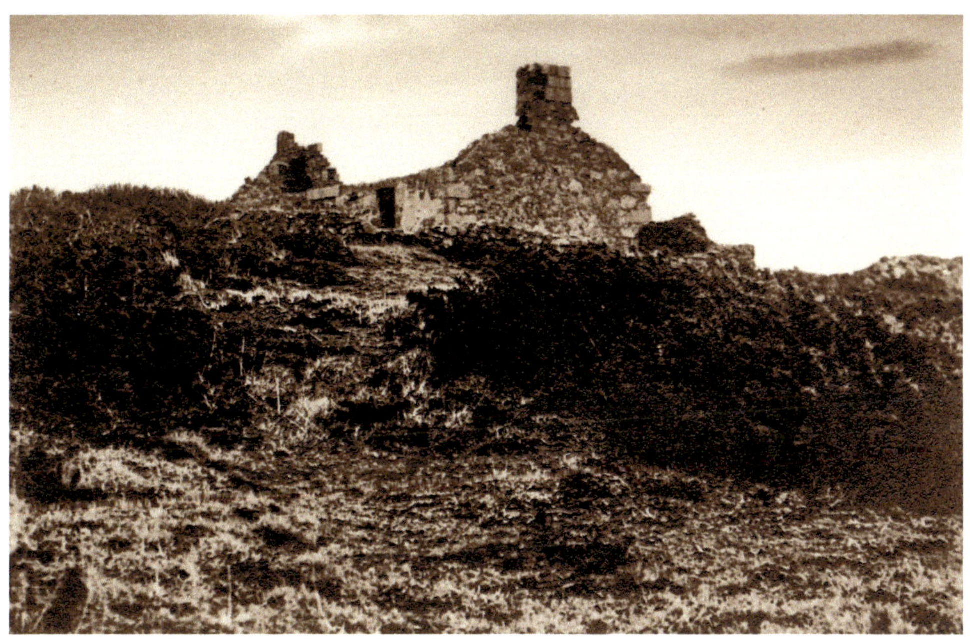

## Mont Herault Watch House

Perched high on a cliff and partially ruined, Mont Herault Watch House looked bleak and neglected in the early twentieth century. The wild cliffs of St Pierre du Bois and Torteval have been fortified at several points in their history, and the watch house was one of the first structures. It was built at some time after 1793 as an observation post and manned by soldiers of the West Regiment of the Guernsey Militia against the threat of French invasion. Now restored, it has a friendlier aspect, nestled among the gorse bushes that grow abundantly in this area.

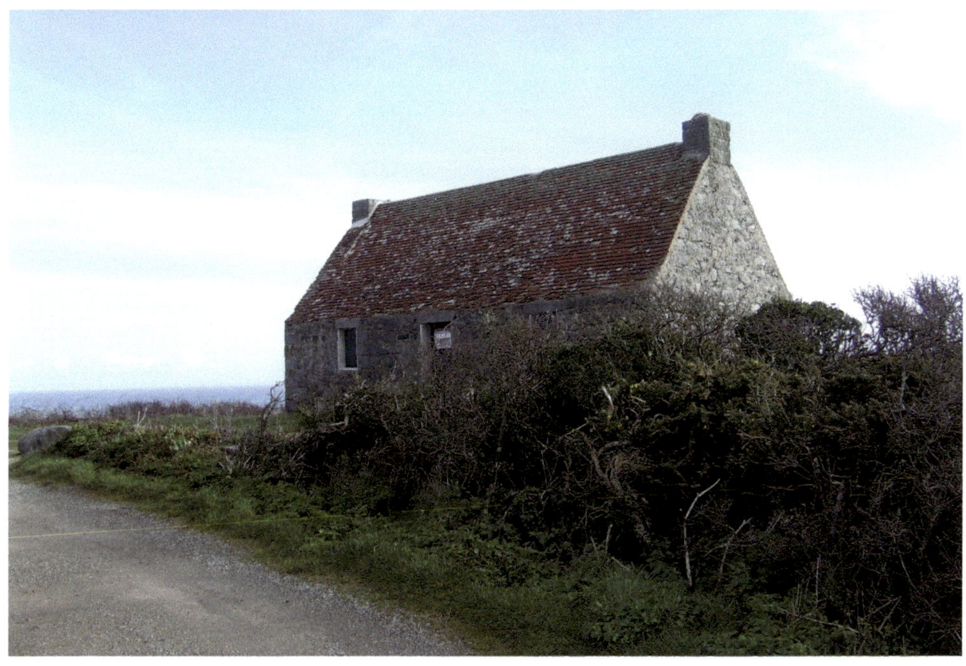

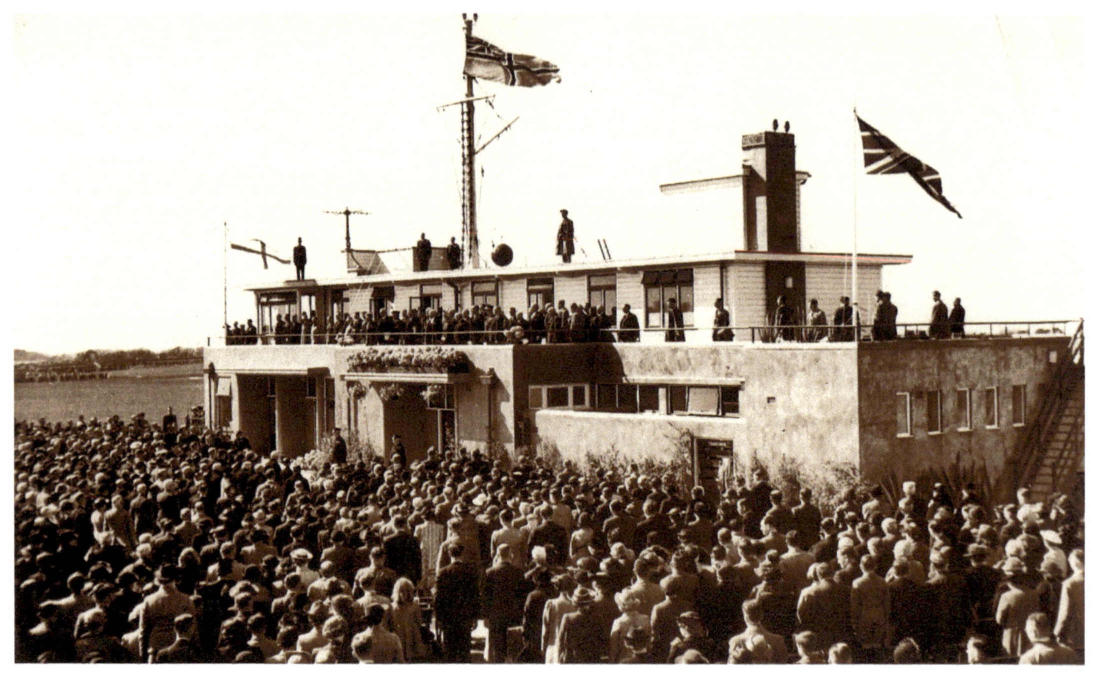

## Guernsey Airport

Guernsey's first airport was officially opened on 5 May 1939 by Sir Kingsley Wood, Secretary of State for Air. The Bailiff of Guernsey, Victor Carey, declared that 'we must take our place in a world of progress...' However, scarcely had regular services been established when, on 30 June 1940, German Junkers troop carriers landed and the occupation of Guernsey began. Regular flights resumed in 1946, but by the early twenty-first century, the building had outgrown itself. This new terminal building was erected between 2002 and 2004 and is designed to transfer 1.25 million passengers every year.

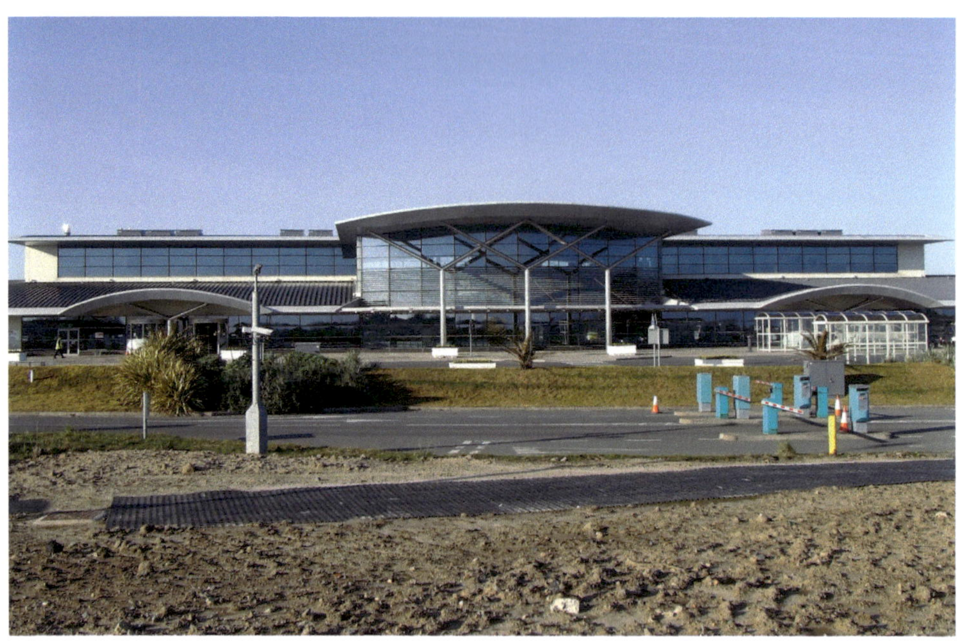

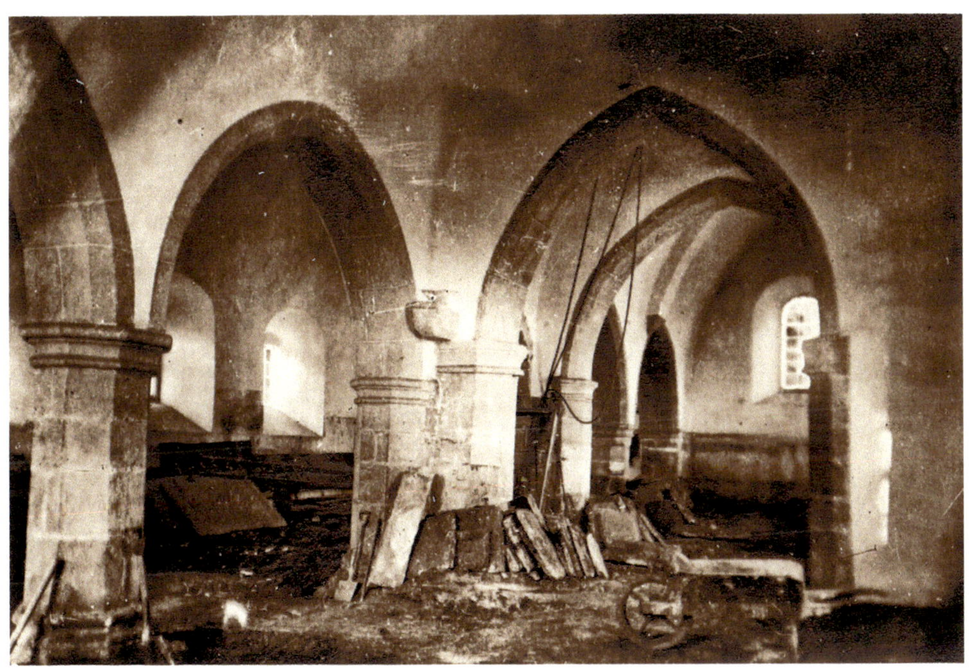

## Interior of Forest Parish Church

The church of St Trinité de la Forêt has stood in Guernsey's highest parish since the thirteenth century. The photograph of 1891 shows the church undergoing renovations to the 'crossing', where the old chancel meets the fifteenth-century north aisle. The happy results of the renovation, plus the care of parishioners, are evident in the modern photograph.

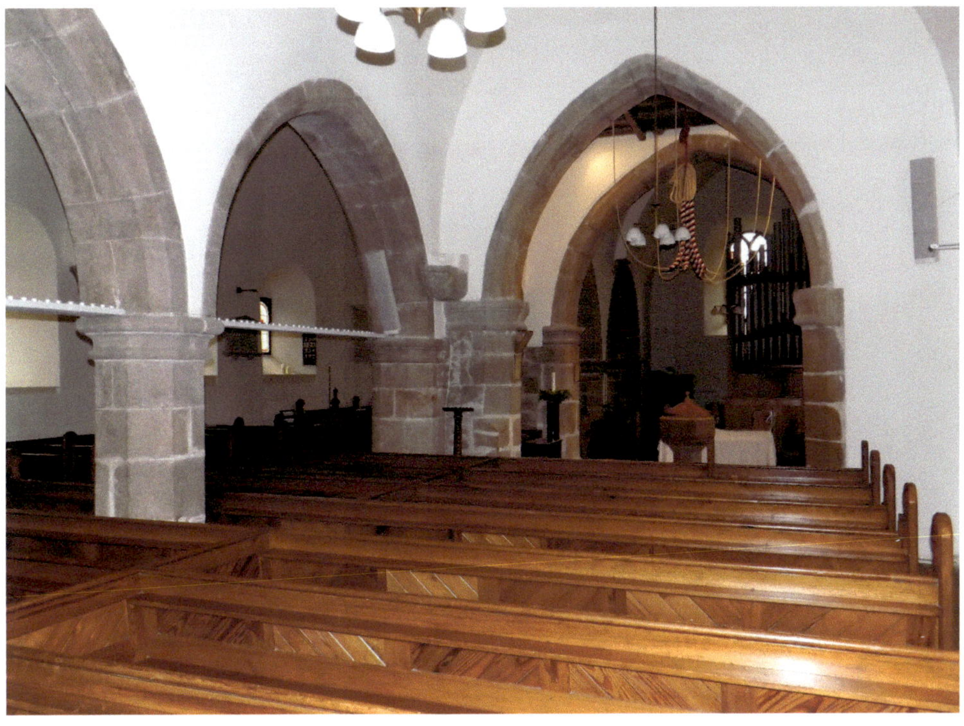

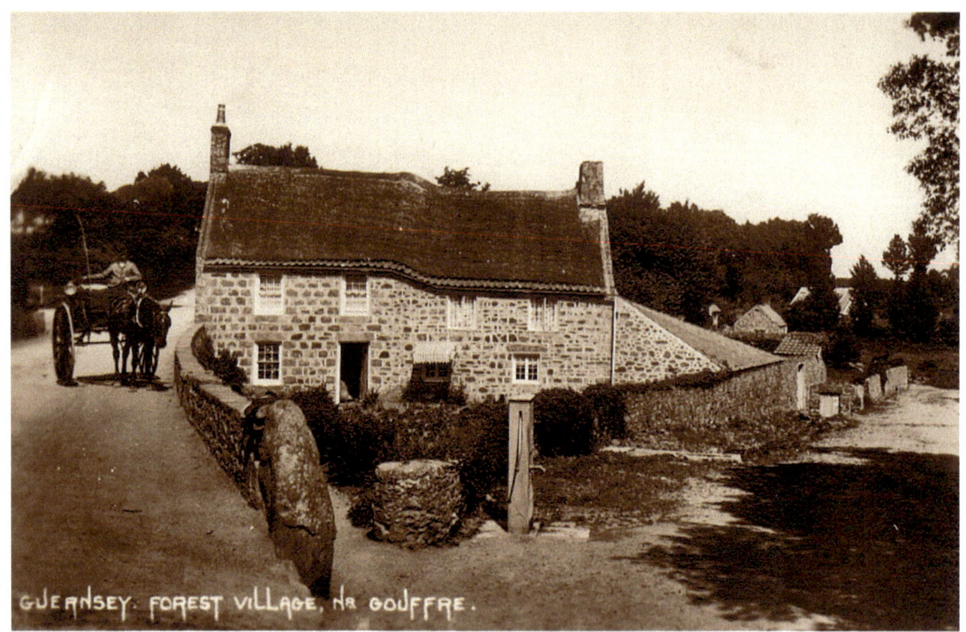


### Le Perron du Roi at Le Bourg

The main road in the Forest parish has changed quite a lot over the years, not least the house on the corner; the traffic is also considerably more frequent than in the postcard of the 1920s. However, it is the neolithic menhir that is of interest here, for that has not changed at all. Standing upright at the end of the curved wall is Le Perron du Roi, a standing stone that once lived on the opposite side of the road and was used as a mounting block (*perron*).

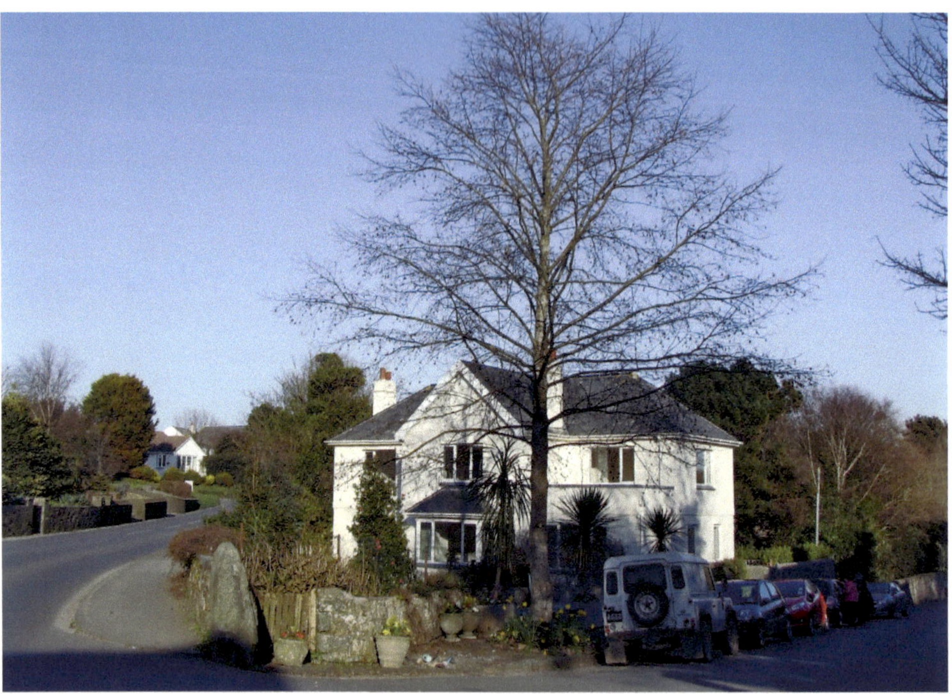

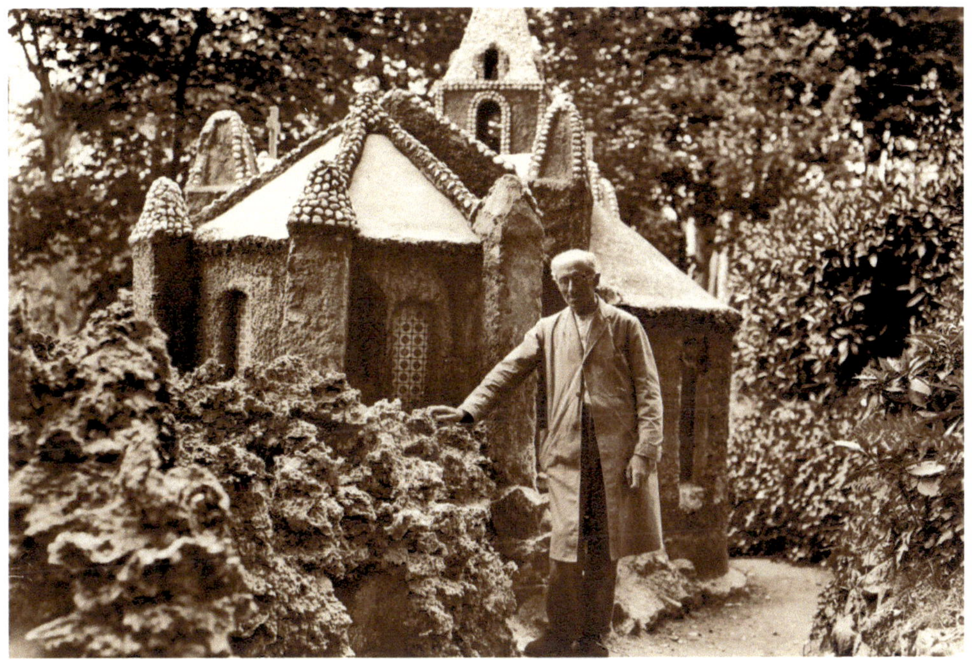

### The Little Chapel

This tiny chapel in Les Vauxbelets is Guernsey's most visited tourist attraction – and with good reason. It is both charming and quirky, representing, as it does, one man's labour of love. Brother Déodat, one of the De La Salle Brothers, who at the time ran a school at Les Vauxbelets, conceived of building a miniature replica of the shrine at Lourdes. The chapel that you see today is his third attempt, and its charm lies in the many thousands of pieces of pottery, pebbles and glass that decorate it.

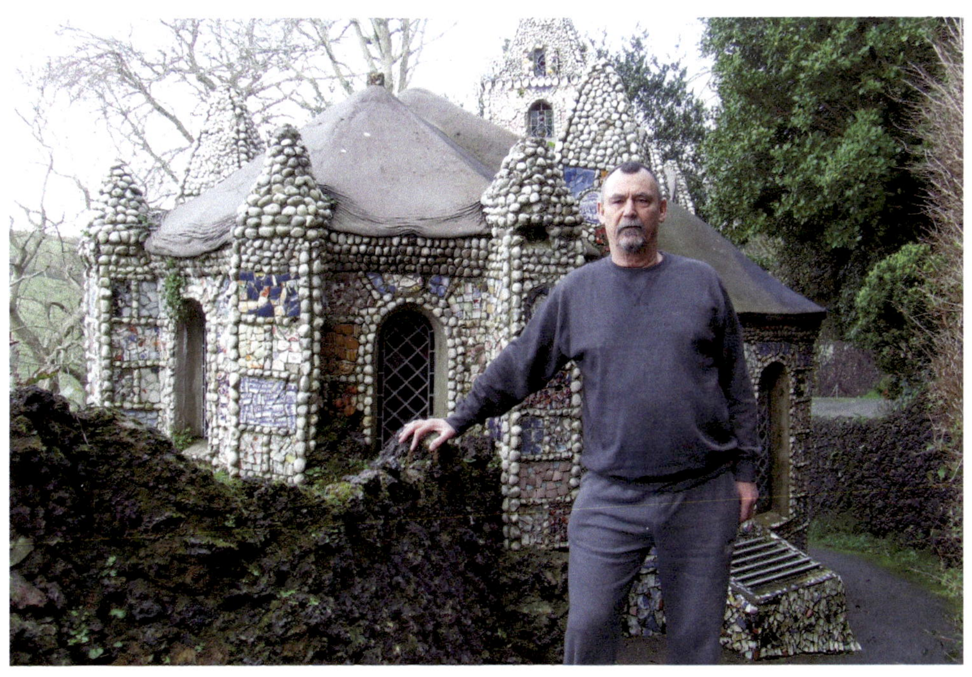

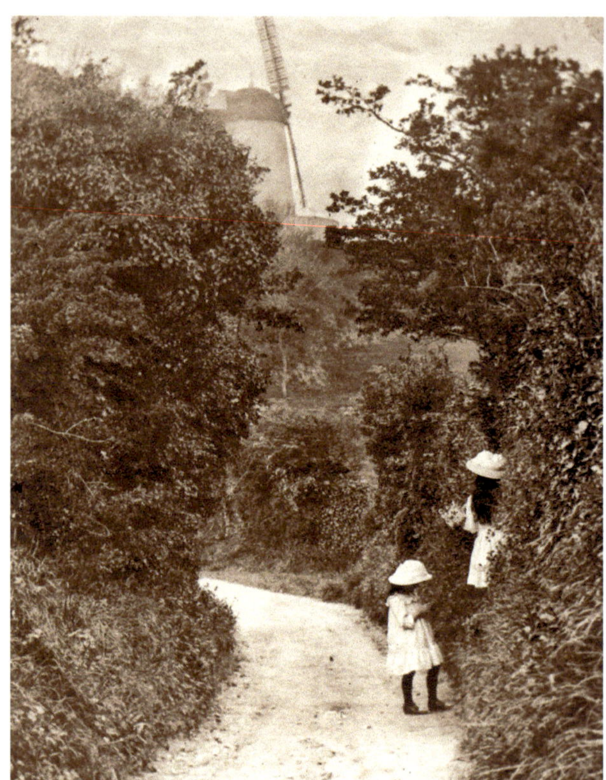



The windmill in Steam Mill Lane, St Martin, was built by the Ozanne family in 1825, and was still grinding corn nearly 100 years later, before falling into disuse. The rural scene belies the fact that it stands right on the border of St Peter Port and not far from the busy thoroughfare of Ruette Braye. Today, the mill has been beautifully restored and is the workshop and showroom of Catherine Best, one of Guernsey's finest jewellers and goldsmiths.

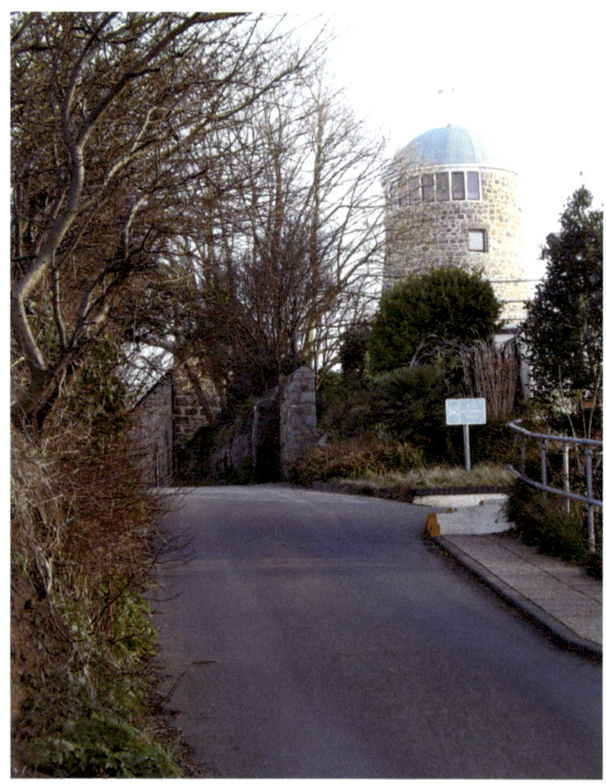

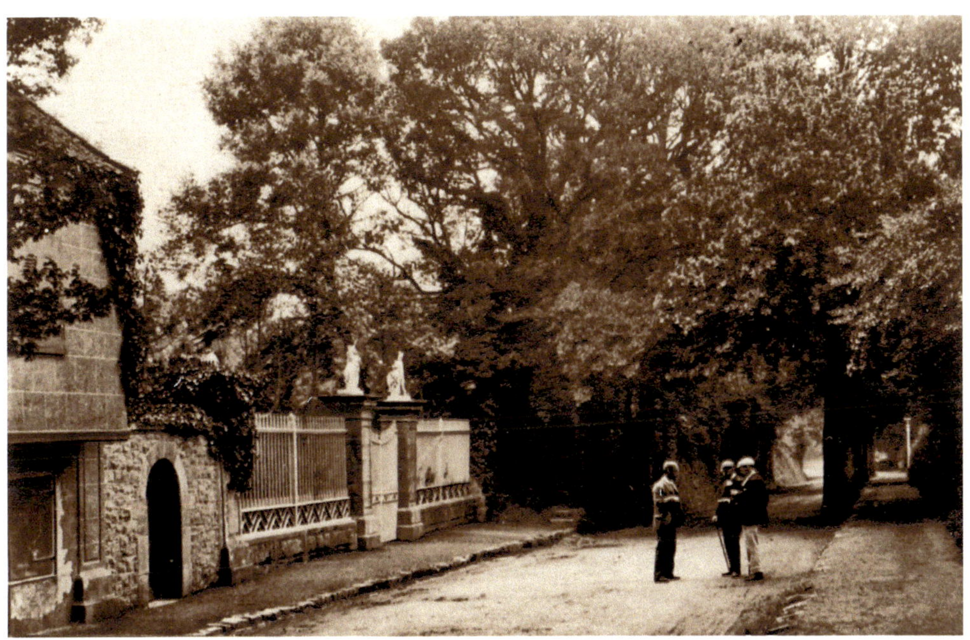

## Route de Saumarez, St Martin

A rare example in Guernsey of trees being taken away instead of planted! Route de Saumarez is the main linking road from St Peter Port to St Martin, and today, a lot of traffic passes along it – having a conversation in the middle of the road would not be recommended. The gentlemen in question are standing outside the gates of Guernsey's mini-stately home, Saumarez Manor. The gates were built in the 1750s by John de Saumarez and display a unicorn and a greyhound, supporters of the family coat of arms.

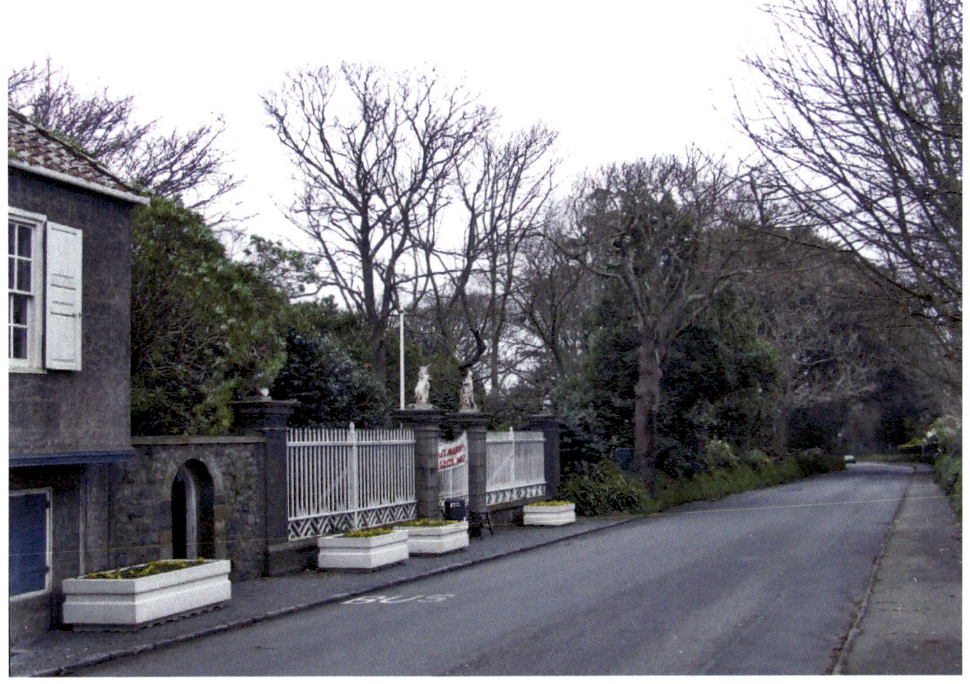

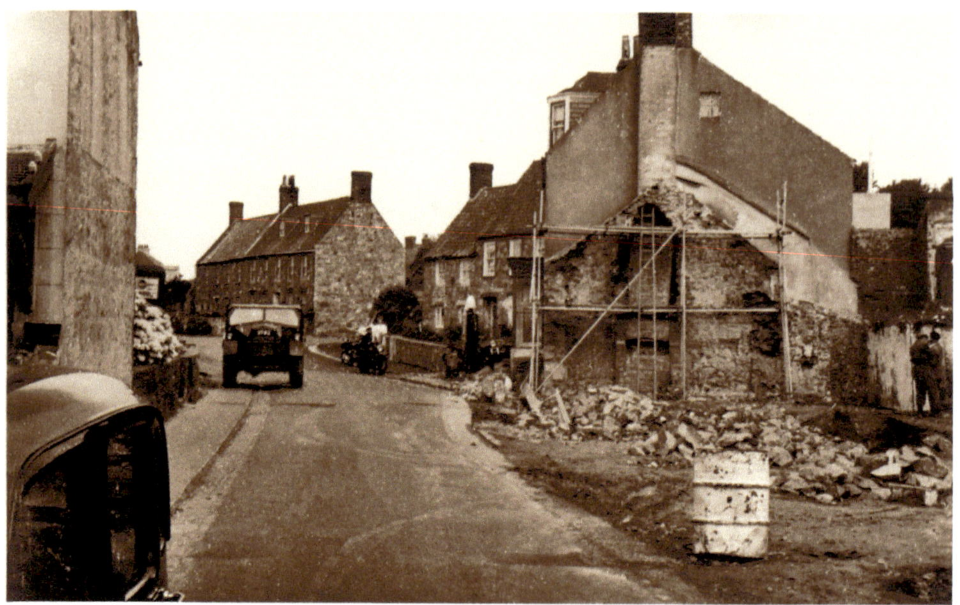

## Grande Rue, St Martin

The major route through St Martin's village, Grand Rue, was slightly widened in 1954 to accommodate the increasing traffic on the island. A row of old Guernsey granite houses were demolished, as this photograph shows, leaving just the fine house on the corner still standing. The shops, a garage, a bank and a supermarket now fill the space the houses left, but the traffic remains a problem!

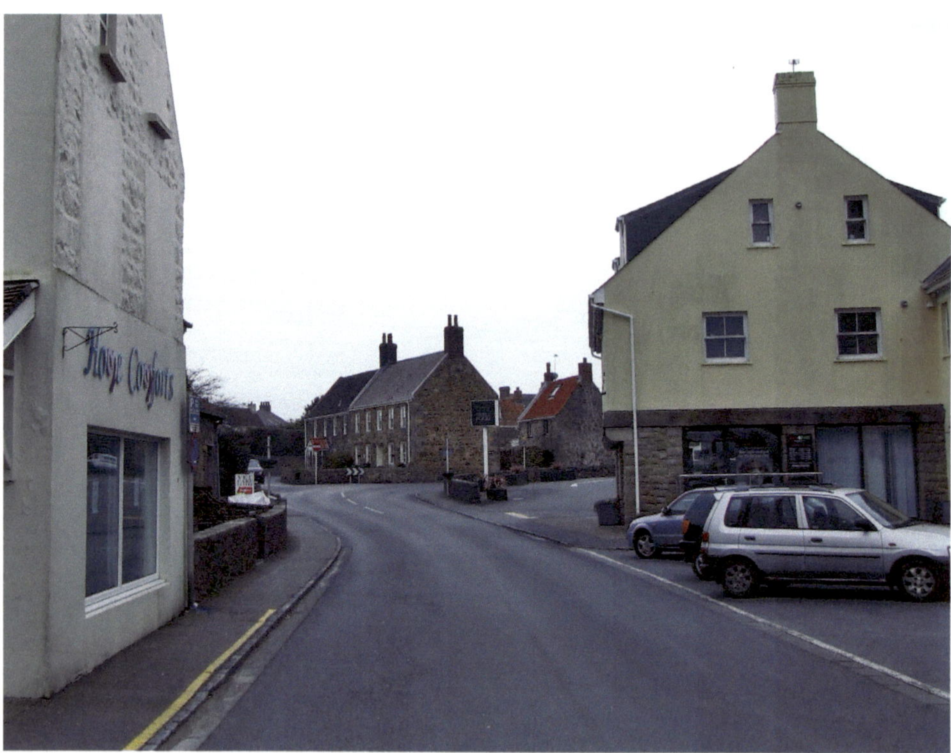

## Doyle Column

Doyle Column at Jerbourg Point has had a rather unlucky history. The first column, built in 1816 in honour of Sir John Doyle, was 75 feet high, but it was built of poor quality stone and had collapsed by 1819. The second column erected in its place and undergoing repairs in this photograph of 1929, was altogether stronger and featured an internal spiral staircase, which led to an admirable view from the balcony. It was demolished by German engineers during the Second World War. The third (and last) version was built of blue and pink granite in 1954 at a cost of £1,400.

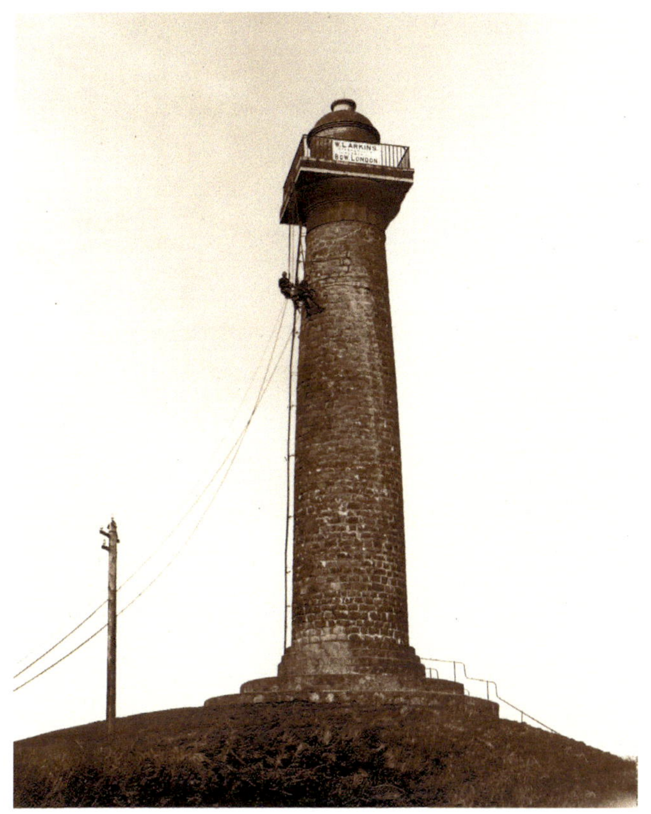

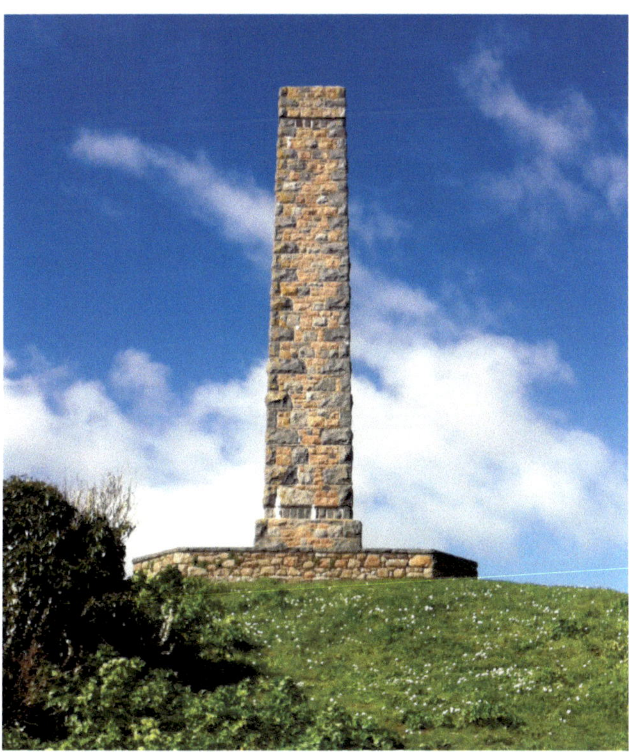

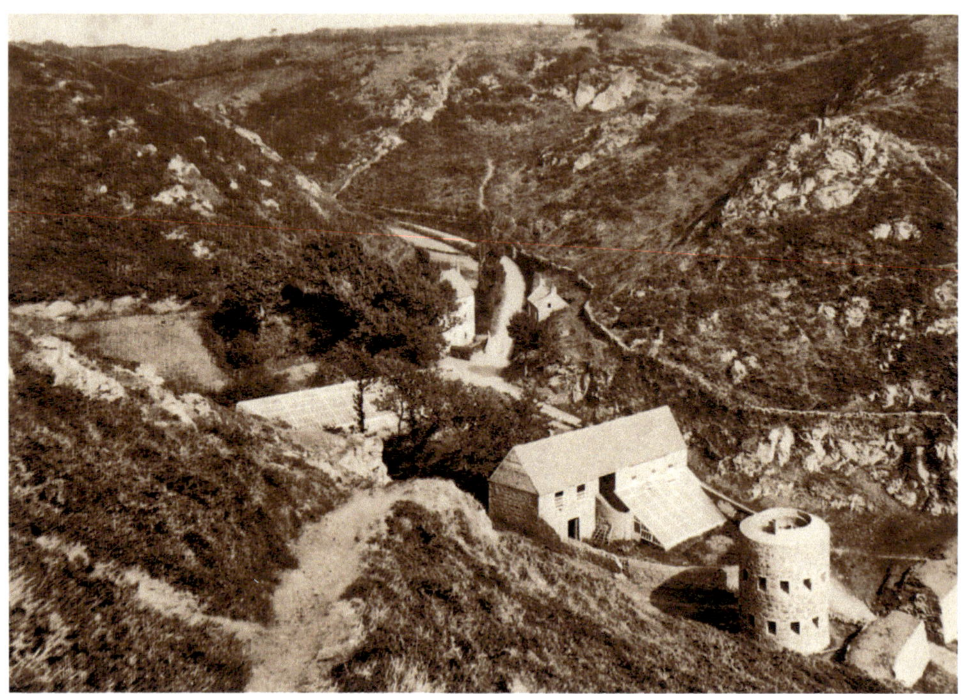

### View of Petit Bôt

'Bôt' comes from the Normand French word 'Bosq', meaning woody, and the deep valley leading down to Petit Bôt bay was once thickly wooded. By the nineteenth century, much of this woodland had disappeared and two mill buildings can clearly be seen. The mill stream still runs down the valley and it was of sufficient size to run two mills: the 'Upper', glimpsed only slightly, and the 'Lower', a more substantial building nearer the sea. The trees have now returned to the valley and the Lower Mill remains as a café.

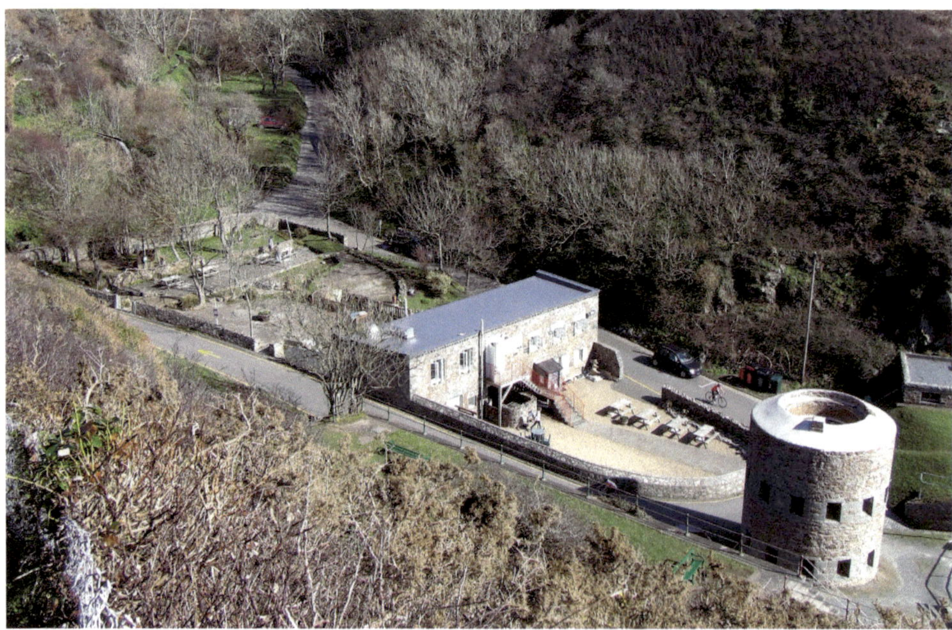

### The Upper Mill Stream, Petit Bôt

The mill wheel turned by the Upper Mill wheel at Petit Bôt was installed at the beginning of the nineteenth century. It was large by island standards, being 9 metres in diameter and weighing several tons. In the 1890s, one of the axles broke and the wheel sank under its own weight to settle in the stream bed. During the German occupation, Petit Bôt was declared a forbidden zone and the Upper Mill house, along with its wheel, was pulled down. All that remains today is the mill stream channel and some of the mill house stonework.

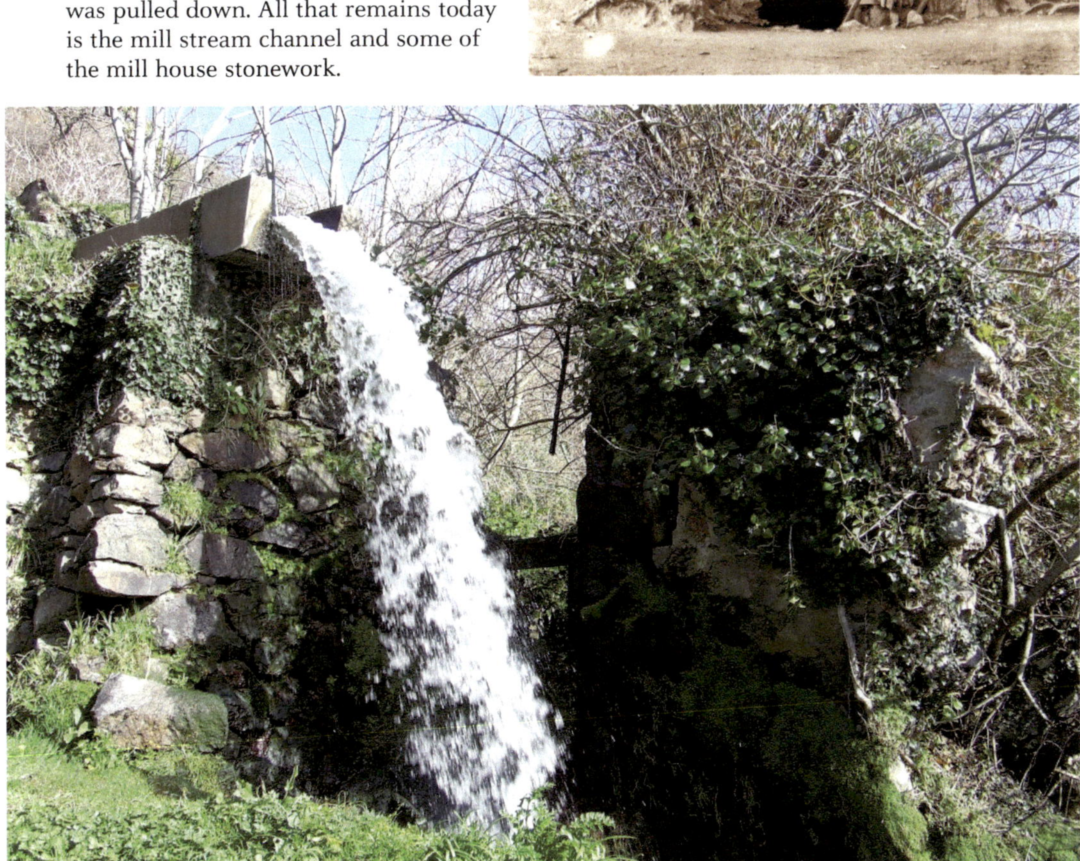

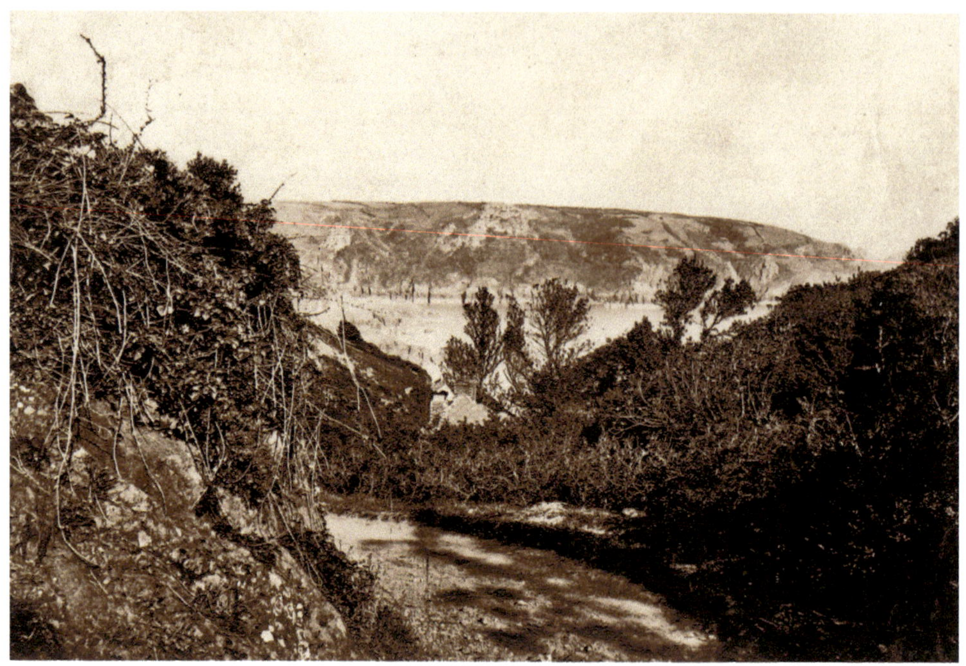

### Moulin Huet Valley

Moulin Huet, on Guernsey's rugged south coast, is green, pretty and replete with wonderful views that inspired Renoir, who painted it in 1883. The 1870s photograph shows the top of the charming cottages nestled under the hill, a scene typical of the narrow valleys of this part of St Martin. Today's scene has scarcely changed, except that we can now appreciate the glorious colour of the sea.

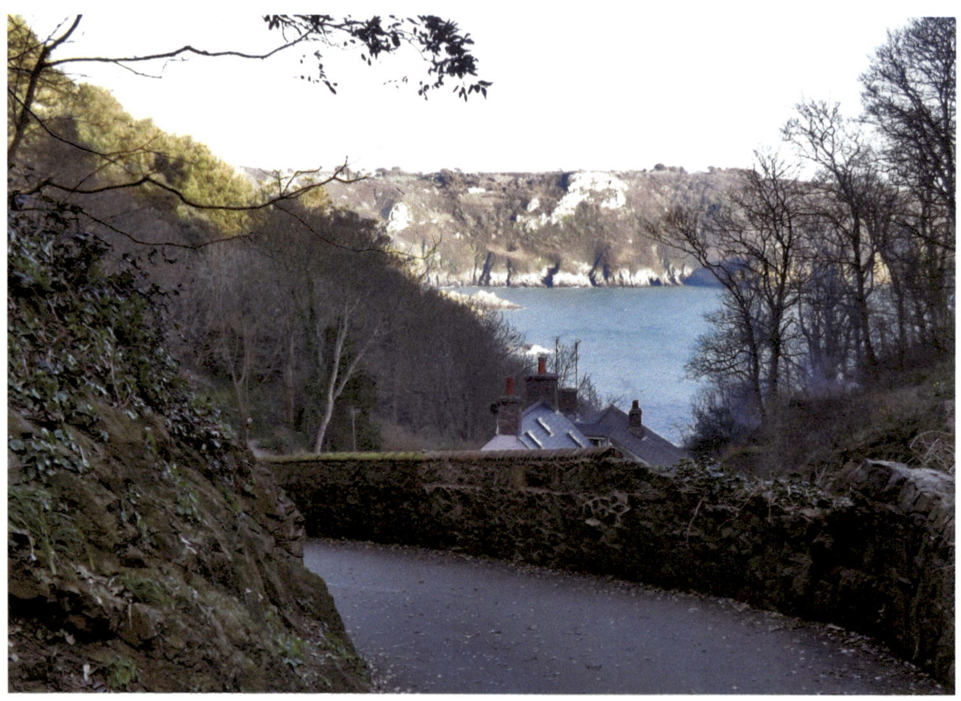

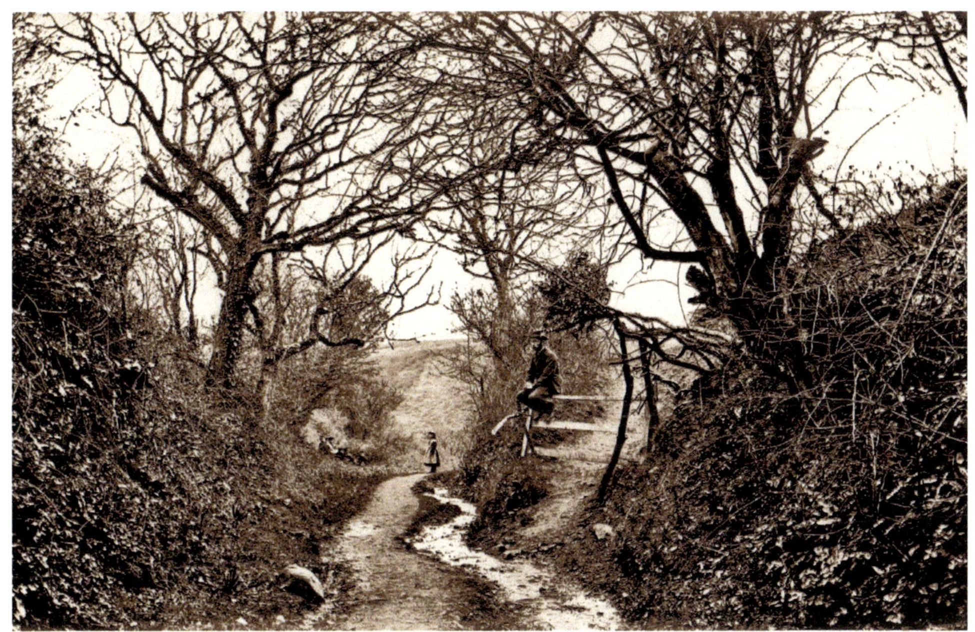

## Moulin Huet Water Lane

La Ruette des Olivets, or simply the Water Lane, has been particularly favoured by photographers over the years, being one of Guernsey's most picturesque areas. It is evident even here that the trees are more abundant in the twenty-first century than they were in the nineteenth. The *douit* (stream) running down the lane towards the sea has been carefully contained behind a retaining wall since the early photograph was taken, so its path is less erratic, and the gate and path on the right have long since disappeared.

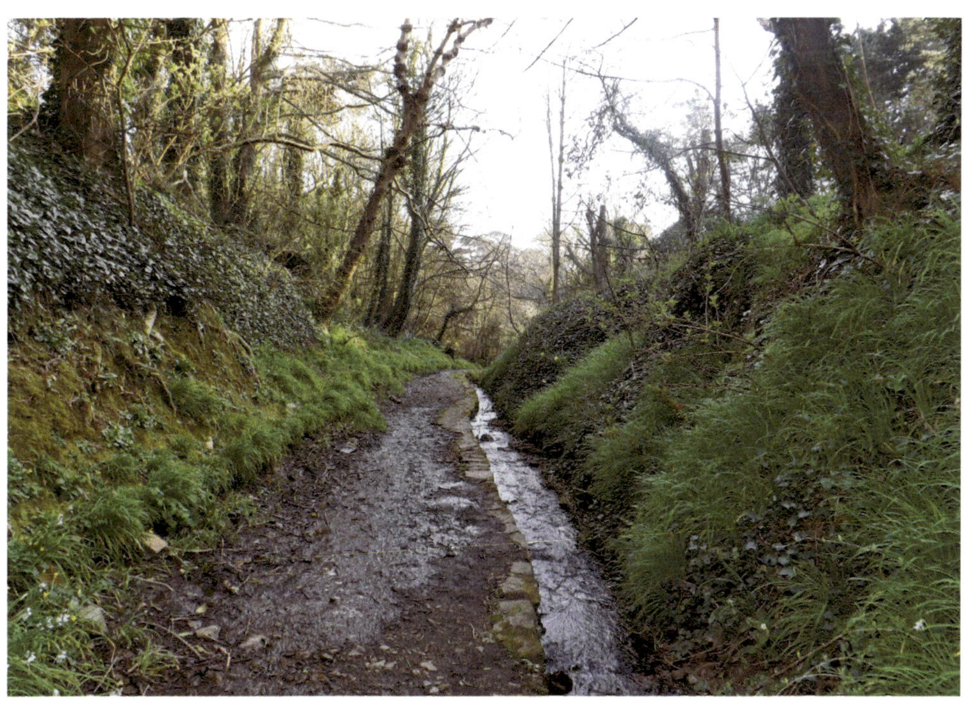

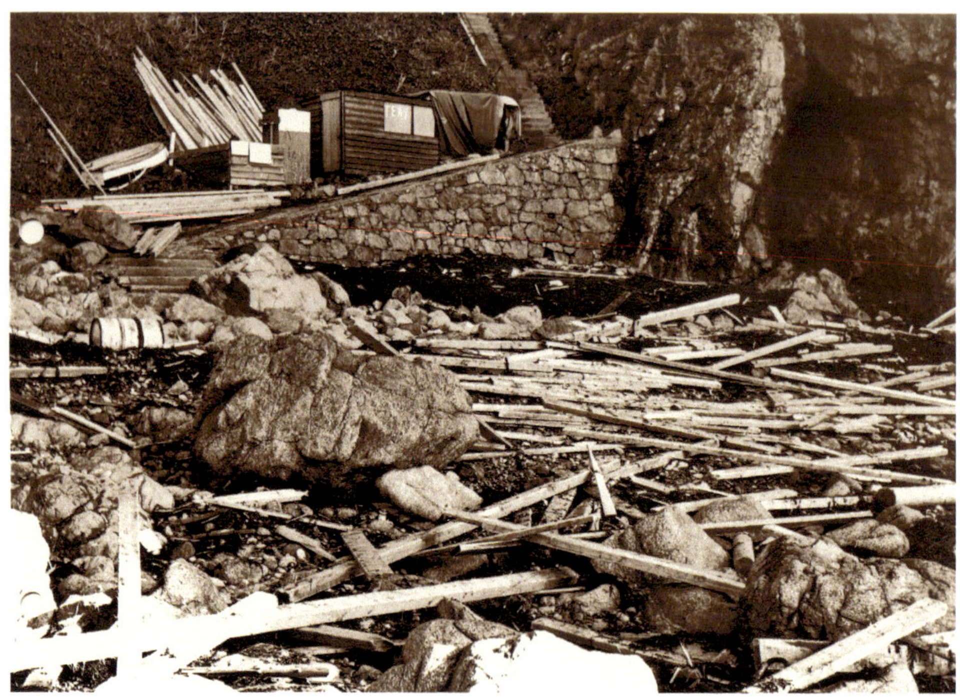

### Petit Port After a Storm

It is difficult to believe that these two photographs are of the same bay – the beautiful and pristine Petit Port covered in oil-spattered timber and rubbish after a particularly high tide in 1978. The tidal range in Guernsey is the third highest in the world, at 30 feet, and it is not unusual for rubbish and seaweed to be washed up on the shores. Rubbish clearance is not an easy operation here as the cliff above the bay is 70 feet high, and must be negotiated by a steep staircase of 321 steps.

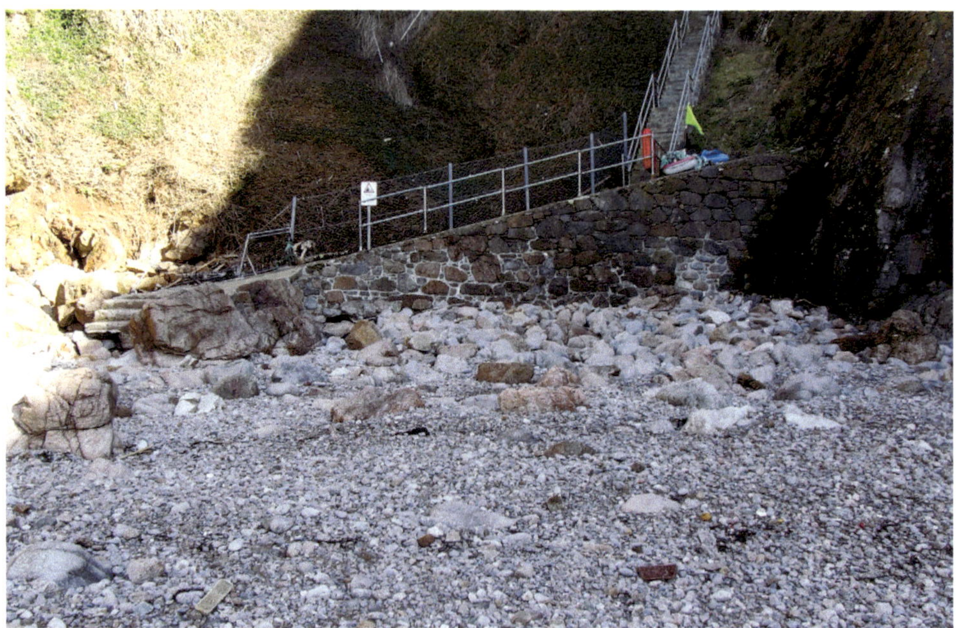

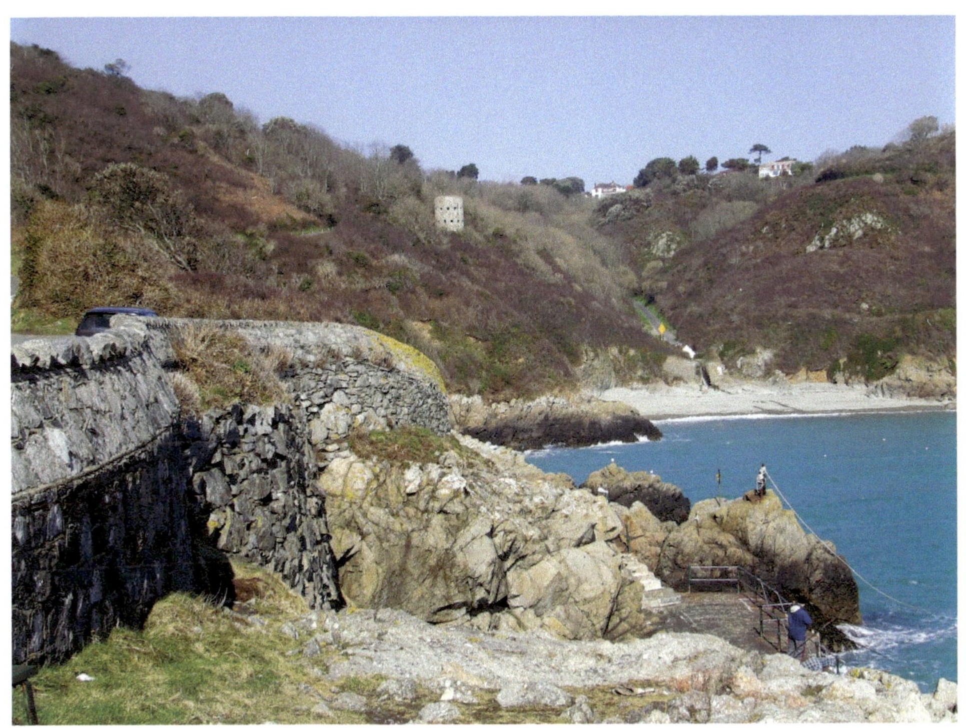

## Saints Bay Harbour

Saints Bay, with its gently sloping sandy bay, has been a favourite spot for families and fishermen for centuries. Overlooking the beach and the quaint harbour is a pre-Napoleonic loophole tower, built after 1778 as part of the ongoing fortification of the island as a defence against the French during the War of American Independence. The nineteenth-century photograph shows a myriad of crab pots clinging to the top of the cliff like barnacles, and the old harbour wall is a rather crude affair at best.

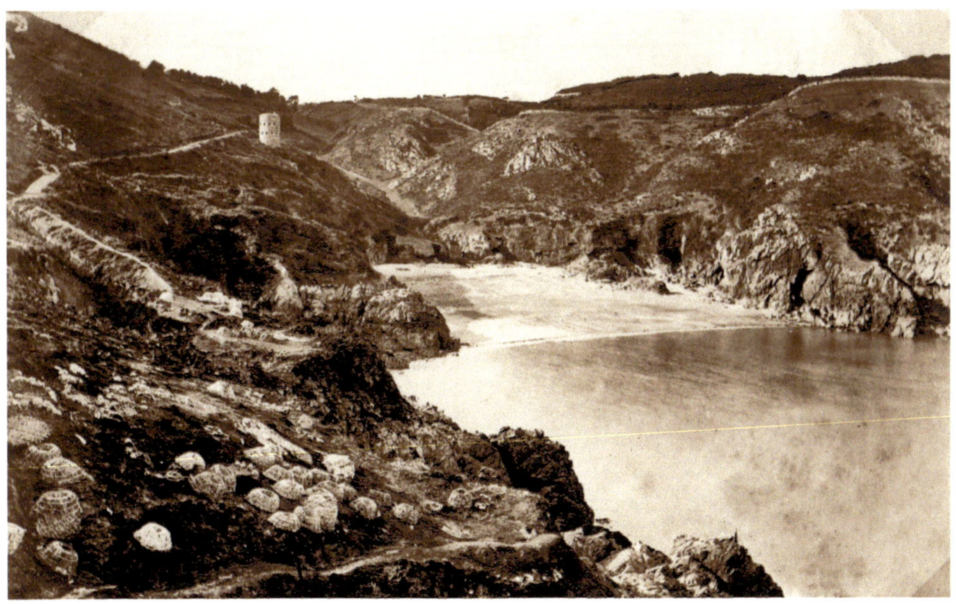

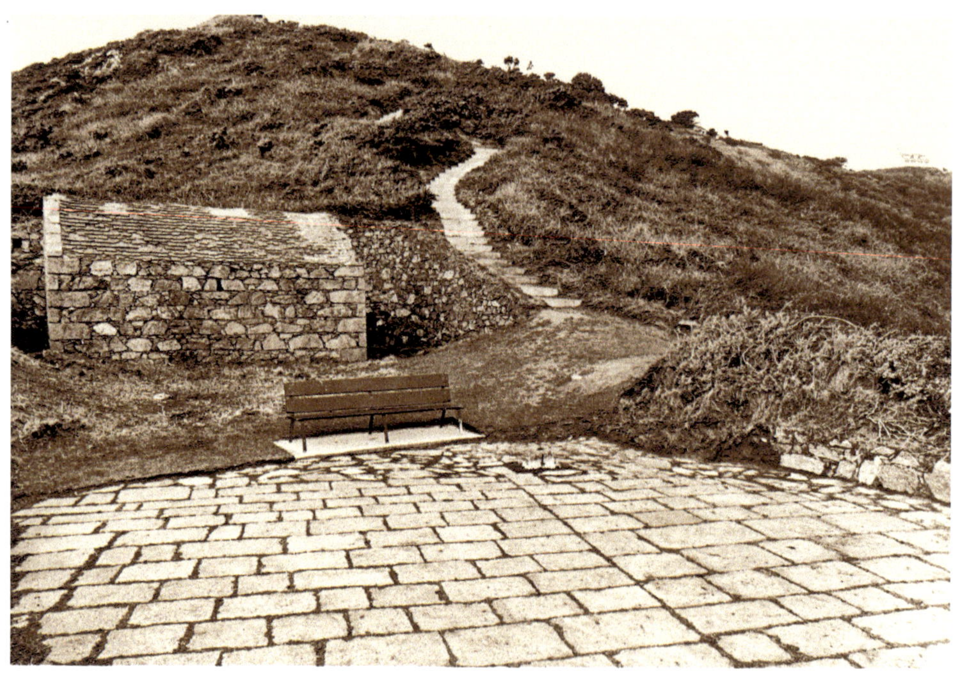

### Magazine, Saints Harbour Steps

About a third of the way up the 304 steps that link Saints Harbour to the top of the cliff, there is a small Napoleonic magazine, which provides a good excuse to halt the climb for a quick rest! There is a fine, paved gun emplacement in front, which provides a lovely view across the bay. During the occupation, Saints was designated by the Germans as a 'Resistance Nest', providing heavy machine gun and casement gun support to the Strong Point of Icart. Now a very quiet corner of Guernsey, little has changed here in forty years.

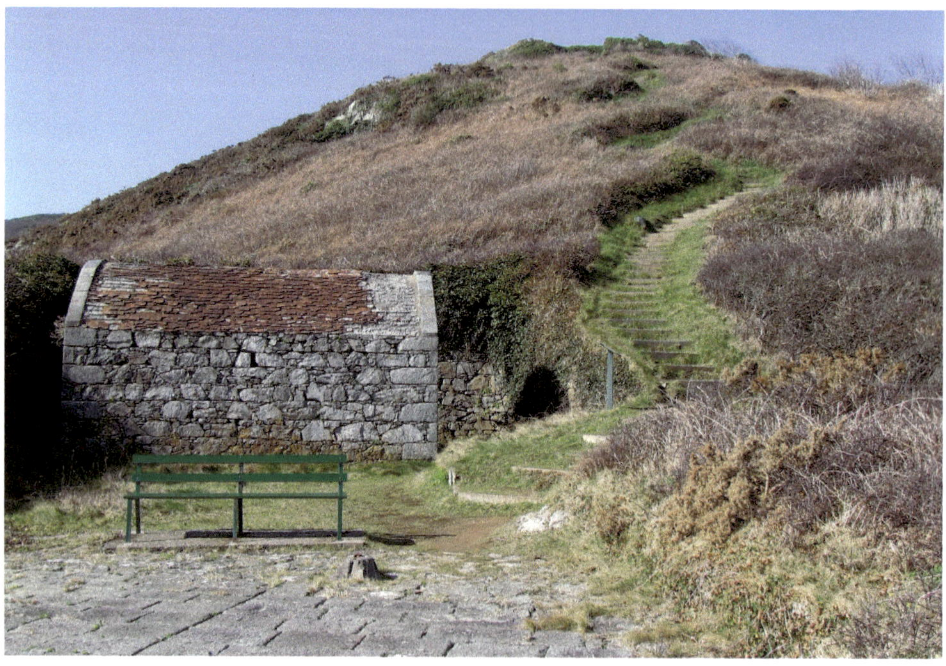

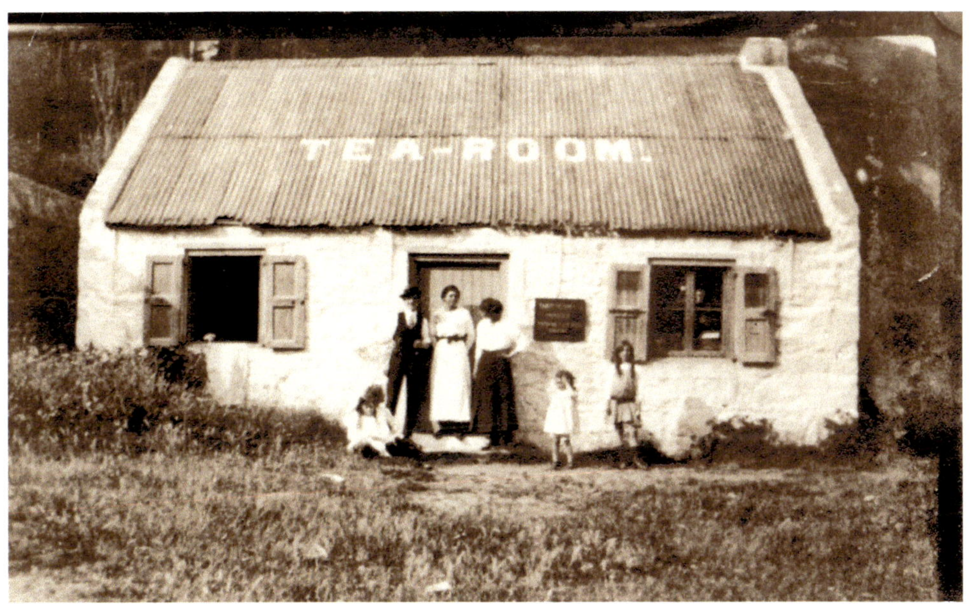


### Fermain Bay Tea Rooms

Fermain Bay is a favourite for visiting boats to drop their anchor and pop over to the tea rooms for a crab sandwich or two. At one time, a ferry took visitors and locals back and forth from St Peter Port Harbour, but since that service ceased in the 1990s, the bay is only accessible by foot or bicycle. As with all island bays, a teashop is never far behind, and this rather primitive one was established by Cecil Ferguson in the 1920s. Today, a very popular café keeps the constant stream of visitors happy.

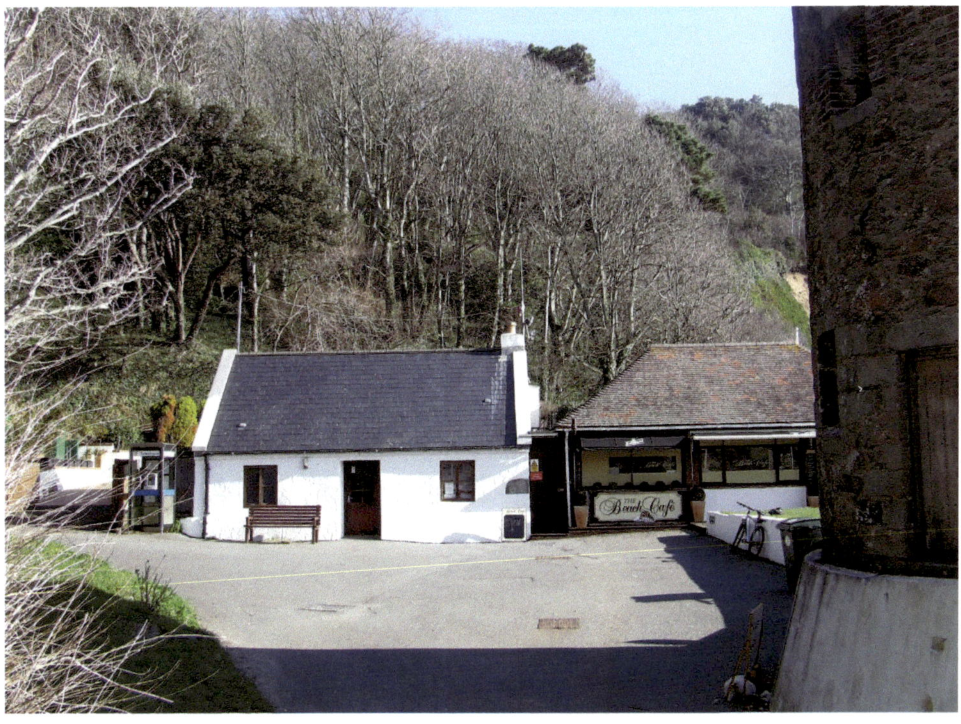

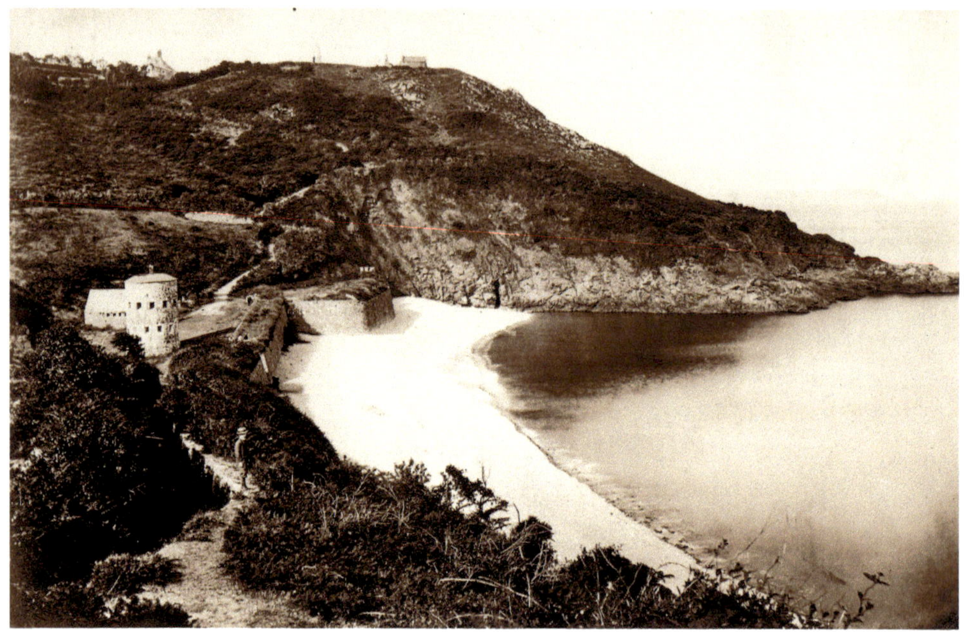



'Fermain' is a Guernsey-French word (more properly *Fermoin*) meaning literally 'iron strong' or 'stony'. It is certainly a place famous for its pebbly beach, and surrounded by granite reefs. *Blacks' Guide to the Channel Islands* of 1878 says, 'nothing can be imagined more charming than the mixture of wild vegetation and rough rocky scenery in this part of the island...' The road may have been widened, and the tea rooms extended, but it has lost none of its charm.

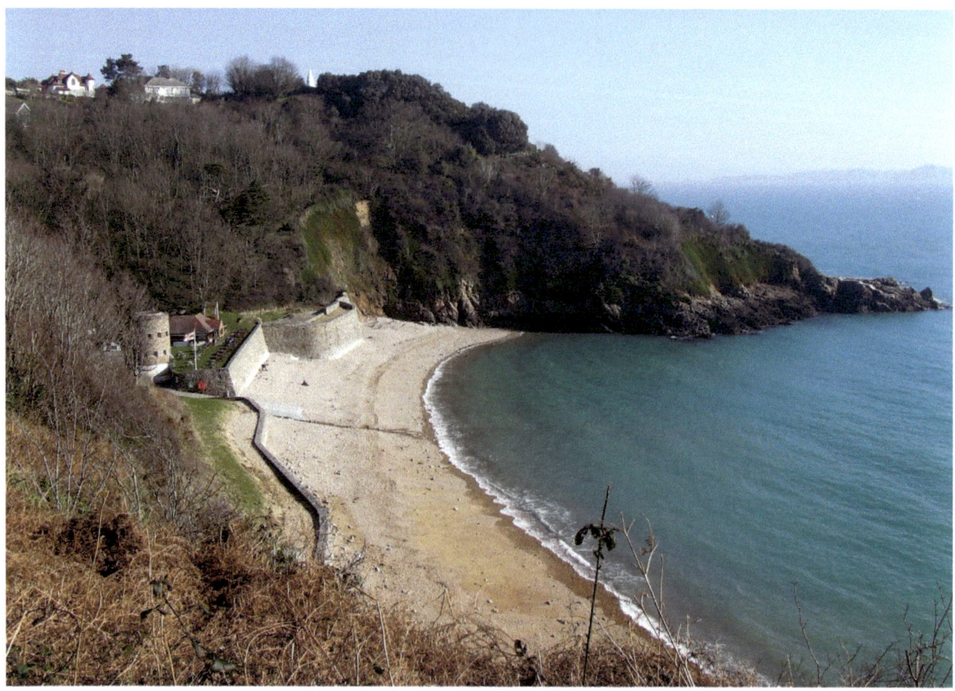

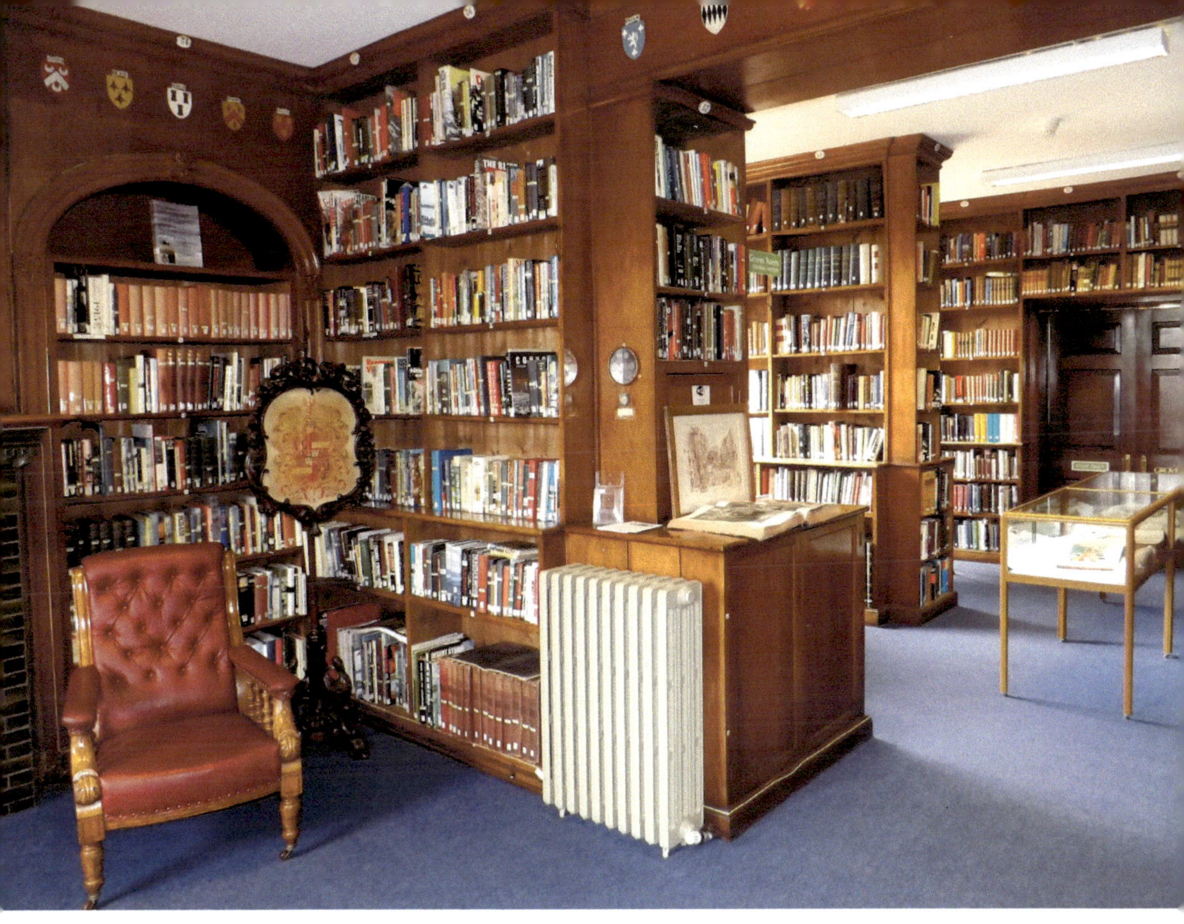

# Library Contact Details

The Priaulx Library
Candie Road
St Peter Port
Guernsey
GY1 1UG

Tel: (01481) 721998
Web: www.priaulxlibrary.co.uk
Email: info@priaulxlibrary.co.uk

# Acknowledgements

Compiling a book of this nature throws you into the path of a wide variety of people and places, and I have thoroughly enjoyed the experience. Some people need to be thanked individually. Firstly, to my brother-in-law Mitchell Sneddon for his photographic expertise and patience with the weather. Thanks to my parents Derek and Marguerite for their support and advice, and particularly my mother for her location finding skills. Thanks also to Tammy, Finlay and Zoë for their helpful comments. Particular help came from the staff and council of the Priaulx Library, James Meller at Rocquette Cider, Andrew Tabel of the Guernsey Dairy, Fiona Malley at St James Concert Hall, Bernie Le Gallais at Seafresh, Neil Sexton at Le Tricoteur, Maggie Falla of the Guille-Allès Library, Trevor Rogers-Davis at Guernsey Cans, and the Bailiff Richard Collas for allowing me to photograph the Royal Court building. The new photographs on pages 15, 16, 19, 21, 22, 35 and 36 are courtesy of Mitchell Sneddon. The photograph on page 44 is courtesy of the Guernsey Dairy.